SHELL GUIDES

edited by JOHN BETJEMAN AND JOHN PIPER

ESSEX

A SHELL GUIDE

A SHELL GUIDE

ESSEX

by NORMAN SCARFE

LONDON FABER & FABER

First published in 1968
by Faber and Faber Limited
24 Russell Square, London, WC1
Printed in Great Britain
by W. S. Cowell Ltd, Ipswich
All rights reserved

SBN 571 08868 6

To Dicky Chopping and Denis Wirth-Miller, Olive Cook
and Edwin Smith, four Essex friends who are
always opening my eyes

While the author is here expressing his personal views,
Shell-Mex and B.P. is pleased to be associated
with his book

ILLUSTRATIONS

5

ACKNOWLEDGMENTS

We've left too little room to name more than a sample of all the Essex people whose laborious studies and whose kindness I've exploited. Philip Morant must stand for the authors of the basic works of Essex history and topography. I'm embarrassed to see his own scrupulous care in acknowledging debts to predecessors in his classic *History and Antiquities of Essex*, 1768. I want to thank Tony Doncaster, whose Castle Bookshop at Colchester is easily the best in Essex, for much useful bibliographical and antiquarian information. George Arnott of Woodbridge I must thank not only for the loan of some scarce books, but also for providing, on *Atalanta*, my first approach to Brightlingsea from the river. The pleasures of discovery in most corners of Essex my parents have shared with me over the years.

At F. G. Emmison's admirable County Record Office, Nancy Briggs and Gus Edwards have been much more than helpful. Nancy Briggs has read the whole Gazetteer and most generously made available her own knowledge of both Essex and its records. In the same way David Clarke, Curator of the Colchester and Essex Museum, has read the Introduction and made several improvements. I've drawn heavily on the work of another friend, Geoffrey Martin's model *Story of Colchester*. Both Harry Wilton of Ipswich and George Harper of Great Warley have read the Gazetteer in typescript to its advantage. Remaining faults are mine.

No editor could be more helpful than John Piper. I'm deeply grateful to him for suggesting the book originally, for straightening out with such deftness and tact many of its clumsier passages, and for equipping it with pictures that truly illuminate the text. Mrs. G. D. Berwick converted my grotesque handwriting into immaculate typescript. Paul Fincham typed the Introduction in addition to so much other help. I'm happy to thank Messrs. W. S. Cowell yet again for their careful and handsome craftsmanship. N.S.

Shingle Street.
August 1968.

6

THE ESSEX ACCENT

THE ACCENTS and character of a place, like those of its people, elude simple definition. A Suffolk man abroad in Essex in the late 1960s, I am relieved to hear country people still talking a very local language, with inflections that express attitudes very similar to those I meet at home. "Tha'ss a rum'n" they still say, affecting mild wonder, exactly as Suffolk people did in FitzGerald's Woodbridge in the 1860s. The word "dag" they still use for a dew, or mist over the marshes. And they have that peculiar East Anglian trick of using the verb "to do" (which they pronounce "dew"!) to express conditions: so that "If you don't . . ." becomes, perversely, "Dew you don't." But the intonations vary, from Stour valley to Thames, and from the Naze to the Rodings. By the time you get to Waltham Holy Cross the pace has quickened: the tempo of thought is more urban than rural. Good Essex Cockneys are born within sound of Waltham Abbey bells.

This wide range of vernacular speech, from East Anglian to Cockney, from seaboard at Harwich to "Home Counties" on the Hertfordshire border, is matched by a varied landscape and a complex pattern of vernacular buildings. Until you know the county it is too easy to imagine that the northward growth of Greater London has spread a sort of urban and suburban dust over the whole county. Yet outside the Greater London boundary, there is an astonishing amount of unspoilt rural landscape; and, by Midland standards, Essex now has no large urban area: Southend is the biggest, with homes for about 170,000 people. After that, five towns hold 50-70,000 each. But two of those are New Towns, Basildon and Harlow, planted since 1945 in the Essex countryside because there was room for them, and because there was a chance to plan them as self-contained communities largely, if not wholly, independent of London. The rest are all old country markets, medieval industrial town-villages, thoroughfare or river-side or seaside towns. Sometimes the thoroughfare-traffic and frequent London train-service have created rather fuzzy suburban dormitories, as they have along the Brentwood-Southend line. But the majority of towns are small and rural, like Ongar and Dunmow, Halstead and Coggeshall – set in smooth brown gently-sloping cornland – or maritime like Burnham, Brightlingsea, Maldon, Walton. One of the biggest and the best, Colchester, not only preserves an old roof-line and a Roman lay-out; it has that characteristic of all the best towns from Rome to Dublin, from Warwick to Edinburgh: you can see the open country from the middle of the town.

Train and motor-car have enormously increased the number of commuters, week-enders and retired people: as a social process, this is certainly nothing new. In 1722, Defoe's interest in this theme led him to observe that "in this part of the country there are several very considerable estates purchas'd, and now enjoy'd, by citizens of London, merchants and tradesmen, as Mr. Western an iron-merchant, near Kelvedon [Felix Hall], Mr. Cresnor a wholesale grocer who was, a little before he died, nam'd for sheriff, at Earls Colne [Priory], Mr. Olemus a merchant at Braintree, Mr. Westcomb near Maldon [Langford], Sir Thomas Webster at Copthall, near Waltham, and several others". In the Gazetteer, some epitaphs are noted for the reason that they illustrate this theme, from Brightlingsea across to Broxted, from Fingringhoe down to Lambourne. Many more await the Essex traveller, in the floor-slabs and wall-monuments of the churches, as well as in the wills in the Record Office, and they go back long before the contemporaries of Defoe.

7

The Kingdom of Essex

With the overgrowth of London during the past century and a half, it has become natural for the country people to think of Londoners almost as enemy aliens, and often they are alien in truth. To get the relations of Essex and London straight it is worth looking back and remembering that for the first seventeen years of Roman rule, from Claudius's arrival in A.D. 43, Colchester was really the capital, the H.Q., from which the rest of Britain was subjugated. Consequently Colchester was the hub of the first great network of military roads whose directness seems such a boon to modern motorists and whose permanent avenues carved through the woodland seemed such a landmark to medieval boundary-makers, whether for parishes or for the limits of the Forest Law.

It was only after their discomfiture in Colchester during Boudicca's revolt of A.D. 61 that the Romans decided that perhaps London would make a better administrative capital. But it seems proper to think of the A12 highway as leading out from Colchester to London rather than the other way round. And it is important to remember that in the seventh century, when Essex was an independent Saxon kingdom, London was its capital, while the remaining kingdoms each had their own capital. In 675, when Erkenwald (see Bumpstead) was consecrated Bishop of the East Saxons, he based himself on London, presumably on St Paul's. After the Danish invasions, Theodred, Bishop of London, revived Christianity. Thenceforward St Paul's remained the cathedral of London and Essex until, in the 19th century, the county was transferred to the diocese of Rochester, then to the newly created see of St Alban's and then in 1913 it acquired its own see at Chelmsford.

In defining the accent it is natural to look, for clues, at the period when the East Saxons established their own kingdom. There is a marked reticence in the Anglo-Saxon archaeological remains: but so there was in the East Anglian kingdom till 1939, when Sutton Hoo suddenly transformed everything. We must keep our eyes open, especially perhaps at Broomfield and Bradwell-juxta-Mare and West Tilbury. St Peter's chapel at Bradwell, after all, remains the most dramatic monument above ground of the early 7th-century Christian mission in England.

Not the least distinctive feature of that old Essex kingdom is the way their kings, alone among the Anglo-Saxon dynasts of their day, laid no claim to descend from the great god Woden: they chose for their ultimate ancestor Saxnot, a god the continental Saxons were still worshipping two centuries later. The first king of Essex was Sledda, whose name may be reflected in early spellings of both Shalford and Shellow. In the same way Sigeric, one of his descendants, may be commemorated in Siriceslea, a royal estate in 1086 whose name has dwindled now to Ryes, a moated site on the Little Hallingbury boundary of Hatfield Broad Oak. Finally, one of their queens, Ricella, is thought to be represented in the name Rickling. Short though Essex is of archaeological remains from this period, many of the place-names help to indicate the story of the first Saxon settlement of the farms and villages. For instance fifteen of the names that end in -ing, like Matching, Messing, Stebbing and Fobbing, probably refer to family-groups of early settlers: the Rodings presumably represent an unusually large band of original colonists, since they occupied so much land. Sheering seems to mean "the army people", and Feering "the people fit for service". At its heyday in the seventh century, the century of Sutton Hoo, the kingdom of Essex may for a time have included Middlesex, and certainly seems to have stretched into East Hertfordshire up to the line of Ermine Street (now the A10). When the earldoms of Hertfordshire and Cambridgeshire were created in the late Saxon period, the Bishop of London retained spiritual jurisdiction over the eastern parts of the new earldoms or counties as far west as

Ermine Street; and so perpetuated this farthest extent of the Essex kingdom for centuries after its kings had been forgotten.

The Boundaries

The Thames estuary, from London out to Harwich, provides Essex's eastern edge: the rest is essentially a political line drawn along convenient natural boundaries in the late Saxon age. The lines along the rivers Lea and Stort, and the less natural boundaries over the chalk downlands in the north-west from Bishops Stortford (where the Bishop of London had his castle) to the Chishills and Chesterford, Hadstock and Bumpstead were drawn when the earldoms of Hertfordshire and Cambridgeshire were created (the cession of the Chishills and Heydon to Cambridgeshire is a recent affair). From Bumpstead, Essex marches with Suffolk, with East Anglia, along the river Stour to its mouth at Harwich. The Stour does as much to unite as to divide Essex and Suffolk. It meanders round Clare and Sudbury and flows through Dedham Vale. It is Gainsborough's landscape, and Constable's. Both were born just on the Suffolk side. Both painted famous subjects across the river: Constable in Dedham and Langham, for instance, and Gainsborough in Bulmer. Apart from the physical similarities and contrasts there are some striking historical and social differences, first noticed by the Essex historian J. H. Round.

Round provoked the question: does it mean anything that when, for instance, Woodham in Essex was divided into three parishes they became Woodham Ferrers, Woodham Mortimer and Woodham Walter, being distinguished from one another by the names of their feudal lords? For when such a division took place at Creeting, say, in Suffolk, or at Burlingham in Norfolk, the new parishes there took the patronymics of their saints: Creeting St Mary, Creeting All Saints, Creeting St Olave and Creeting St Peter; likewise, Burlingham St Edmund and Burlingham St Peter. There are a few exceptions, but the general rule is clear. Does not this suggest basic differences of social structure between Essex and East Anglia? What is important, in relation to this boundary, is that these differences reveal themselves at once, very close to either bank of the river Stour – where Belchamp took its names in the Essex way (the dean and chapter of St Paul's were lord of the manor, not patron saint), while on the Suffolk side Bures, Holton, Stratford and Capel took theirs the East Anglian way. What this shows is that an Essex parish tended to coincide with a single manor and tended to take the name of its (usually Norman) lord in perpetuity. A Suffolk parish rarely did any such thing. There, names like Monks Eleigh or Earl Soham are exceptional, and this must be because there was rarely a sole lord of the manor in the parish – usually there were two or three or four. There are records of something like thirteen different medieval lordships in the parish of Cavendish just across the Stour from Belchamp. When you remember, too, that Essex had only about 400 medieval parishes compared with Suffolk's 500, it becomes obvious that ownership was divided among significantly fewer people, and that a much closer identity existed between parish and manor, which in turn suggests a greater independence of spirit in East Anglia. This becomes clearer when we see the impact of the Normans and their establishment and maintenance of the Forest of Essex. At Great Canfield to this day, you can still feel you are arriving at a Norman-French feudal village.

Essex Physiognomy

"The major characteristic of Essex soils is their great variety over the county as a whole and within small distances." So wrote my namesake, N. V. Scarfe, in 1943.* The son of an Essex farmer, he did much to clarify the general picture of the shape and formation of the county. I think it is best to start as he did

* *Land Utilization Survey of Britain: Essex*, edited by Dudley Stamp.

9

The Essex landscape: near LITTLEBURY

by imagining oneself in the Saffron Walden neighbourhood. West of Walden, at Littlebury and Elmdon, one is immediately aware of the chalky open downland: here at the surface is the great bed of chalk that cups the whole region of the Thames estuary, the so-called London Basin. What one has to imagine is this thick bed of chalk sloping down under the surface so that beneath Chelmsford it lies at a depth of 360 feet, and at Southend as much as 400 feet from the top: but then suddenly it comes swooping up to the surface in a steep slope that breaks out at Purfleet

and Grays Thurrock on the *north* bank of the Thames, before sloping off to the Downs of Kent.

This great deep trough of chalk lying underground between Saffron Walden and Thurrock is extremely old – perhaps 70 million years or more. The general line of the trough appears to point from London out towards Harwich, in roughly the same direction as the A12 London–Colchester road. This road itself provides a rough line of useful demarcation. Generally speaking, to the south and east of this road the chalk trough has been filled right up to the present land surface with a great layer, 400 feet thick in places, of London Clay. At Ingatestone this thick layer of London Clay crosses the A12 and runs across the whole southern edge of Essex through Kelvedon Hatch to Epping and Nazeing.

London Clay is not to be confused with the Boulder Clay that covers so much of the rest of Essex. London Clay, as its name rather suggests, is darker (blue weathering to brown), colder, even heavier and more difficult to drain, and very much older. It may be several million years old, whereas Boulder Clay is perhaps no more than 80,000. This broad foundation of London Clay all round southern and eastern Essex, from London out to Harwich, explains all the striking differences between the coast of Essex and that of Suffolk. East of the A12, Suffolk is made of light sands and gravels, and so presents to the long-shore sailor or prospective early settler an inviting, fairly steeply shelving, clean, bright, shingly beach. Essex's shoreline is mainly of low muddy creeks and marshes, beloved of wildfowl and oysters, and their catchers. This is partly the alluvium deposited by the Thames and its more modest neighbours, Crouch, Blackwater, Colne and Stour. But behind the alluvium is London Clay. It is exposed in river-valleys and in the low cliffs of Westcliff, Frinton, Walton and Harwich. In the north-east area at least, it numbers among its less tedious ingredients septaria and local conglomerate building-materials to be noted in later paragraphs.

Return now to the vantage-point of Roughway Wood, Chrishall, near Saffron Walden. Nearby at Littlebury, Strethall and Elmdon, the rim of the ancient chalk trough was exposed at the surface. But here at Roughway Wood, and right away to the A12 in the east and Harlow in the south – to the edge of the London Clay in fact – a varying but not very thick layer of Boulder Clay has been deposited during the relatively recent Ice Ages, when Paleolithic men were hunting Paleolithic beasts in these parts, and grunting to one another about the excessively savage weather. This Boulder Clay now provides about half the face of Essex – virtually everything to the north-west of the A12, between Marks Tey and Ingatestone. Not all that different from London Clay to look at, or to work, it has one very important difference. Being tumbled about by a glacier it has acquired a good deal of chalk. This lime-content makes it much more suitable for the growing of barley and wheat, turnips, clover and indeed grasses, than the London Clay which has nevertheless for centuries provided good grazing.

As we stand at Chrishall, we can imagine this apron of Boulder Clay spreading away below us, sloping gradually down to the south-east. All the rivers of Essex seem to fan out through the fields away from this north-west corner. Why did this glacial Boulder Clay stop where it does? Apparently it came up against a line of old low hills that still form a distinctive and delightful skyline to the south-east as one drives along the A12 or travels along the main Colchester–Chelmsford railway line. Its ridge rises to Tiptree and Wickham Bishops and again to Danbury, and then it swings west to Fryerning and Kelvedon Hatch to High Beach. This range of hills is largely moulded in London Clay by ice-action and weather: their caps are of "Bagshot" sand-and-pebble beds, and they are sometimes described as a zone of "Bagshot Hills".

A more remarkably picturesque series of these outlying hills, for one doesn't associate hills of any kind with Essex, runs roughly parallel with the Tiptree–Danbury line, nearer the coast. It provides the platform for a series of spectacular hilltop churches which are oddly little-known: starting with St Nicholas', Laindon (in Basildon New Town), the series takes in Pitsea, Fobbing, Rayleigh, Ashingdon, Canewdon, Cold Norton, Latchingdon and Purleigh. It is particularly suggestive that on the hilltop at Purleigh, where the Bell Inn seems to share the churchyard with the church, the villagers used to welcome the

dawn of May with a hymn from the top of the tower. Presumably they had done something of the kind ever since Christianity replaced the worship of Saxnot and the other pagan gods. One wonders why it stopped? Was it another of the old links that broke with that most lamentable human cataclysm the First World War?

Not only do these roughly parallel zones of "Bagshot" hills appear to have acted as a barrier to the drift towards the south-east by the cap of Boulder Clay: they themselves seem to represent the valley-walls of a course of an earlier river Thames, running out along the more north-easterly lines of the upper Crouch, the Blackwater estuary and Hamford Water. This theory is supported by the presence of the southern rim of the chalk-lining of the London Basin at Purfleet on the *north* side of the present Thames. It is also perhaps borne out by the remarkable earthquake of 1884, the most serious of its kind in Britain for about four centuries. It struck precisely this "trough" area, signalling a mysterious underground shift of the foundations of Essex into a more comfortable position, perhaps a fault relating to the very sharp downward slope here of the chalk-lining. The buildings most shattered (twelve or thirteen hundred of them, including twenty churches) lay between Colchester and the mouth of the Blackwater.*

The London Clay has its excitements, and also its compensations: oysters, hilltop churches, and exotic building-materials. At the foot of those small eastern hills lie the marshes from Walton Backwaters, Mersea, Wigborough and Tollesbury to Tillingham, Paglesham and Canvey Island: the sensation of steep descent to Canvey from the Hadleigh

* *Report on the East Anglian Earthquake of April 22, 1884,* by Raphael Mendola and William White, 1885.

The Essex Boulder Clay landscape:
Tye Green, ELSENHAM

heights is always a surprise. Canvey marshes are now more historical and tragical than pastoral. Two islands, Horsey and Northey, are more arable than pastoral. Osea Island in the Blackwater was well-known to Londoners in Defoe's day "for the infinite number of wildfowl – duck, mallard, teal and widgeon . . . they tell us the island seems cover'd with them at certain times of the year . . . and they go from London on purpose for the pleasure of shooting." These marshes still provide good sport, much of it refreshingly described by Mr. Wentworth Day. As the *Victoria County History* said at the beginning of this century: "The bags now made will not compare with the sensational records handed down by tradition. Colonel Russell of Stubbers and his henchmen, 'Gabe' Clark and Amos Taylor, Linett of Bradwell, the Mussetts of Mersea and the Handleys and Hipsys of Maldon were the wildfowlers whose achievements are remembered."

Those of us who find the delicate sea-flavour of oysters delectable do not necessarily want to know the whole complicated process of cultivation as set forth in volume two of the *Victoria County History*.* There is a regular ceremony early in September involving the Mayor of Colchester, in chain and cocked hat, in the first dredge of the oyster fisheries at Brightlingsea. 1967 had a bumper harvest, and the fishery now looks so prosperous that a helicopter is hired to keep watch against the poachers.

A curiosity of the marshlands, the so-called Red Hills are shared by Essex with Kent, Lincolnshire and elsewhere. After fifty years of antiquarian speculation about these mysterious reddish platforms, the rather obvious conclusion has been reached that in England the sun by itself was a quite inadequate extractor of salt from sea-water. Fire was needed, and even before Roman times the brine seems to have been either boiled or poured over heated stacks of clay rods. In the Middle Ages the brine seems to have been concentrated by methods that have also left their puzzling remains. These marshland sites, from the Stour round to the Crouch, are very evocative. At the time of Domesday Book the salt-pans seem to have been confined to the marshes between the Stour and the north bank of the Blackwater, including a group of six at Wigborough and thirteen at the Tolleshunts, but otherwise not usually more than one in each place. The *Royal Commission** volumes list Red Hills in twenty-two of the coastal parishes.

The London Clay provides Essex's most distinctive features: the Boulder Clay the most attractive farming landscape. The primitive forest grew equally well on both: as witness the splendid oaks and hornbeams of Epping in the London Clay, Hatfield Broad Oak in the Boulder Clay. But when the oaks were cleared and the fields made, a process retarded in much of Essex by the artificial restrictions of the medieval Forest Law, the lime-content of the Boulder Clay made its fields much more nourishing to both corn and grasses than anything that could be done with the London Clay.

The farmers quickly became conscious of such geological differences. Domesday Book reveals much the densest concentration of plough-teams to the square mile in the chalk downs and the Boulder Clay of north-west Essex and the glacial loams of the Tendring district. Meadowland, too, was distributed mostly over the north-west half of the county, and related to streams like the tributary of the Stort at Parndon and the upper Chelmer at Tilty. And of course the recorded population in 1086 was thicker (between ten and fifteen to the square mile) on the ground there than anywhere in Essex except the small Colchester–Mersea district.†

It is clear as one travels over Essex that, for all its local soil variations, the Boulder Clay

---

* See note at the head of the Gazetteer.
† See *V.C.H. Essex*, Vol. I, and H. C. Darby, *Domesday Geography of Eastern England*.

* Abbreviated to V.C.H. hereafter.

covering the north-western half has features which link it very closely indeed to the central two-thirds of Suffolk and to Hertfordshire. As in Suffolk, the essential characteristics are scattered farmsteads, fields very early enclosed, deep ditches to drain the water from the heavy "three-horse" clay, and for similar reasons moats to keep the walls of the farmhouses dry and the farm stock easily coralled. The *Royal Commission on Historical Monuments* recorded them in two hundred and eighteen of the four hundred Essex parishes. I have counted about three hundred moated farmsteads (or farmsteads with remains of moats) altogether, noticeably spread over the north-western half of the county, particularly from the Rodings and the Easters up to Wimbish and Bumpstead and thence across to Easthorpe. One of the most complete is at Claverings Farm in Halstead Rural. But there are outliers in the London Clay at East Horndon and Basildon, at South Ockendon apparently in valley gravel and Tolleshunt d'Arcy between glacial gravel and London Clay. A consequence of the field ditches and their priority over the roads in the eyes of the East Saxon farmers is a set of country roads with an almost unparalleled series of right-angled bends. It's no use trying to drive quickly from Birdbrook, say, to Saffron Walden, or from Mistley to Harwich. But if you have plenty of time to meander, these roads have much more pleasure to offer the sightseer than the military precision of the roads the Romans left.

Some of the most attractive of the large "scattered" parishes of north-west Essex developed Greens for common grazing, and as in Southern Suffolk these are often called "tyes". Felsted developed no less than nine Greens. Many of these parishes owe their fame to their having developed village-centres for early commercial or industrial reasons – usually forming a cluster of buildings not far from the church: as at Bardfield, Finchingfield, Wethersfield, Thaxted, Castle Hedingham, Coggeshall – the list prolongs

itself delightfully, and it is a function of the Gazetteer to describe what is known of such developments. The word "End", as in Audley End, is especially used in Essex to describe the later hamlets that developed away from the main settlement of the village. There are 150 of these Essex Ends – almost without exception in the Boulder Clay of north-west Essex, and scarcely one example is found over the Suffolk border. These Ends are a corollary of the closer unity in Essex between manor and parish that we found in the earlier section on *The Boundaries*.

In Thaxted and Bardfield and Finchingfield and elsewhere, windmills survive. A greater profusion of watermills now characterises Essex, partly because they are more easily converted to modern uses. One of the many services rendered by Chapman and André's map of Essex*, is that they distinguished between the corn mills and the fulling mills (and for that matter the oil mills for crushing oil from seed) that survived in 1777 along the many streams of Essex, and so gave us an idea of the extent to which cloth was still being made in Essex in its last stages in this area. The way the local textile industry has been carried forward into the present through Courtaulds may be seen in the Gazetteer under Pebmarsh, Braintree and Halstead.

The date of the digging of all those moats and ditches has surprisingly never been properly determined by the simple spade-processes of modern archaeology. Being regularly cleaned out, homestead-moats are not likely to yield their origins readily. But at present we are not even sure whether they are mostly early medieval or late. One thing that must have retarded them is the Forest of Essex.

Norman Essex and the Forest
It was not just the Romans and the East Saxons who linked London to Essex at least politically. The Normans when they came controlled Essex much more tightly than East

---

* Published in 1777 and reprinted by the Essex Record Office in 1950 and 1960.

Anglia. William the Conqueror himself expressed this by building the keep of Colchester castle on a plan that was half as big again as his White Tower of London, which itself ought perhaps to be thought of as an Essex castle! Norfolk and Suffolk had been implicated in rebellion against the Conqueror as they had against the Romans, and in Domesday Book both Norwich and Ipswich were largely in ruins. But Colchester was all right, with over 400 houses recorded, which presumably implies at the very least two thousand people. Another contrast between East Anglia and Essex that Domesday Book revealed is that the percentage of free men to unfree in Suffolk was as high as 41 per cent (with 7,666 free men, Suffolk had over half the free men in England!): in Essex the proportion of free men in 1086 was as low as 7 per cent. It was the considered judgement of the historian J. H. Round that: "There is no county perhaps that bears more clearly than Essex the imprint of the Norman Conquest."

What are the more tangible remains of "the imprint of the Norman Conquest"? Colchester and Hedingham have been mentioned. In splendour, Hedingham "hall-keep" falls just short of the royal keep at Orford, but it is one of the most impressive remains in England of Norman baronial power. And if one wants to imagine for oneself something of the dignity and the military problems of being one of the leading Norman barons, half a day spent exploring the interior of Hedingham keep will not be wasted. In terms of fine building, just as at Orford, the church at Hedingham says as much as the castle. Both are well preserved. Of the other castles, the great Mandeville mound at Pleshey is impressive; its outer defences include the entire village. At Rayleigh, too, the mound Suain built is not to be sniffed at: nor is the H.Q. of Count Eustace (of Boulogne), at Ongar. Nor should one ignore the mound that the railway so much disfigured at Witham. It was built, presumably, for Edward the Elder in 912, but it is equally

presumptive that it served as the court of Count Eustace's "Honour". This is not the whole list of Norman fortifications: the ruin at Walden is not impressive, but the effect of the bailey on the shape of the town is, with the market on the broad platform below the castle gate. The small castle-mound at Mount Bures is undignified, but De Sumari's at Elmdon and Mandeville's at Rickling and Peverel's at Stebbing are certainly not.

As for Great Canfield, I know of no small group of motte-and-bailey, church and manor-farm so redolent of the whole Norman situation. It is chiefly from the Domesday account of Essex that we know of the Norman reintroduction of grape-growing in England. Missing their home comforts, the new Norman lords established at least nine vineyards in this county – at Rayleigh, Hedingham, Belchamp, Great Waltham, Stebbing, Debden, Mundon, Ashdon, and Stambourne/Toppesfield. At Stambourne the square Norman church-tower is itself almost like a young keep. Of the other Norman square towers the most notable are at Boxted, Boreham (central), Corringham, Finchingfield, Felsted, Great Maplestead and Great Tey, the last also suggesting a small keep.

The most impressive Norman church buildings to survive are monastic: the front of St Botolph's, built for the first English Austin canons, at Colchester, and the noble nave built by the Bishop of Durham at Waltham Holy Cross. But it should be recorded that no less than a score of round Romanesque chancel-arches still stand in Essex (one or two of them obviously rebuilt). The view east through the arch in Canfield church is moving. And the schemes of contemporary paintings in the church at Copford are interesting, repainted though most of them are. The Romanesque chancel-arch at Stansted seems inspired, for the church stands on a Roman site. Stansted takes its surname from the Montfiquets. Together with the

WIMBISH: Broadoaks

18

office of Forester of Essex, it passed with its castle to them from the Gernon family who held in Domesday Book, when there was woodland enough here for 1,000 swine.

On the dark subject of the Forest of Essex, the main trouble has arisen from the fact that the word forest has two meanings: it means at once an actual belt of woodland and (in strict legal terminology) an area, whether wooded or not, in which a particular law applies – the Forest Law, designed to preserve the King's hunting in the area by such technical rules as trespass on "vert and venison". To know what actual woodland existed in the Conqueror's day we look at Domesday Book and see a great deal of wood spread over Boulder Clay and London Clay alike, but considerably thicker in the west than in the east. This is borne out by many place-names, such as Waltham, a forest farm-settlement, and Hatch, a forest-gate. We saw that the north-western half of the county was also that with the most cornland and meadow, so there is no question of continuous forest. On the other hand, Elsenham (which has a round chancel-arch) and Takeley together had woods enough to feed 3,500 swine. Over the centuries the areas of woodland have been greatly reduced, yet it is possible to see in the remaining woods of Epping, and Hatfield Broad Oak, and the vestiges near Writtle and Colchester (Mile End) the main nuclei of the Norman Forest of Essex. Royal statements declaring the whole of Essex "afforested" seem to have been no more than attempts to impose severe legal restrictions that men would have to buy themselves out of. In 1204, for instance, "the men of Essex" raised 500 marks and 5 palfreys to secure the disafforestation of the whole county north of Stane Street (the Colchester–Dunmow–Stortford road). However, it seems doubtful whether royal woods were ever established there, or even whether the whole royal pack of foresters, verderers, regarders and wood-

PLESHEY, the moat

CASTLE HEDINGHAM

wards was ever let loose on that land north of Stane Street; which makes Stane Street in a way a more real medieval boundary between Essex and East Anglia than the Stour valley.

Several picturesque stories survive in the records of the Forest courts – of five poachers with bows and arrows and two with greyhounds hunting the King's deer on Thomas the Martyr's day, 1239, near Chigwell; of a hind being hunted with much hallooing (*magno clamore*) through the streets of Colchester, even the Jews joining in, till it broke its neck trying to leap the town wall (1268), and so on. Incidentally, the Forest of Hainault acquired that romantic name only in the eighteenth century: it was previously Hind-holt! For all the severity of the Forest laws, the ways of life of the villagers in the woodland are agreeable to reconstruct in the imagination. It is the greatest pity that the ancient rights of woodcutters which survived until the nineteenth century were then extinguished (see Loughton). Only the horn-beams themselves, with their strange attenuated appearance produced by the loppers' axes, now remind one visibly of that life. That, and a few records, such as the parish-marks actually used by the reeves of the Forest-parishes to brand their cattle before they were turned out to graze on the forest wastes. The letters of the alphabet, crowned, eight inches high, were used for this purpose, from A to R: A for Waltham Holy Cross, B for Nazeing, and so on to R for Stapleford Abbot.

"In Hainault only a haze of thin trees
Stood between the red double-decker buses
and the boar-hunt".
Denise Levertov

The Building Materials
With so much forest, timber was the first and most obvious of the Essex building materials, and the first builders the carpenters. Yet the earliest buildings that have survived are of stone. The stones of Essex include none of the grander limestones. There is chalk at the surface near Saffron Walden, and it has been used not only in clunch cottages at Hempstead, Great Chesterford and Debden, but also in the 13th-century undercroft of the dormitory of Beeleigh Abbey, and in the clerestory and interior of the great church at Saffron Walden. One wonders if those 13th-century stone doorways in the screens-passage of Little Chesterford Hall are of this very local stone: also the stonework beneath the plaster at Priors Hall, Widdington, presumed to be also of the 13th century?

Flints form within the chalk bed, and are found loose in the chalky Boulder Clay. Flint is the hardest, most intractable of all building materials, though in the rubble walls in which it often finds itself it depends for stability on mortar, very vulnerable to frost. In Suffolk and Norfolk, flint and freestone are combined together in what is called "flushwork", delicate patterns in which the two materials

form a level "flush" surface as close and fine as gauged brickwork, and in which elaborate canopies and tracery are simulated. In Essex, flint is mainly used as rubble for walls, but sometimes there are fine dark flush-flint walls: the tower of Brightlingsea church is the best example, a noble building by the highest East Anglian standards, its west face elaborately composed, the stages of the buttresses linked by stepped string-courses to the window-sills: the buttresses themselves provide the main decoration. Dedham tower, too, has noble dark-flint stages and in its angled buttresses a strong suggestion of Redenhall in Norfolk: only the flushwork is lacking.

The best flint flushwork is in the gatehouses of St John's Abbey, Colchester, of c. 1480, and of St Osyth's Abbey, which has almost identical decoration, but built on a more ambitious scale. There is other good flushwork in Ardleigh porch, Great Bromley's beautiful clerestory and porch, and (Victorian) the transept at Liston. There is much well-used flint: Fingringhoe porch for instance, though its beauty lies almost entirely in the quality of the flint itself, the way it has weathered, and the engaging top-heaviness of the chequered parapet: truly rustic. Marvellous texture achieved by different means – the even mixture of a yellow septaria in with the rough uncut grey flints – is seen in the west wall of Hatfield Peverel church. Here the effect depends largely on the contrast of colour, which brings us to two more of the stones of Essex.

These two are known, egregiously, as septaria and pudding-stone. Septaria crops up in the London Clay bed, mainly in the north-east corner of the county. It takes the form of lumps of an argillaceous (i.e. clayey) limestone, ironstone or the like: parts near the centre of these lumps are cracked, and these cracks (the *septa* that give the stone its name) have filled with mineral calc-spar, or sometimes pyrites. The London Clay bed is old by East

WALTHAM ABBEY, the nave

Anglian standards, and the septaria, which looks like petrified clay and varies in colour from ginger almost to Saffron yellow, is reasonably hard. At Colchester the Romans used it to make their town walls, the Normans to erect their keep, and it may be seen to have survived the weather of several hundred winters pretty well. (Its qualities are displayed to advantage in the keep at Orford in Suffolk.) The people of Harwich walled their town with septaria, but that wall is gone. Defoe says they also paved their streets with it, and that the effect was "as clean as those pav'd with stone"! Its great merit from our point of view is that it adds a pleasant variation of colour and texture to the fabric of many ancient church walls, where such qualities do much to redress the lack of well-carved freestone. These churches are mostly to be found in the peninsula between the Stour and Colne estuaries (at Lawford, Ramsey, Walton, Kirby, Frinton, Clacton, Great Bentley,

EARLS COLNE church tower, embattled with the de Vere mullet (star), in flushwork 🖝

ST OSYTH Abbey: stone and flint flushwork, and stone carving

Thorrington and St Osyth.) Down towards the Blackwater, it was used at Peldon, Wigborough, Tollesbury, Goldhanger and Tolleshunt Major, and farther south at Steeple, at Stow Maries and even at South Shoebury. The remains of the Tudor house built by the Darcys on the site of St Osyth's Abbey show what successful effects could be achieved by combining septaria and freestone in a sort of flushwork. It seems extraordinary that the fabric of this most imaginative building was never copied. Septaria, on the other hand, came into its own at the beginning of the nineteenth century. Hundreds of thousands of tons of it were dredged up off Harwich and used to make the stucco for Nash's London.

Pudding-stone is a geologically-later, and inferior, building material. It is what is called by geologists a conglomerate; a sort of natural concrete, in which pebbles, often with a mixture of ironstone, are held together like currants in indigestible pudding. Iron stains these pudding-stones anything from an orange russet to chocolate. There is no question of working such stones. But large lumps of them have been used in Norman church walls, and those walls still stand. Like septaria, pudding-stone's main asset is its colour, adding interest to dull rubble. A classic case of this is the tower of Lawford church, where it is combined with septaria, and flint, and brick of three different shades, giving the kind of pleasure one gets from a Victorian patchwork quilt.

From conglomerates it is a near cry to "clay-lump", which is Boulder Clay watered, with straw trodden in by an obliging horse, and then left to dry out in a wooden mould, but not fired. The trouble with this building-material is that it is readily soluble in rain, and needs a coat of lime-plaster for protection. That was soon provided, and there are naturally a good many examples of this use among the cottages and farm-buildings of

ST OSYTH Abbey: fragment of the Darcy House north of the Dormitory range

north-west Essex: a pleasant cottage in White Roding is the first example that comes to mind.

There is one more stone, Kentish rag, from the quarries near Maidstone across the Thames. It is a chalky-looking "young" limestone, of slightly rough texture, and varies in colour from a silvery-grey to the grey of a grubby elephant. That ancient "Essex" building, the White Tower, provides a famous example of its use. In fact the stone has been little used in Essex, but where it occurs it usually does itself credit. It is noticed most between Thames and Blackwater in church towers. Harwich breakwater is built of it; so is the Pugin chantry-chapel at Thorndon Hall, and the prom at Clacton.

The Romans left vast quarries of brickwork behind them in the towns, for which the Anglo-Saxon farmers, who succeeded them here, had small use. It is really only after the Norman Conquest and a conscious revival of Romanesque ideas that brick-making started up again. The *use* of bricks in building was well enough known by the Saxons. The delicate brick arcading round the upper stage of Holy Trinity, Colchester, is demonstration enough; but clearly there were plenty of old Roman bricks to hand. That was c. 1000. After the Normans came, the intersecting arcades on the front of St Botolph's Priory-church at Colchester could similarly be constructed of Roman bricks. Most of the Romanesque work shows the builders well aware of the value of regular shapes and sizes in building-materials, which is one of the chief assets of bricks. Roman bricks occur in the quoins and the arches of Saxon and Norman buildings (all either churches or

castles: no houses have survived*). But though there is so little building-stone there is not the least shortage of clay or brick-earth. If the Saxons didn't make bricks, it must have been less that they couldn't than that they preferred to live as many of their present-day successors do, in timber structures. After all, they went on making pots, and Saxon Hatfield Peverel (to give it its Norman name) undoubtedly made use of brick loom-weights measuring $4\frac{1}{2}$ in. $\times$ 2 in., a very un-Roman size.

Whether the remarkable 12th-century arcading of Polstead church (in Suffolk, but not far north of Colchester) is made with Roman or with Norman bricks is less important than that it clearly demonstrates the value to the Normans of bricks in making such an arcade. When the Cistercians took over Coggeshall Abbey from the Savignacs in 1148, and faced the job of making not only arcades but vaults, brick was the primary material on which their whole design was based.† There is evidence in the seating recesses and windows of the guest-house that these bricks were made for their precise purpose. They are moulded for the job. And there is an historic line direct from them through the fine 16th-century ornamental corbelling of, say, Feering Church, or Layer Marney Tower, to the spectacular brick-laying of the façades in Dedham of "Shermans" and the Old Grammar School.

Immediately after Coggeshall, the story is still fairly obscure. In Colchester the churches of St Martin's and St Leonard's-at-Hythe, and in the neighbourhood those of Stanway All Saints (now part of the Zoo) and Fordham, all contain bricks that from their part in the structure look as if they must have been

* J. S. Gardner: *Journal of the British Archaeological Association*, 1955.
† Except the Norman cellars at the corner of Pelham's Lane, Colchester.

St Botolph's Priory COLCHESTER.
Roman bricks re-used in the west front

made in the fourteenth century. None of them is of such a full-blooded red as Coggeshall Abbey, but they vary from a rather anaemic pink through buff to yellow. It must be said that the traditional brickwork is rarely a good warm red. With a few exceptions – for example at Feering and at Peldon – it has more of a bluish, purplish tinge, a slightly bruised, cold colour. This is so from Toppesfield down to Theydon Garnon, from Thorpe-le-Soken and Gestingthorpe down to Ingatestone. Among the most notable exceptions is Antony Goud's beautiful early-Georgian tower at Terling.

Two decorative brick features are characteristic: battlements, and the corbel-tables under them. Knowing that such features occur in the Netherlands regularly from the twelfth century one wonders for a moment whether here is a motif that was a direct reference by the fifteenth- and sixteenth-century builders to local Norman castellation. It seems more likely that the fashion was set by the Montgomerys of Faulkbourne Hall, which has a continuous following not only in neighbouring churches – Great Baddow and Feering – but also in Hadleigh Deanery in Suffolk, and Layer Marney.

Brick step-gables and curved "Dutch" gables are rarer than in Norfolk and Suffolk. There are only about ten curved gables; none very spirited. A few "crow-stepped" porches, as at Pebmarsh church and Colne Engaine, are echoed in house-porches, as at Little Warley. Diapering (a pattern of dark-blue or black burnt bricks set into the others) is common in fifteenth/sixteenth century work. It is usually diamond-shaped, but there are variations. It is beautifully effective in Layer Marney Tower. At Thorpe-le-Soken, "The Abbey", of 1583, has had its brickwork entirely whitewashed. Painting and colour-washing brickwork is a waste of a good texture. It is a bad habit, among some good ones, that the Civic Trust has inadvertently encouraged ever since the days of their celebrated pilot scheme at Magdalen Street, Norwich. In the eighteenth

century very good use was made of "white" bricks, as well as red. Sometimes they are silvery-white, as at Canewdon Hall or in Johnson's handsome Shire Hall at Chelmsford; sometimes a cross between pale yellow and grey, for example at Shearing Place in Steeple Bumpstead; sometimes a fairly full-blooded ochre, for a recent example some flats, "High View", at Chigwell.

There is nothing remarkable about Essex tiles, unless it is that the roofs they cover are often spectacular in sweep, as at Old House Farm, Little Sampford, and Brett's Hall, Tendring. There seems to have been no enthusiasm for pantiles, as there was in North Suffolk and Norfolk. Steepness of pitch was designed to throw rain off thatch as fast as possible in the days before thatch gave way to roof-tile. Tile-hanging is not at all a common traditional form of wall-protection in Essex. The best example is at Newney Green, Writtle. Shingling, on the other hand, that is the use of *wooden* "tiles", is very characteristic of Essex, especially for the cladding of church-spires.

The Tudor chimneys of Essex include some very elaborate decorated brickwork: at Layer Marney and St Osyth's Abbey notably. There are dozens of other examples. Grange Farm at Radwinter has diaper-work and corbelling in the stack. The Elizabethan parson of Radwinter, William Harrison, wrote: "There are old men yet dwelling in the village where I remain which have noted three things to be marvellously altered within their sound remembrance: One is the multitude of chimneys lately erected, whereas in their young days there were not above two or three, if so many, in most uplandish towns (the religious houses and manor places of their lords always excepted, and peradventure some great personages), but each one made his fire against a reredos in the hall, where he dined and dressed his meat".

In a county with so much woodland, timber provided most houses from very early times, as well as ecclesiastical buildings. Apart from

GREENSTED-JUXTA-ONGAR

all romantic and aesthetic considerations, much of the economic wealth, the real estate of the county of Essex, is bound up with its profusion of sound timber houses. At Greensted-juxta-Ongar stands the only wooden building in England that has survived from the Saxon period. It is a mile west of Chipping Ongar, and lay on a medieval road south from Bury St Edmunds through Stambourne, Finchingfield and Dunmow to London, an Essex version of the Pilgrims' Way: another ran parallel through Chelmsford–Braintree–Halstead. As it is unique, we cannot be sure how characteristic this church is of middle, or late, Saxon timber-building – even in Essex. But when we look at its walls we cannot help imagining the stockades erected by the Normans around the tops of those castle-mounds – as shown in the

wonderfully detailed picture of Dinan castle stitched into an early section of the Bayeux Tapestry. In Essex, from such castle-mounds as Stebbing and Ongar as from elsewhere in Britain, all trace of Norman close timber-building has vanished,* and we have to go as far as Leicester castle to see an example of their timber aisled halls. The reason for the disappearance of Norman stockade-work is the transitory defensive nature of the building. Only great Norman stone houses stand – chiefly at Colchester and Hedingham.

Two stone houses of the thirteenth century survive, at Little Chesterford, and Widdington. Mr. Cecil Hewett in three learned articles,† concludes that there were "two major schools of carpentry" in Essex from the thirteenth to the fifteenth century, and he produces some persuasive evidence for the early dating of some of this timber-work. For instance, Navestock belfry he finds clearly datable within the period *c.*1040–1260, with the more precise possibility of some time in the second quarter of the thirteenth century. He shows Navestock's links with Norman–French carpentry. Of all Essex's old buildings, her stout timbered belfries are the most impressive and curious. They are fairly closely grouped in the south: with the exception of Magdalen Laver, all stand to the south of the line Maldon–Chelmsford–Ongar–Chigwell; and Magdalen Laver is not far north. They are grouped between Mundon and Sutton in the east, through North Benfleet, Ramsden *Bellhouse*, the Hanningfields, Stock, Margaretting, Mountnessing, Doddinghurst, Blackmore, Navestock and over to Chigwell and Magdalen Laver. The implications of this close grouping are clear in terms of influence, and it is surprising to find them so widely spaced in time by Mr. Hewett. Their main features are great vertical posts, grouped in various ways and braced ingeniously and elaborately to take the swing of

* A piece of Pleshey's stockade is at Colchester Castle.
† *Archaeological Journal:* cxix (1964), and *Medieval Archaeology*, vi/vii (1964) and x (1967).

bells as well as the pressure of winds. These braces in most cases involved "outshots" – heavily timbered extensions round the base of the belfry on those sides where the existing nave-structure affords no buttressing, no help in tying the base of the vertical posts. For instance, at Mundon the belfry was built, apparently in the early 16th century, outside the west wall of the nave, which serves as support to the east side of the belfry. The "outshots" are thus confined to the north, west and south sides of the belfry, surrounding it on those sides by what Dr. Pevsner calls "aisles". Apart from the interest of the carpentry within, the results in the external appearance are very striking. Instead of a stepped effect between the diminishing stages rising from outshot base to tip of pyramidal roof or spire, the junction between stages is made by a sloping roof of shingling or tiles, often hipped or squinched to the shape of an octagon in plan, so that the rainwater is thrown well clear of the walls by a series of projecting aprons. The result is a building of unfamiliar shape – like some kind of simple pagoda without the curves, and not unrelated to the timbered "stave" churches of Norway.

The earlier dates suggested by Mr. Hewett are: Doddinghurst *c.* 1220, Navestock *c.* 1250 (checked by carbon-14 tests to 1133–1253), West Hanningfield first half of the 13th century, and Stock *c.* 1245–1315. Margaretting he puts at about 1450. My main doubt concerns West Hanningfield: if it *is* really as early as the first half of the 13th century I cannot help wondering why it came to be placed so exactly mid-way along the west wall of the combined nave and south aisle, which was not added to the nave before the first half

MAGDALEN LAVER

of the 14th century. My other query concerns Ramsden Bellhouse, where the belfry is certainly a late-medieval structure, but the surname is very much earlier. It seems almost too great a coincidence, here, that the place should have got its surname from a family whose name, Bellhouse, owed nothing to a belfry on this site.

Mr. Hewett puts some very early dates on a number of other Essex wooden buildings. From their joinery and "structural concept" he thinks two barns at the Hall of Belchamp St Paul's belong to the twelfth century: (interesting in view of the meaning of Belchamp's name). The most wonderful barns to look at are those of the Templars at Cressing, where he would date the wheat-barn back to *c.* 1275. The structures of aisled barns are curious, for they embody the shape of many early timber houses. These are known as "aisled halls". There are the remains of no less than ten of them, embodied in houses that have been modified to suit later requirements. To visualise these houses, it is therefore easiest to begin by looking at a barn with this aisled form, that is with two rows of free-standing internal timber-posts, just like the piers of an aisled church. Church arcades are usually of stone, but there are timber ones at Shenfield, Theydon Garnon and Upshire.

All the aisled houses date from the 14th century, or in one case a little earlier. The form goes back to Anglo-Saxon times, and even earlier. They are at Little Chesterford Hall; Tiptofts, at Wimbish, *c.*1350; St. Claire's Hall at St Osyth; Stanton's Farm at Black Notley; Fyfield Hall; Wynter's Armourie at Magdalen Laver; Bourchier's Hall at Tollesbury; Baythorn Hall at Birdbrook; Widdington Hall; and Priory Place at Little Dunmow, which Mr. Hewett thinks probably dates from the second half of the 13th century. As William Harrison noticed, chimneys were mainly the creation of his own 16th century, with the increase in brickwork. Before the building of chimneys, these large open timber halls were necessarily open to the roof which contained the louvres to let out the smoke from a central open fire. For convenience and privacy small rooms, in two storeys, developed at each end of the hall: a service end (buttery, pantry, etc., as is seen still beyond the "screens passage" in so many Oxford and Cambridge college-halls), and a private "solar" end. These had already developed in the 14th century in St Claire's Hall. Fyfield Hall seems to have been built originally without extensions, in the most primitive form. At Little Chesterford, the aisled hall is an extension from the earlier stone one.

The aisled form seems not to have been used in houses after the 14th century. Already in that time Gatehouse Farm, Felsted, Great Codham Farm, Wethersfield, Southchurch Hall (now a public library) and Lampetts at Fyfield were being built without aisles. Mr. Harry Forrester* notices a number of good 15th- and 16th-century barns, however, that have aisles: from one at the Red Cow Inn at Chrishall down to South Ockendon Hall, from Great Walley Hall in Fairstead and Power's Hall, Witham, out to Bury Farm at Felsted and Guttridge Hall at Weeley. Mr. Forrester's book provides very useful sketches of the different types of 15th-, 16th- and 17th-century timber-framed houses, showing how one can quickly learn to read much of the general plan and date of such a house from the outside. For matters of detail, like the earliest form of such a house before it underwent alterations (after all, so many of them were remodelled to conform with standards of later centuries), a close look at the roof-timbers and floor-framing is necessary. One familiar development in the houses of two or more storeys is the projection of the floor-joists of the upper floors out through the line of the ground-floor wall, so that the upper rooms are said to jut or jetty or over-sail, on the structural principle of the canti-lever. An example familiar to travellers along Stane Street is Houchins Farm, Coggeshall,

* *The Timber-Framed Houses of Essex.* Chelmsford, 1959.

where the jettying occurs in two upper floors: another example is the King's Head, Chigwell. All this made an impression on Celia Fiennes when she travelled through Essex in 1698. At Colchester just fifty years after the siege, she described the "well pitched streets which are broad enough for two Coaches to go a breast, besides a pitch'd walke on either side by the houses, secured by stumps of wood and is convenient for 3 to walke together; their buildings are of timber of loam and lathes and much tileing, the fashion of the Country runs much in long roofes and great cantilevers and peakes." (She also noted the "great burdens" of grass and corn that characterised the Essex "woodlands".)

"Loam and laths" is a reference to the method of filling in between the vertical *studs* (posts) of these box-framed buildings. It was a long time since there had been enough timber to spare in Essex forests to build such solid walls as those of Greensted church. Most medieval house-carpentry was *half-timbering*, with the oaks reserved for main structural functions, and the rest of the walls filled with "loam and laths", or "wattle and daub". This is illustrated in one of the rare building-agreements relating to Essex oak, though the building itself was to be a Bucklersbury shop. In 1405, John Dobson a London carpenter was to build a great shop and over it two storeys, the first jutting front and back, the second jutting only towards the street: he was to cut the necessary timber in the wood at Hadleigh belonging to the Chapter of St Paul's, and to work and frame it there. The Chapter would then arrange transport of this prefabricated shop to London, where it was to be ready for tiling and daubing in just under a year. (Another detailed building-agreement relates to the seasoned-oak roof, ceiled with English boards, to be built for the choir of Halstead church by John Taverner of Halstead, presumably still in position above the boarding of that ceiling.)*

* L. F. Salzman, *Building in England down to 1540*, Oxford, 1952.

The trouble with the daubing of half-timbered buildings was quickly discovered to be the way the mud cracked and shrank in summer and dissolved in the rains all the year round. A remedy was soon found to be the provision of a lime-plaster coat over the outside and inside of the half-timbered walls. Where the stud-work is at all irregular, we can be sure the builder intended the walls to be plastered over from the first. Where the stud-work is regular, plastering may not have been initially intended, but there is plenty of evidence from, for instance, the wonderfully detailed estate maps of John Walker, now in the Essex Record Office and done *c.* 1609, that by then most of the timber-framed buildings had been plastered over. At the hamlet of Newman's End, Matching, the timber-framed buildings on Walker's drawing include six single-storey cottages a medieval hall-house with 2-storeyed cross-wing, and a 2-storeyed jettied house as well as half-a-dozen barns and farm buildings, all wholly plastered over by 1609. At White Roding, Mascallsbury had already been plastered by 1609: it was subsequently enlarged in a number of interesting ways, and finally given a yellow-brick front early in the 19th century. But the history of its growth can be made out in detail by comparing maps with the present internal framework. S. Cosin's map of Aldham in 1639 is one of a very few that show timber-framed houses (the two that then lay close to Aldham church, on its former site) with the studs showing. An early Tudor painting on the north wall of the nave at Tilbury-juxta-Clare shows the studwork of a house, but one in which the filling had been done in brickwork – bricknogging – which was of course not subject to the deterioration and the draughts in the way that daub was.

The comfort brought about by this plastering, as well as its own beautiful decorative quality, is described by William Harrison and especially appropriate since he was writing at Radwinter. "In plastering likewise of our fairest houses," he says, "we use to lay first a line or two of white mortar, tempered with hair, upon laths, which are nailed one by another ... and finally cover all with the aforesaid plaster, which, beside the delectable whiteness of the stuff itself, is laid on so even and smoothly as nothing in my judgement can be done with more exactness. The walls of our houses on the inner sides in like sort be either hanged with tapestry, arras work, or painted cloths, wherein either divers histories, or herbs, beasts, knots, and suchlike are stained, or else they are ceiled with oak of our own, or wainscot brought hither out of the east countries, whereby the rooms are not a little commended, made warm, and much more close than otherwise they would be." The trouble with our age here is that, with a misguided belief that we are recovering features of historic interest, we have for decades now been peeling off the plaster and exposing the poor pale bleached stud-work, rendered horribly spikey by the nails with which the plaster was keyed, or pitted where those nails have been removed: the texture is usually very unpleasing, and we have merely demonstrated an ignorance of age-old building practice (see Thaxted for perhaps the most trying examples, but most Essex villages display

GREAT COGGESHALL: Houchins

CLAVERING: Cottages beside churchyard *GREAT COGGESHALL: Paycocks*

at least one harrowing example). Which makes it all the more important to visit Tewes at Little Sampford, where not only is the plaster intact, indeed faintly pargeted: the timbers inside have preserved their natural texture and colouring more perfectly than any I have ever seen.

The two finest pieces of Essex parge-work are at Colneford House on the Earls Colne/White Colne boundary and The Sun Inn, Saffron Walden. For two centuries, weatherboard (or clapboard) has provided a serviceable alternative overcoat for timber-framed buildings in Essex, especially near the coast. See Leigh, for instance.

Who were the medieval carpenters whose work remains among the chief glories of Essex today? Only one of them is at all known to us, and he remains alas hazy. The life of Thomas Loveday, who flourished between the years 1503 and 1536, has been reconstructed as much as may be by Mr. John Harvey.* Between 1505 and 1510 he was building Little Saxham Hall in Suffolk, for the Solicitor General: it was based on the model of Horham Hall, Thaxted (and was demolished in the 18th century). In 1515 he was one of the leading burgesses of Sudbury in Suffolk. Next year he contracted for much of the woodwork at St John's College, Cambridge, of which his stalls are still to be seen in the (Victorian) chapel. It is likely that he was carpenter of the hammerbeam roof of St John's College hall. He and his wife Alice have their names carved in the roof of Gestingthorpe church, along with Petir Barnard and his wife. This suggests that they were donors, but there are similarities with St John's which indicate that he may have been carpenter of it as well. (I don't feel with Mr. Harvey that it is "heavy and cumbrous".) Mr. Harvey names other roofs in the neighbourhood that from their style may be

Loveday's work: Sturmer, Steeple Bumpstead, Stambourne and Wimbish, and one may add the south aisle at Sible Hedingham. The double hammerbeam roof at Castle Hedingham is surely his. He died and wished to be buried there in 1535, not far from his old Sudbury home. And we are left wondering who did those fine hammerbeams at Great Bromley and in the porch at South Benfleet.

What cosiness, after the medieval discomforts, William Harrison depicted in his book. It is a very strange coincidence that in the 19th century Eden Nesfield, one of the Victorian architects who cared about local traditional building methods, should have done so much work himself at Harrison's old parish of Radwinter. But Essex abounds still in such original small comfortable early-and-late Tudor rooms as the rector's study at Great Yeldham, its ceiling richly engraved with the emblems of his patrons, or the parlour at Simpkins Farmhouse at Lindsell, or the panelled solar with chamber over and powder-closets at Walker's Farmhouse, in Farnham.

Mr. Alec Clifton-Taylor* makes the point that "structurally the timber-framed house was, far more closely than any other, the forerunner of the steel and reinforced concrete framed structure of today". And we saw how John Dobson was pre-fabricating a London shop in Hadleigh woods in 1405. The old building trade that goes on in Essex with the most complete continuity from the earliest times to our own is roof-thatching. Nor is it a dying craft. Essex has thirty thatchers at work today. It is good to think of three generations of them, the Shelleys of Hockley, their very name linking them with a parish in the ancient woodland, and all to be seen working together on the same Essex roof: father, son and grandson.

* English Mediaeval Architects, 1954.

* The Pattern of English Building, 1962.

Pargeting at the old Sun Inn, SAFFRON WALDEN

GAZETTEER

Abbreviations are usual ones, like points of the compass and main styles of medieval architecture (E.E., Early English, for most of the 13th century; Dec., c. 1290–1350; and Perp. going on into Tudor). R.C. sometimes shares its usual meaning here with the Royal Commission on Historical Monuments which, in four heavy vols. 1916–23, included an account of almost every building in Essex erected before the year 1714.

Italics have been used, as consistently as possible, to draw the traveller's attention to named houses, and sometimes churches, embedded in the text. In Basildon italics have also been used to draw attention to Neighbourhoods, and in Harlow they are used for Clusters and for the old submerged parishes.

Places are listed under their substantive names: Abbess Roding and Aythorpe Roding will be found under Roding, South Weald and North Weald Bassett under Weald. This has the advantage of grouping together places with much in common; it also helps to bring out any significance the name may have for the enjoyment of the present place. The numbers in brackets refer to the numbered square on the map at the end of the book where the place is to be found. As the map shows, this Guide covers the whole area governed by the Essex County Council at the date of publication. Some twenty ancient Essex parishes, from North Ockendon to Walthamstow, have lately become part of Greater London, but nearly 400 parishes remain.

Abberton and **Langenhoe** (13). Amalgamated in 1962, when *Langenhoe church* was demolished. Standing with the *Hall* on edge of marsh, it had been wrecked in the 1884 earthquake and rebuilt. "Red Hills" in the marshes are platforms composed of the reddened remains of the firing of pre-historic salt-works. *Abberton church* achieved lakeside situation when four miles of reservoir were made by damming Layer Brook. Reservoir pleasantly "natural"; indeed, a wild fowl ringing station. Tudor brick churchtower so purple that black-brick pattern ("diapering") in belfry-stage is hard to see. Neglected painting – Madonna, child and young St John; also smelly ship's lantern burning since 1964. Wooded valley of Roman River embowers *Abberton Manor*, formerly Badcock's Farm.

Abbess Roding *see* Rodings.

Abridge *see* Lambourne.

Aldham (10/13). Hall timber-framed, with steep roofs and chimney-stacks above Roman River. Engaging group of buildings at Ford Street, where A604 crosses Colne: *Shoulder of Mutton* is a good example of an Essex timber-framed house with white traditional weather-boarding. Another house pargeted, 1706; another, with timber frame exposed, now serves as village hall.

Church rebuilt (Hakewill) 1855, half mile from site of old one. Porch and two medieval doors retained. Flinty in good Essex tradition, but spire egregious in being entirely freestone. Light, dignified interior contains gravestone (rescued from old churchyard, 1966) of Philip Morant, stalwart compiler of *History of Essex* in two stout folio vols., 1768. Especially good on Colchester.

Alphamstone (10). Alfhelm's "ton" before Domesday. Farming parish. All but one bay of the unusually well framed long Tudor barn at *Clees Hall* shipped to the United States between the Wars. Church perched up above Lamarsh brook. Chancel partly of Tudor brick. Graffito says it was "repared wyth New tymber worke By me nycholas le Gryce p' son, A° 1578". Rest of chancel refaced in black flint by late Victorians (Sir A. Blomfield). Nave stuccocoated. Prominent wooden belfry: three early Tudor bells. Open timber Elizabethan north porch, approached through brief limewalk. Nave north wall has windows of 12th, 14th and 15th centuries; the last with pieces of its original glass. Purbeck font with late Stuart cover. Fourteenth-century slip tiles in chancel. Pleasant canopied effect at W. end produced by slender early 19th-century support-poles and frieze beneath belfry. Good screenwork in south aisle arcade (? part of

Blomfield restoration). All needs care.

Alresford (14) pronounced Arlsf'd. Green slopes down to creek of Colne river, brimming at high tide. Beside it *Plumpton's Farm*, weatherboarded among fruit trees. Slopes disembowelled at gravel quarry, with loading-pier in creek. Little church with bell-turret humped above quarry and potato fields, cement-covered except at Roman-brick west quoins. Untidy interior much Victorianized. Colourful hatchments in plaster-ceiled nave. *Quarters House*, augmented 1951, remains the "beautiful little fishing house" Constable described in 1816. It lies beside stream in glade of Hall park. Constable's picture of it hangs in Melbourne, Australia.

Althorne (16). Shameless caravans disfigure open slopes south to Crouch at "River View Farm". Perp. church of handsome texture, especially tower (black flint and grey rag in equal amounts, trellis pattern in tall battlements), presumably given by John Wilson and John Hill, for whom prayers are asked at west door. Chancel of ripe, red Tudor brick (Victorian window): this and two fine south nave windows probably date from 1508, for a brass of Wm. Hyklott says he paid for the workmanship of the wall[s] of this church. Font, of *c.* 1400, astonishingly intact, carved with figures like puppets, vigorously enacting baptism of a King, martyrdom of St Andrew (the Patron), etc.

Ardleigh (11). *Crockleford* is in a most attractive valley with white weatherboarded little watermill that was once a fulling mill. Widely scattered farmhouses: *Mose Hall* and *Gatehouse Farm* are two good medieval examples. *Vinces Farm* has a celebrated Bronze Age site. Another 15th-century house, much restored, stands at the central crossroads diagonally opposite the church, which has brown ironstone conglomerate tower and exceptionally well designed flint flushwork S. porch, both of the late 15th century. Inscription on porch asks prayers for "John Hu[n]te at the wode, Alice his wife", and (presumably) their two sons. Engaging tall stonework beasts at corners: impressive doorway and door within, spandrels show Adam and Eve "at the wood". The rest of church, presumably including the incongruous brick-and-flint flushwork tower-parapet, is by Butterfield; 1882–3. Nave interior newly painted, walls russet, stone-dressings cream. Dark nave paintings look like the handiwork of the Master of Braxted, Ernest Geldart. The south-east chapel was added in 1958 to the memory of Father Flynn, with two pieces of modern metal "sculpture" by Ivor Roberts Jones: Madonna and St Francis. Gilt and marbled monument to Barbara Lufkin, 1706, in porch. New Swedish houses nearby.

Arkesden (2), three syllables. A pretty, thatched, timber-framed, plastered or clap-boarded, tree-shaded settlement of B.B.C. commuters, along the Wicken stream. Church with monuments. Richard Fox brass, in armour, 1439. Recumbent priest divided between two broad alcoves. Large coloured stone altar-tomb with debased acanthus columns and Richard Cutte and wife recumbent, 1593. He boasts descent from builder of Horham Hall, "Treasurer of the most honourable household of mighty King Henry 8"; she was daughter of Edward Elrington,

chief butler of England to Edward VI and Queen Elizabeth; each kneeling child has the name and marriage alliance inscribed on a label. *Wood Hall*, a house of 1652 much altered and enlarged, has an oak doorway of 1652 with Cutte arms in the spandrels. Distinguished grey and white marble, in fine condition, carved by Edward Pearce, displays busts of John Withers and wife, 1692; he looking like the young Charles II, she already an early Georgian beauty. *Rockells Wood* was described by Morant, in 1768, as "the joy of fox-hunters".

Ashdon (2). Hilly ash-shaded village with cluster round *Rose and Crown* at the road junction in brook bottom: complete with Conservative Club and Labour Hall. Original wall decorations preserved in ground-floor room of early 17th-century Rose and Crown; arabesque panels in red, white and black paint. Church on the higher ground to the south is best seen from the south side of the churchyard; clerestory given its brick windows by Thomas Cornell, 1527, almost too late to throw light on the rood: east of this, a broad, tall gabled chapel, *c*. 1320, is lit by a large 15th-century south window; presumably the guild chapel of "Our Lady Brotherhood" endowed by John Chalne, clerk. Chapel sensitively restored, with brick flooring, 1939, by Sir Albert Richardson: notable roof, and figures with shields on label-stops of east window. Large tomb-chest in chancel: early-Tudor Tyrell of Little Warley and Ashdon Place (Waltons). *Guildhall*, on the south side of the churchyard, has been stripped of its external plaster, but inside retains hall-screen at one end. *Waltons*, at Bartlow End, or Little Bartlow, is an impressive red brick remodelling, *c*. 1730, for Sir William Maynard of the Tudor house of the Tyrells, which remains embedded in it. Furthermore there are two adjacent Tudor outbuildings with splendid chimney-stacks, like yeoman farmhouses, one red-brick, one timber

and plaster; by contrast on the neighbouring ridge, a post-mill; dark-timbered with neglect.
Bartlow village is in Cambridgeshire, but the plastered *Old Forge* and little yellow brick *railway station* stand on Essex side of the Granta. Public footpath through sycamore and ash saplings leads suddenly to four astonishing tumuli – the *Bartlow Hills*. The tallest rises abruptly to a height of 45 ft. They are rather hard to see, for growth of scrub. Three more stood parallel west of these. They were part of some Romano–British headquarters, *c*. A.D. 100. The mounds contained walled tombs. Grave-goods of glass, decorated bronze and enamel, dug out in 1832–40, were carted off by the Maynards to Easton Lodge (Little Easton) just in time to perish in their fire of 1847.

Asheldham (13). Dec. church stands next to three-storey cream-washed brick *Hall* of *c*. 1820. Tower coloured by yellow septaria, grey flint and a few red Roman bricks: brick battlements cemented. Fourteenth - century masons' marks on north doorway. Prehistoric camp 600 yards W. of church might be mistaken for broom-covered modern gravel workings.

Ashen (3). Ash trees, and views to Clare. *Hall*, a simple farmhouse with neat symmetrical Georgian bays, looks up a long straight lane, turning its back on the Stour valley. Church dedicated, like Birdbrook's, to Augustine of Canterbury, stands near the Red Cow Inn. The patched 14th-century tower, with two bells of *c*. 1333, is flanked by a fine Tudor brick stair turret with battlements and corbel-table. Ancient S. door; 13th-century ironwork. Tallakarne monument, 1610. A seat is carved with "This hath bin the churching, the mearring (marrying?) stoole and so it shall be still. 1620". Good unsigned marbles with long inscription to John Piper's son, Stephen, 1721, the first surrounded by trophies and reciting his qualities in Latin: Colonel of

1st Life Guards under William III and Anne.

Ashingdon (16). Scene of Canute's decisive victory over Edmund Ironside, 18 October 1016. To this hill he returned in 1020 bringing bishops, abbots and monks to consecrate the church of stone and lime he had built for the souls of the slain, including Ulfkittel, the heroic E. Anglian leader, "and all the flower of England". Present little church has no features earlier than *c.* 1300 except its noble site looking across to Canewden. Is it possible the old stone fabric was destroyed for its association with a wonder-working image? In an age not famous for scientific enquiry, Bishop Baldock (1304–13) set a commission to investigate the properties of an idol that was causing crowds, especially childless women, to crawl daily up this hill on their knees. Present small tower mostly grey rag, topped by tiled pyramid. Georgian brick S. windows; early Tudor brick E. wall. S. doorway only six feet high, and very narrow. Good interior timbering: three great tie-beams arch-braced to oak piers. Nave ceiled till 1951. Silver coin of Canute found in churchyard: replica here, original now at Prittlewell Priory museum. *Hall* has tall curved 17th-century gables.

Audley End *see* Walden.

Aveley (8). Above the broad Thames, but no longer picturesque as when the Lunatick Club met by 18th-century moonlight, and when Constable stayed up at *Belhus*, with the Barrett-Lennards in the late summer of 1813. That large Tudor house, "Gothicized" in the 1740s and '50s, is gone. Its vast Capability Brown landscape remains, approached by mass housing of South Ockendon and by a pair of good new schools, (County Architect). The most remarkable survival here is *Bretts*, a plastered, timber-framed moated house, perhaps going back to the 14th century: home of the Celys, whose business was exporting Cotswold wool and whose papers,

1475–88, were edited in 1900 by H. E. Malden for The Royal Historical Society. No trace of the medieval market at Aveley, which is a mere unit of the Urban District of Thurrock. Vast building and quarrying operations bared the skeletons of two prehistoric elephants in August 1964. Church exterior is farouche; but take three steps down into N. porch, and two more into N. aisle of a building in which the sense of continuity is cared about. Cream-washed stone and well-preserved oak roofs. Round-headed Norman arcade of S. aisle is echoed by round, timbered chancel arch of uncertain date (Royal Commission volume, 1923, says, "No chancel arch"!). Spandrels of arched braces of nave roof have traces of medieval colour. Elegant Jacobean pulpit, 1621, with sounding-board and, serving as back-board, the marble to Dacre Barrett-Lennard who died in 1724. In the N. chapel, two interesting pictures: in the reredos, a Crucifixion, and in the front of a chest serving as altar, an Adoration. Floor of chancel a pleasant jumble of Victorian tiles, old pamments, ledger slabs and brasses. A highly regarded Flemish brass, 1370, shows Ralph de Knevynton with an astonishingly long waist and short legs.

Baddow, Great (6). In 1818 "chosen by many respectable families", and by 1848 "one of the handsomest villages in Essex", it still retains handsome features though ceasing to be a village and fast merging with Chelmsford. In the S.E., along Southend Road are two good examples of the former residential village: *Pitt Place*, older in rear, has smart Georgian brick front, painted white and set off by clipped ivy; and *No. 58*, a green-painted weather-boarded cottage, stands in a neat kitchen garden. Farther south, in this corner of the parish, among orchards, *Great Sir Hughes*, a beautiful Caroline house, was replaced between the Wars by a neo-Georgian one. *Little Sir Hughes* is a good old farmhouse with a fine Georgian bay-windowed front. *Mascalls* is a

neat Georgian white brick house nearby. *Houghtons, Adstocks* and *No. 41* are other good survivors in Southend Road. Baddow has much more to dread from bungalows than ever it had from such a pleasant Victorian industrial building as that used by "Woodworkers" – Italian Gothic polychromatic brickwork.
Rich red early-Tudor brick makes the best single visual contribution to Great Baddow, and is the dominant note in the church at the heart of the place: it offsets the square grey tower and pointed lead spire superbly, and is echoed by later landmarks. The red brick is mainly concentrated in the clerestory, and laid with occasional black bricks in a diaper pattern, the surface cleverly broken by a crisp corbel-table beneath finialled battlements. Tudor brick battlements are repeated above the Decorated S. aisle.
Within, the spectacular pulpit has its main panels decorated with false perspective, a delightful Renaissance conceit. The immensely tall backboard is dated 1639 and surmounted by a tester prodigiously ornate, "Jacobean", as exotic as something from Angkor. A monument of 1753 is to Amy and Margaret Gwyn, maiden sisters, and Ann Hester Antrim, beloved by them as a sister. Sir Henry Cheere's marble portrays them in "virtuous retirement" amid garlanded urns and pretty rocaille. Helen Sydnor's monument is lettered well; 1651.
W. of church, in High Street, Georgian triple bow fronted *Bryants Stores*. Ahead, *The Vineyards* shopping-centre is a vast new pile of shops, flats, offices, banks, restaurant and car-parks in four main wings (1966: Stanley Bragg & Associates). Textures, colours and siting good. Nothing "Essex" about it, and the tallest block has firmly subdued roofline comparing feebly with church spire and flamboyant clerestory. To test these new buildings in their setting, contrast them with the group at the foot of Tabors Hill, the long range of *Valley Cottages*, the *Westminster Bank*, the *Manor*

GREAT BARDFIELD

House and – just opposite at *No. 6 High Street* – the Victorian white brick, white paint and glass of the Doctor's house with its delectable ironwork fencing.

Galleywood. St Michael and All Angels, 1873, beside pleasant rough-grown common once a military camp, still bears itself with assured air of a Victorian middle-class suburban church. Yellow brick, with red brick dressings, stone spire richly crocketted at base. A familiar landmark for miles around; given, like its fellow at Widford, by Mr Pryor of Hylands (Writtle).

Baddow, Little (6), divided from Gt. Baddow by a tongue of Danbury, to which it is closer in spirit. *Hammonds Farm*, white brick, with projecting round classical porch, looks over flat Chelmervalley fields and rising woods to Danbury spire. *Church* and *Hall* stand together. Timber frame of Hall exposed. Fireplaces of main chimney left in mid-air when old wing removed. Church porch floored in black and white polished stone. Big St Christopher. The monuments provide the chief interest of the church; especially that of Henry Mildmay, 1639, in a stone with lovely brown vein, his two kneeling wives, one young, one old, magnificently carved. He took part in the Irish wars. They lived at *Great Graces*, a red brick

Elizabethan house now reduced. An external chimney stack disfigures handsome curved gable. From here, *Grace's Walk*, a mile long, leads straight towards the spire of St Mary's, Chelmsford. The church also contains two remarkable oak effigies, early 14th-century, protected by a low iron rail: man and woman, her dress and headdress exquisitely draped. Thomas Hooker, puritan lecturer at Chelmsford, had a school here before fleeing to Holland and Massachusetts. *Congregational chapel*, 1707, was founded *c.* 1670 by one of the Barringtons for a minister ejected for noncomformity from Boreham. *Tofts*, a Barrington house, was rebuilt *c.* 1815 by General A. Strutt. *The General's Arms* is pleasant pub in woods. *Old Riffhams* nearby, a beautiful small house ingeniously remodelled in red brick in early 18th century, stands close to road on land falling steeply; on road front, first floor treated as ground floor, and attic as first floor: hence two dummy windows and comic curved gables concealing inconvenient foot or two or roof-ridge. *New Riffhams*, see Danbury.

Bardfield, Great (3). Little old market-township in rich open farming country sloping very gently N. and S. of the stream of

the Pant. Well seen from the S., from track leading to *Champions*, with water-mill below, tower windmill on ridge beyond, and church to the right along the ridge. Church crouches on skyline in most views of the village; from the bridge at Bridge End, and from Crown Street beyond the *White Hart*, which has had some of its 15th-century timber frame exposed. The richest variety of medieval timber and Georgian brick houses and shops is in the broad sloping High Street, scene of medieval Tuesday market. "Borough" court held in Town House (on north corner of junction with Thaxted road). A small single-storey *Cottage Museum* (25 ft. by 10 ft.), has a thatched roof, single tie-beam, open to rafters, and contains a very large brick chimney-stack. *Place House*, on the same side, with Tudor brick windows, brick nogging and carved corner bracket, was the home of William Bendlowes. His initials and ? 1564 are carved on a bracket. An inscription on a window in the house and on a brass in the church show he was proud of a period of 73 days when he was the sole Sergeant-at-Law. He founded a very late chantry, in Mary's reign. The church is famous for its late 14th-century stone screen between nave and chancel, later than

BASILDON NEW TOWN: Brooke House at the Town Centre

Stebbing's. It has much window tracery of the same period, and a south doorway of handsome proportions, containing lovely original door. Chancel tie-beams elaborately carved 1618 with E. Bendlowes' initials and motto. The design of the organ-case, said to be by Pugin, seems consciously related to the screen.

South of church, *Hall* with dovecote. South of town, *Bushett Farm* is a medieval hall-house. *Great Lodge* is a remaining corner of a vast house of the 1620s. It has a late Georgian interior with very pretty curved staircase, and grand adjacent barn converted to modern uses: *Park Hall*, three-storey, early 19th-century, cream washed, has an ornamental bridge over a garden-brook.

Bardfield, Little (3). The church has a famous massive Saxon tower of flint and pebbles and clunch. It rises in five stages, each slightly recessed. Symmetrical pattern of louvres. (Battlements and Decorated west window are late

Victorian). Handsome organ-case of *c*. 1700. Georgian almshouses. Several good timber-framed houses of 16th and 17th centuries. Nice gabled hotel next to church.

Bardfield Saling *see* Saling.

Barling (16). Grey ragstone tower stands boldly with a boarded spire above the saltings, creeks and the neighbouring cornfields at the end of the road from Mucking Hall. Stone much weathered. Checkered frieze on W. face. The handsome early Tudor arcade to the N. aisle, with concave-sided octagonal piers, adds to the already unusual sense of height and space for a church of these parts. Pulpit, too, contributes. It is of Georgian panelled oak, with tester raised on tall back of Stuart-late voluted oak. Two exquisitely carved shattered fragments of small alabaster figures: a bishop with staff, book and rosary, and another priest. Nearby a large cottage is dated, in pargeting, 1627 (R.C. has "167(8)").

Barnston (5) (locally "Bans'n"). On ridge above the Chelmer. The well-kept church has a Norman nave. There is a medieval graffito of a man's head in a hood outside the N. doorway. The E.E. chancel has an ambitious double piscina. The church rears a white cupola bell-cote beside the dovecote of the *Hall*, which is Elizabethan and earlier. Along the ridge, *Barnston Lodge*, white brick, imposing and apparently Georgian, has too prominent a hipped roof. Plastered, timber-framed *old rectory* is fronted with charming "Wyatt" windows. *Aptonfield Farm*, Hounslow Green, is a medieval hall-house.

Bartlow *see* Ashdon.

Basildon New Town (9). Basildon is complicated. Its U.D.C. grapples with an area that stretches as far afield as Buttsbury, Wickford, N. Benfleet and Bowers Gifford, which preserve some independence, even some identity, and

48

appear under their own names in this Gazetteer. At the core of the U.D.C. area, the more compact "urban fence" of BASILDON NEW TOWN was "designated" in 1949. The major part of seven historic parishes is undergoing a translation into New Town of 140,000 under the Development Corporation's latest master-plan, of 1965. Near half-way in 1967.

Basildon's transformation is inherently different from Harlow's. Harlow had a two-years' start, with four almost uninhabited parishes in surrounding very rural landscape. Basildon's seven parishes already had 25,000 people, living in hair-raising scatters of shacks and gim-crack bungalows; the land in something like 30,000 ownerships, and all part of N. Thames-side industrial and commuter region. Since the opening of a more direct railway from Barking across to Pitsea in 1888 and the division of Pitsea Hall Farm into "plot-lands" in 1901–3, elderly and wage-earners alike were lured here from the East End by the hope of cheap rates and rural bliss, also by free rail-tickets and notorious champagne-lunches at land-developer's expense. The landscape itself is beautifully moulded, and this too the New Town Development Corporation inherited, a real compensation for the burden of having to negotiate with all those owners. There are gently sloping fields, and more sensational views over Thames, especially from Pitsea Church Hill and Langdon Hills. So far, the architect–planners have steadily enhanced this landscape. The one rival they have erected among the neighbouring hill-top churches is a triumph of design: *Brooke House*, 14 storeys, at the Town Centre. And at March 1965, 3,550 shoddy buildings had been abolished.

It is easy to criticise the 1951 master-plan. There were only 2½ million cars owned in Britain then; and the Corporation's proposals to provide 25 per cent car-accommodation (1 car-space between 4 households) were slashed to 15 per cent! There are over 10 million cars now, and they are increasing fast. Housing is now being planned with 200 per cent car-space (1 for family, 1 for visitor). Similarly with housing densities. Whatever the architect–planners wanted, people coming out from East End expected "garden-suburb" housing; the majority still do. Early, indeed most, Basildon Neighbourhoods are thus unexciting two-storey dwellings provided with adequate shrubbery, but inadequate motoring arrangements. With the new plan to increase the town to 140,000, the density has risen from 15 or 16 dwellings per acre to 19. It is now seen that there must be wider variation in quality of housing if Basildon is to be more representative of English society, and the overall density will revert to 16.

The shape of the town is an E.-W. oblong, 6 miles by 3. Its ungainly E.-W. width was governed by existing shackery, and the lines of main road and rail. Because of the great width, the Town Centre was placed literally at the centre, where the site happens to be level. Plenty of interest in the surrounding natural features: most dramatic, the well-wooded Langdon Hills at S.W. edge of town, rising to 387 ft. From here a discontinuous rim runs across the S. edge of town, with views S. over marshes to Kent, N. over Basildon and beyond, and rising to Pitsea Church Hill in the south-east: the medieval hill-top tower of St Michael, Pitsea, in the S.E., and the medieval hill-top spire of St Nicholas, Laindon, in the N.W., are two of the most eye-catching eminences to be found in the vicinity of any English town. The gables and sharp little spire of Laindon preside over the long N. descent to the Town Centre, and, at a discreet distance, over the Town Square itself.

Town Centre: traffic-free: car-parking at ground-level adequate in 1967. Enter from W. the so-called Town Square, the best new central piazza in England. Success depends on the impressive breadth of the paved deck-area between flanks of shops N. and S.: sense of leisure created without reducing bustle at shop-doorways; dignity and grace are added by 14 storeys of flats, *Brooke House*, perfectly conceived and placed (Anthony B. Davies with Sir Basil Spence). Human scale is restored immediately alongside by playful figures in a fountain that sends up the right amount of spray to catch the breeze perpetual near tall buildings. F. E. McWilliam's small bronze personification of Homer with dove on shoulder is no longer to be seen in glazed entrance-hall of Brooke House: so many young came in to play with him that he was removed to Gifford House, the Development Corporation's H.Q. out at Bowers Gifford. Small sunken square N.W. of Brooke House contains the trim main Post Office with agreeably tent-like ceiling over counters. Sense of enclosure not yet complete in Town Square, but three new buildings are on the drawing-board for the W. end, where St Martin-of-Tours' church looks lifeless, like an empty hangar. At this end, a spherical clock like a rigid steel balloon is not very effective: Keay House, partly U.D.C. offices, is one of those drab buildings that the designer has felt constrained to decorate with external mosaic; admission of failure, especially here where the mosaics are already faded and tawdry! Market Pavement leads off S., curving well round to the Market Place, very lively on *market-days*: Tuesdays, Fridays and Saturdays: jellied eels and Leigh cockles.

New buildings to see outside the Town Centre; these are conveniently near the main Roundacre roundabout. At *Ghyllgrove*, immediately N. of Town Centre, first turn left from Broad Mayne brings you in to The Gore: excellent textures, colours and shapes of high-density 2-storey housing by Brett, Boyd & Bosanquet: *Pomfret Mead* and *Neville Shaw*, for instance, have what is almost unique in New Towns, the nostalgic feel of a good-looking town-street. Perversely, new-townees prefer "common-or-garden" suburbs. Butneys leads from The Gore to edge of *Fryerns*: on this edge *Tangham Walk* became famous, apparently because such sensitive grouping and use of building-materials is so rare. The other example of first-rate handling of site and materials is at *Lee Chapel South*: just S. of Roundacre roundabout, turn right up The Knares, and past the neat pub turn left into *Botelers* (name of one of three Basildon manors): here Tayler and Green have introduced detached houses with low pyramidal roofs, interspersed with small terraces; their grouping, concern to provide some privacy, and their "detailing", are immaculate models of how to do these things. Easily the most beautiful single new building to see so far, 1967, is Yardley's factory by John D. Morgan and David C. Branch, at the corner of Miles Gray Road in *Industrial Area No. 2* (immediately N. of Ghyllgrove): massing, and use of tall light vertical louvre blades, like Venetian blinds on their side, make marvellous use of this corner site. How one wishes St Martin-of-Tours at Town Centre showed something of this quality.

Drive towards Town Centre from N. down Upper Mayne, shows most interesting experiment in denser housing on right (to W.), in *Lee Chapel North* and *Laindon East*. Pleasant variations of housing textures and grouping in Lee Chapel North visible from Upper Mayne and Laindon Link, and good urban grouping at e.g. *Boytons*. Drive W. along Laindon Link provides salutary shock on reaching ramshackle bungaloid B.1007. But here, in Laindon East, *Danacre*, *Northey*, etc., a shade austere, are nevertheless instructive examples of dense house-building: Anthony Davies, architect, using Siporex, a gas-concrete material favoured in Sweden. Two areas to watch over next five years, where at last Buchanan's traffic principles seem to have been assimilated: one between W. end of Laindon Link and Laindon Station; the second, if the scheme is passed by the Ministry, is the area known as *Hawkesbury*, after old Hawkesbury Manor farm.

Old sites of Basildon. Basildon's

name and its village church survive: S. porch *c.* 1450 carved with bear and ragged staff, and dragon, in spandrels: late-Elizabethan brick chancel, gift of Arthur Denham, 1597: nave repaired in brick 1702, date on weather-vane; church now among two infant schools and recreation-ground off Whitmore Way. *Barstable*, now a Neighbourhood, is thought, from foundations reported ploughed up in 18th century, to have been a former village. *Dunton:* mostly-Victorian red-brick church with shingled spire and clap-board belfry, locked like most Basildon churches: Hall S. of churchyard. *Lee Chapel*: medieval chapel on E. side of Laindon, long since disappeared. Gives name to two Neighbourhoods. *Laindon.* Not only is St Nicholas' spire a fine landmark, it crowns one of those massive "Essex" medieval timber belfries. Furthermore, very unusual 2-storey chamber stands W. of it, framed *and solidly walled* in oak: possibly a 17th-century re-building (for school) of a medieval priest's house. Church much restored, but 15th-century S. porch preserves remarkably rustic spandrels carved with dragon, scallop-shell and beast pierced by patriarchal cross. Locked. *Langdon Hills. St Mary's,* late-Victorian ragstone fabric, with "Norman" W. tower, a grim building, ill deserves its incomparable situation, perhaps the best view-point in Essex. To the west, Old Church Hill descends, a hedged country lane, long and steep. Half-way down, *All Saints*, terribly sorry for itself, its small weather-boarded spire wide open to the weather. The early 16th-century brick chancel and nave are putting a good face on things and still weather-proof, but in 1967 within the homely 17th-century brick porch, the early 19th-century Gothick panelled door hangs, crumpled, from one hinge – smashed in. This interior is still one of the best examples of an unspoilt church in Essex. Come in. The W. gallery was put up in 1811, to obtain 65 additional sittings. Clerk's pew and pulpit also made *c.* 1811. The rest of the

interior took its character at the Restoration of Charles II. Nave plaster-ceiled (crown-post struts also plastered) and tympanum over rood-beam painted with Royal arms in blues and greens, 1660, when the rood-beam was carved with that quotation from Proverbs, 24, which the parson of Messing (q.v.) had had painted on the Royal arms in his church a generation earlier to so little avail: "My son, feare thou the Lord and the King", etc. Here the message is signed John Elliett, Church Warden. His name and Thos. Richardson's also appear in parge-work on N. wall of nave. Sturdy rustic rails round three sides of the altar are also of this date. The earlier, 1621, brick N. chapel (signed with R.E.'s initials) contains box-pews and Georgian Creed and Commandment boards. Funds must be raised. With a vast new population gathering just over the hill, it seems great folly to allow this beautiful object to disintegrate: one day they will appreciate it.

Nevendon preserves a good core of old houses near medieval church (drastically restored in 1875), especially Nevendon Hall and Frampton's farm. *Pitsea*: St Michael's church, approachable only on foot, occupies one of the most staggering situations of any English church, on the top of a knoll, with views all round over Kent and Essex. Unluckily the foreground is mostly taken up with pylons at present, and the church, rebuilt in 1871 after a fire, has an utterly dull interior. But from below it presents a fine spectacle. Pitsea Creek must surely develop as sailing-base for the newcomers. *Vange*, with a very early settlement-name, meaning fen-district, also occupies part of the New Town's southern ridge, from which its small towerless church, with Norman fabric, overlooks the Thames. Early 19th-century panelled south door locked. Key at parsonage, near the Barge Inn, on the corner

All Saints LANGDON HILLS (BASILDON NEW TOWN)

opposite St Chad's new church. St Chad's by Humphrys & Hurst, has the light interior qualities of their church of St Paul, Harlow, but not its exterior grace.

Battlesbridge *see* Rawreth.

Beach, High *see* Waltham.

Beaumont-cum-Moze (14) united in 1678, when Moze's eleven farmers could no longer repair their ancient church. It stood southeast of *Old Moze Hall* down beside Hamford Water (Moze means "marsh"); its site is marked out by two oak trees and a nasty little concrete cross; its fabric was demolished to repair St Leonard's, Beaumont, Norman French, "fair hill", *c.* 1175). *Beaumont* church was largely rebuilt to the design of C. Hakewill, *c.* 1854, with small pyramidal stone bellcote guarded by angels north and south: handsome from the west against a sunny sky. Tall west lancets throw pleasant light into the cosy, cluttered interior. The *Hall* has pairs of curved Dutch gables, more Norfolk than Essex. Tall brick rectory with mansard roof.

Beckingham *see* Tolleshunt Major.

Beeleigh *see* Maldon.

The Belchamps (3/10). The spelling, a Norman French rationalization of Anglo-Saxon "Belc-ham", is a very early reference to a "homestead" with a roof of "timber-beams".
Belchamp Otton (once owned by "a son of Otto") has a church dedicated to St Ethelbert, an 8th-century King of East Anglia. The Norman S. doorway stands within a 15th-century porch. Brick-floored interior, well kept. The west end is specially delightful, where 17th-century posts carved with guilloche ornament support the small belfry, and where a small gallery stands against the north-west wall of the nave. Box pews. Curled communion rails. *Church Cottage* has thick walls, like a fort.
Belchamp St Paul (granted in the

10th century to the Dean and Chapter of St Paul's) had a December cattle-fair on *Cole Green*, the site of an ancient chapel. *Shearing Place*, on the slopes down to Clare, has an irresistible white brick front (yellow and grey tints) with central semi-circular bow. The church, rebuilt in the 15th century, stands beside a large open lawn with oaks. Gargoyle on bell-tower staircase. A board inside gives details of the restorations of 1853–1912. "High Church" at present. A visitation in 1297 found the chancel ruined but a wooden altar with images of St Giles and St Edmund in the loft at the west end; also eleven more images, and the great rood. Misericord seats, almost the only ones left in Essex (? from Clare priory), with carved seated figures (two original, two "reproduced"). Elizabethan brasses in chancel are wrongly re-set in one slab, so that the engraved group of children do not tally with the 1591 inscription. There are tablets to three long-serving Pemberton vicars, 1702–29, 1781–1811, and Rev. Edward Pemberton, who died in 1859, "devoted, faithful and affectionate pastor" nearly fifty years. The second is by a Braintree sculptor, John Challis.
Belchamp Walter is the best of the three, in gentle, secluded landscape, where Aubrey de Vere had planted a great vineyard by 1086. Church and Hall on opposite sides of lane. Large lofty nave, *c.* 1325. Fifteenth-century open-timber S. porch and W. tower with checkered flushwork battlements, wobbly weather-vane on cupola above stair-turret, and tall W. window with three black plaster panels above. Two similar panels on the E. face of the tower-arch bear the (inaccurate) arms of great-grandparents of John Raymond who bought the manor early in the 17th century. Robert Taylor, senr., signed the monument to another John Raymond, 1720, with cherubs sitting on a gadrooned shelf. A John Raymond began the present Hall that year. The spacious nave is cream-washed, except where red outlines of 14th-century painting have

been restored. The Virgin suckling her child opposite the S. door has an anatomy so medieval that one begins by wondering when bottle-feeding began. Further east is a detailed Last Supper and a martyrdom by bow-and-arrow (of SS. Edmund or Sebastian). Other fragments include the Wheel of Fortune. In the N. wall is the lavish cusped arch erected for the (missing) tomb of Sir John Botetourt, *c.* 1325, of Mendlesham in High Suffolk, who married the Fitz Otto heiress and presumably had the nave rebuilt: the arch is literally stiff with foliage and shields (and one small animal). Graffito of 1574 on one shield.
The *Hall*, 1720, was restored for the Raymonds in 1966 (Donald Insall), is of two storeys, nine bays, pilasters, rubbed red brick predominant over white. Rustic flint brick and rubble piers to entrance-gates include medieval fragments (see the Royal Commission volume). Nice Victorian flint and brickwork in *Church Cottage*. Ivy-grown gateway-folly west of Hall. *St Mary Hall* has a tall brick chimney-stack with detached shafts: its whitewashed pargeted front bears a crest as on the Hall gates.

Belhus *see* Aveley.

Benfleet, North (9). Lanes full of suburban housing. The church, much rebuilt, stands beside big fish ponds. Inside the west end, a Norman window and the stout Tudor frame of the former bell tower. Tablet beside porch commemorates Jn. Cole, wounded at Waterloo at the celebrated command: "Up Guards and At 'Em". *Great Fanton Hall*, a Jacobean house altered *c.* 1787 (date plastered on E. front), represents a large Domesday manor belonging to Westminster Abbey.
Benfleet, South (9). West side heavily suburban. Steep slopes to the south have spectacular views over Canvey to Kent. Oysters and jellied eels on sale. Impressive church near the causeway to Canvey. The churchyard has a brook along the north side, and seems to

be on the site of the fort prepared by Haesten, the Danish leader who concentrated most of his forces here in 893 and lost them to King Alfred's English. Remains of many burnt ships were found when the railway was made. The church's stout square W. tower carries a little spire. The fabric is of flint rubble with a spatter of red brick; a Tudor brick buttress props the W. end of the S. aisle. Windows of the N. aisle are very good early Tudor work. The handsome 15th-century timber S. porch is roofed with hammer beams. The church's interior is also impressive. Two large blocked Norman windows looked west, but the W. wall is lumbered with the dominant organ-gallery, by Nicholson, who also designed the pleasant screen (1931) with its delicate tracery.

Bentley, Great (14). The church, approached from the vast village-green, shows good details of the building practice of its day, about the 1130s. The chancel was extended eastwards, and the tower and porch added, probably in the 14th century. The stone used is mostly dark brown ironbound conglomerate, with a few bands of almost yellow septaria. The whole interior is white-washed. Here Constance Spry's devotees are active. The altar occupies the centre of the parquet-floored chancel. A pretty monument names Peter and Mahala Thompson of Brook House (she was christened in 1801).

Bentley, Little (14). The church has an "E. Anglian" 15th-century flint tower, beautifully flecked with an occasional red brick. The S. wall of the nave, S. porch and a step-gable over the chancel arch are all in red brick, part of an expensive Tudor repair. The nave is basically Norman, the chancel basically E.E. Simple arch-braced hammerbeam roof: every angel's head sawn off, but wings folded back. The Royal arms are displayed in the unrestored porch. A restored Georgian rebuilding of a Tudor parish hall stands beside the church tower. South from the churchyard, there is a thatched

octagonal "lodge". The small white-brick, white-shuttered early 19th-century Hall stands just north of substantial ancient red-brick garden walls – all that survives of the great Jacobean palace of the 2nd Paul Bayning, who died in 1629 worth £153,000.15s. His son, Paul, buried in the vault under the N. chapel here in 1638, left his daughter married to the 20th and last De Vere, Earl of Oxford. Bentley Hall was pulled down and the whole Bayning fortune sunk with that of the De Veres. Fragment of Victorian summerhouse on overgrown moated inner "island" garden.

Berden (2). The Post Office has a little Georgian bow shop-window. A timber-framed house and its well-house with wheel have replaced the Austin Priory. The *Hall* is very imposing: Tudor brick, with three sharp gables on each of four sides, beside a most interesting tall Tudor brick well-house. The church's interior feels bare but contains two fine E.E. windows with stiff-leaf caps in chancel, whose mason's name, Gefrai Li Mathun, is carved N. side of chancel arch. Brasses. Mural tablet to Thos. Aldersaie, 1598, "by avauncement an esquire". Panels of medieval screen form seat for player of Georgian organ. Moated mount, presumed Norman from finds: now part of blissful garden of thatched (weekend) cottages known as *The Crump*: "397 ft. above sea-level" grooved on brickwork of external bread oven. Just west of here, at the Hertfordshire boundary, is one of the few places where Essex rises above 400 ft.

Berechurch *see* Colchester.

Bergholt, West (10). *Cook's Mill House*, down beside the Colne, is of trim Georgian red brick: the fulling-mill itself has gone. *Hall*, middle Georgian, 3-storeys, 7 bays wide, white paint and red brick, looks prosperous beside the church which in summer stands knee-deep in sheep's parsley. The medieval fabric, brick floored, with Georgian altar-rails

and west gallery, owes its present neglect to its remoteness from the village – full of uninteresting 20th-century housing.

Bicknacre *see* Danbury.

Billericay (9), one of the new nebulous local-government areas; is also one of the rare words for which Oxford Dictionary of English Place-names attempts no explanation, beyond showing its emergence *c*. 1313. A century ago, it was a small market-town and chapelry in the parish of Great Burstead. Now vastly outstripping its parent, the name Billericay appears on 1964 1-in. O.S. map as far away as Nevendon, divided by the width of the Southend road from Basildon's factories. Because it took a lead in promoting Basildon New Town, it finds itself within the local-government boundaries of Basildon Urban District. Physically quite separated by Burstead's nice countryside from the "designated" boundaries of the New Town, Billericay may one day regain administrative autonomy.

Burstead's name provides the clue to its early settlement, meaning pre-Saxon "fort". Roman station and burial-ground unearthed in 1847 "on a high hill between Gt Burstead and Billericay" (? Bell Hill). Ancient entrenchments at Norsey Wood and down at Blund's Walls Farm, emphasizing the early development of the site as a strong-point between headwaters of Wid and Crouch, explain the growth of Billericay as a market-town on high ground. A crowd of peasants dug in here in the great revolt of 1381.

The distinguished small late 15th-century red-brick tower of St Mary's and the spread of late-medieval buildings along High Street to the south, mark a response to the grant of a market to Billericay in 1476. High Street is a lively, compact mixture of old and recent building: *Cater Museum* at No. 74. St Mary's dates from *c*. 1343, but the main body of the building is late-Georgian, with green-painted galleries on cast-iron columns. The excellent brickwork of the tower was extended across the aisles to form a *façade principale* – possibly in 1880. The town has good Georgian buildings. Just opposite the church, *Chantry House* was associated with the Pilgrim Fathers. Modern sprawl, but cheerful aspect. Mayflower Secondary School, new, is very handsome. Burstead, Ramsden, etc., see separately.

Birch (13). Great and Little Birch are now one. Originally, in Domesday, it was spelt "Bricha" meaning newly-broken-in land. At Great Birch, the 1850 "Dec." church is by Teulon. Clad in brown pebbles, it still has a good atmosphere of a model Victorian church inside. 1737 bell from former building. Monument to young Lt Bridges slain in Indian Mutiny. Others to the Round family of *Birch Hall*, which is now demolished, though the family still own local lands, as becomes the kinsfolk of J. Horace Round, the formidable historian of *Feudal England, Family Origins*, etc. Tall, red-brick, ivy-hung fragment of church-tower of Little Birch near site of former Hall, and superb lake full of lilies.

Birchanger (5). "Birch-slope", but now a suburban settlement above Stortford. Church much rebuilt. Tympanum of Norman S. doorway carved with small capering lamb identifiable by length of tail – at first sight a fifth leg.

Birdbrook (3). Its nice name refers to the stream of the upper Colne, though the parish stretches north to the Stour at Baythorn End. *Baythorn Hall*, timber framed, its front stripped and patterned with wind-braces, its side brick-nogged, has a central aisled hall attributed to the late 14th century. *Baythorn Park* looking across to Suffolk, was given its dignified front in 1801 by George Pyke, namesake apparently of the original builder in 1668, who is said to have used materials from a still earlier house opposite the Swan Inn. Parish full of interesting houses and cottages. Notice,

from the churchyard, the uncompromising late Georgian extension to the old low timber-and-thatch *Plough*. Topiary next door, at *Yew Tree Cottage*. Early Norman date of nave and chancel betrayed by red herringbone work: extensions both E. and W. in 13th century shown by lancets in E. and W. walls – the three in the thick W. wall, deeply recessed, throw a charming light on the baptistry. There a tablet claims that Martha Blewitt of the Baythorn Swan had nine successive husbands before she died in 1681, and that Robert Hogan married his seventh wife on 1 January 1739. Handsome marble funeral casket to George and John Pyke, 1760, signed J. Pickford and W. Atkinson. Very pretty urn against flame-coloured marble, by King of Bath, to James Walford 1743. Thomas Walford, the local historian, has a decent memorial by Lufkin, 1833. He landscaped his house, *Whitley* (recently rebuilt), erecting in a nearby wood a hermitage of ragstone, unsquared timber and treebark; now gone, or well hidden.

Blackmore (5). Spectacular 15th-century bell-tower above rich dark cornfields – one of a series of displays of highly original medieval timber-engineering that runs most notably through Mundon, West Hanningfield and Margaretting to Navestock. More, even, than Navestock, Blackmore tower resembles a Norwegian stave-church or an oriental pagoda. It rises in three diminishing rectangular stages, each linked to the one above by a splayed pent-roof, the top linked to a small octagonal shingled spire, the bottom anchored in its own north and south aisles: two stages are boarded; the bottom, formerly plastered, is now unluckily stripped.
The rest of the church is interesting enough: choir and nave housed within the mid-12th century nave of former Priory of Austin canons. Inside, the whole appearance of the west end (from one pier east) is of round-headed Norman masonry on a fairly grand scale. Contents include a cresset stone (for floating a group

of wicks in oil: a medieval chandelier); alabaster effigies of Thomas Smyth and wife, 1594, recumbent on tall tomb-chest which is a convincing early 20th-century reconstruction from old fragments of marble and trophies; and a slab in the chancel to a Royalist rector of Runwell, 1660, "persecuted to the day of his death by Gog and Magog".
The canons were granted a fair at their house, 1232. Priory dissolved in 1525. When Henry VIII retired here on pleasure he was said to have "gone to Jericho". Hence the name *Jericho Priory* sometimes attached to *Blackmore House* which nevertheless was built *c.* 1714 apparently several yards from site of priory. Some early Georgian windows, facing-bricks and a staircase with barley-sugar balusters survive; the rest of the fabric is late Victorian.

Bocking *see* Braintree.

Bobbingworth (5), usually called "Bovinger". Since 1789 the Capel Cure family have lived at *Blake Hall*, an early 18th-century house extended in 1822 by Soane's brilliant pupil George Basevi, and again *c.* 1840. (Basevi fell from Ely west-tower in 1845.) Fine staircase, probably from Schomberg House, Pall Mall, introduced early in the 20th century. Library wing knocked into service as R.A.F. ops room 1940–48. *Blake Hall Station* on Ongar line (1865) is just in Stanford Rivers parish. *Bilsdens*, south of Blake Hall park, late medieval, re-fronted late in the 18th century, was the home of Bournes whose Elizabethan and Caroline brasses are in church. Chancel and tower-porch 1840, gault brick, by a "Mr Burton": nave 1680 refaced 1818, red brick. Made-up two-decker pulpit and box pews. Wireless station (not without wires) dominates S.W. of parish.

Boreham (6). Village above Chelmer river. *Boreham House* imposing and rectilinear, with

BRADWELL-JUXTA-COGGESHALL

BRADWELL-JUXTA-COGGESHALL: the chancel through the screen

ornamental canal running straight out towards A12 and the main Chelmsford–Colchester railway, has been known for generations to thousands of travellers: the fashionable and ingenious Thomas Hopper added the wings in 1812: the basic design, including magnificent Entrance Hall and Saloon, was by James Gibbs, 1728, for Benjamin Hoare, youngest son of the banker. Sir Elijah Impey with fifty servants dined here during the trial of himself and Warren Hastings. Now Ford's Tractor & Equipment Training Centre, might have its formal front avenue restored. Hoare also owned New Hall, until 1737, and is said to have brought fine marble and other materials from there. *New Hall*, built by Henry VIII as a great quadrangular house, was granted by Elizabeth to Radcliffe, Earl of Sussex, who remodelled one side of quad as it survives: the rest was demolished *c.* 1737.

South front composed of six superb 2-storey windows, the main windows characteristically on first floor a seventh bow is embedded in small remodelled east wing, *c.* 1737). Over the entrance (middle bay), runs an unstinted tribute in Italian to Elizabeth I – "wisest queen on earth, brightest star in the sky, a virgin generous, learned, godlike, elegant, just and beautiful". It was not composed by the latest occupants, who have been nuns ever since canonesses of Holy Sepulchre arrived from Liège, 1798. Their chapel contains arms of Henry VIII from his house here, carved in stone, and framed in fine, very Georgian trophies.

In the village centre, its porch sensibly prolonged the whole way out to the street, the church is irregularly assembled about a 3-storeyed Norman central tower (with 17th-century battlements). The S. aisle was given a good flushwork Edwardian face. The aisled nave, of several periods, includes the remnant of a Norman altar-recess and a brick tower-arch, round headed. Narrow chancel, 14th-century, much occupied by organ, with south chapel of *c.* 1589 to house monument of that date. On it lie three Earls of Sussex with their feet against couchant monkeys wearing hats: the Great Chamberlain, 1542, and two Chief Justices of all Forests, Parks, Chases, Warrens, etc., south of the Trent, 1567 and 1583; all in need of care. In churchyard, the mausoleum of Lord Waltham of New Hall, based on the Athenian "temple of the winds" in 1764 was pulled down in 1944, its roof needing repair. Tufnell vault in porchlike structure, *c.* 1805, north of chancel. The Old Vicarage is notorious for cultivation of Alpine plants.

Borley (10). The churchyard is inhabited by a weird grove of fifteen yews, magnificently shaped. The north-east corner of the nave is occupied by Sir Edward Waldegrave's six-poster tomb. Imprisoned in 1561 for having mass at Borley Hall and refusing the oath of supremacy, he sickened and died that year in the Tower. His widow was a daughter of the Rector of Melford, across the valley. One of their daughters is shown kneeling in the chancel, in 1598, and also on her parents' tomb. Gainsborough's uncle, Humphrey Burroughs, Rector of Borley, lies before the altar. The celebrated "haunted" *rectory* was lately demolished. The early 17th-century *Hall* raises a tall chimney stack beside the delightful brick and weatherboard watermill on the Stour.

Bowers Gifford (9) is in Basildon U.D., but not the part "designated" for the New Town. Its remote little church is as romantic as its name, except when the S. Benfleet electric train rockets past the churchyard. The grey ragstone W. tower is tipped by a substantial slate-grey shingled broach-spire, and propped by one massive S.W. buttress. Studded early Tudor S. doors. A panel of armorial glass has an inscription about Henry VII of England. A brass knight, probably Sir John Gifford, 1348, has lost a leg and his head but retained his fine shield.

Boxted (10). Heath to south, winding lanes, high hedges and mature orchards spreading to Horkesley. Views across the Stour, notably from Lower Farm, to Stoke-by-Nayland tower. A house of attractive early 19th-century white brick, with pink-washed gate-cottage, stands E. of the church. A granite 1890 mausoleum, like Edward the Confessor's shrine, lurks in the churchyard. The Norman W. tower, of rough conglomerate and much recent mortar, is topped and embattled in good Tudor brick. Inside, the crude, pointed aisle arcades have been cut through the thick Norman walls: queer, rather exciting effect, all beautifully whitewashed

and lit with clear glass dormer windows, one dated 1604. Monuments include one to Sir Richard Blackmore, 1729, who spent his last seven years here: a schoolmaster and physician ("His boys grew blockheads and his patients died" wrote a friend), he was appointed Physician in Ordinary to William III and wrote no less than six epic poems, one admired by Locke, another by Dr Johnson, all unread by us. A special Act encouraged Elizabethan clothiers here and at Langham.

Bradfield (11). *Hall*, the step-gabled house of Sir Harbottle Grimston, a leading Essex Parliamentarian during the Civil War, was replaced by a plain new farmhouse in 1955. The 13th-century rubble church tower is crowned by a stout Georgian brick parapet and corbels perhaps made of septaria-stucco: a late 14th-century bell is said to be inscribed: "I am Koc of this floc wit Gloria tibi Domine". Large transepts of 1840. Tablet to a Crimean adjutant. Cement exterior does not mislead. South-east of the church-yard runs the ribbon wall of *Bradfield Place*, a Georgian 3-storey private convalescent home for elderly gentlefolk: it has pleasant Trafalgar balconies.

Bradwell – juxta – Coggeshall (6). With Elmstead and Lindsell in Essex, it is among the best preserved small country churches in England, though box pews, a Georgian pulpit with tester, a west gallery and remains of a parclose in the nave were removed, alas, as lately as *c.* 1932, the date of the crude oak altar-table. All else is wonderfully evocative: oil lamps, old chest, brick floor (including some medieval slip tiles at west end), a Norman stone font on a Tudor brick pedestal, expressive 14th-century red-and-pink wall painting. Fifteenth-century screen tracery is crowned by a dramatic survival – rustic boarding, like a great tympanum, that formed the E. side of the former rood loft. Even more dramatic, beyond the screen, a pair of Jacobean funeral monu-

ments serve as an extraordinary reredos to the altar, their round Renaissance marble arches neatly and unconsciously echoing the round Romanesque inner splays of a pair of Norman windows in the E. wall above.

The fabric of the church, basically Norman, is well seen outside. Pleasant irregular 14th-century window-tracery in the nave walls has especially good painted figures of *c.* 1320 on inside splays; the best in S.E. window: of Thomas's Incredulity on the left (larger than life) and St James the Greater, with book, staff and scrip, on right. High on the N. wall, a small head presumably represents that of Christ perched on Christopher's shoulder.

The twin Renaissance monuments behind the altar were put up by Sir Henry Maxey (died 1624) in memory of himself and his wife, and his parents. His mother, a great heiress, disinherited the children of her first marriage in favour of her second husband's (Maxey) children. Sir Henry's brother William, commemorated in marble on the N. wall, combined puritan habits and "Joshua's resolution" with loyalty to Charles I. The inscription says he called his children up "by 5 of the clock in the morning and caused them to demand his blessing upon their knees". Later "he appeared from his closet to discharge his public duty as Justice of the Peace . . . He was most for peace. He was one that reverenced the orthodox clergy of Ingland. He died in his good old age a true subject to Charles the First and no rebel." William his third son served Charles I in all his wars against his rebels, and was Major-General of his horse at the Siege of Colchester. Henry his second son was Adjutant-General of horse, and lived to complete this monument "for the perpetuating of the memory of his dear parent". Royal arms of Charles II. Various other monuments.

Bradwell – juxta – Mare (13) occupies the north tip of Dengie peninsula, at the mouth of the Blackwater. Notabilities include

BRADWELL-JUXTA-MARE: St Peter's chapel at the wall

foundations of a great 3rd-century Roman fort of "the Saxon Shore"; St Peter's-at-the-wall, the most completely preserved of the group of small churches of the 7th century, associated with the re-introduction of Christianity to Southern England (the others are in Kent, with one possible exception in Suffolk); the old rectory (Bradwell Lodge) with a very fine *pavillon* extension of the 1780s; and a massive uncompromising mid-20th-century nuclear power station.

The fort is presumably "Othona". When Bishop Cedd organized a Christian mission to the East Saxons here in the 650s (roughly the time of the Sutton Hoo ship-burial further up the coast), Bede called the place Ythancestir, and "a city". In Domesday Book it had become Effecestre; in 1212 it was just "Walle". St Peter's-ad-Murum is not merely "at" the wall, the foundations of the middle of the nave *cross* the middle of the former west wall of the fort, which stretched for 522 ft. None

of this side of the fort is visible, but some of the S. wall is, near a picturesque, tumble-down marshman's cottage, where a shed records the height of the terrible tide of 1953. St Peter's apse and south porticus are visible in outline at ground level, but nave walls retain their original height, about 24 ft.: they owe their survival to their use as sea-mark. Observe this nave: its Kentish fellows are reduced almost to foundation level. Notice deeply splayed windows of red Roman brick: sills 14 ft. above ground: buttresses running up to sill-level are original, despite unbonded appearance.

Bradwell's own name appears in the 12th century, reference to "Broadstream" of the Blackwater or to the brook on Tillingham boundary: it consists of a pleasantly curved quiet old village street, beside the parish church, and "Waterside", now dominated by the power station. Small Georgian lock-up in churchyard wall. Tablet on red-brick church-

tower affirms the tower was built in 1743 (architects, S. Anderson and T. Gough). Brass inscription to John Debanke, Elizabethan rector 40 years. As early as 1291 this living was very rich. A friend of Gainsborough and Garrick, the Rev. Sir Henry Bate Dudley, who reclaimed 250 acres of marshland and had the sense to encourage the hollow drainage of heavy land, employed John Johnson (later the architect of public buildings in Chelmsford) to add an irresistible *pavillon* to his Tudor country rectory in the 1780s. A roof-top belvedere embodies all the chimneys in plastered "colonnade" effect. The elegant entrance hall is vaulted, the library oval. Recently home of Tom Driberg, M.P. for Barking, author of *The Best of Both Worlds*, it is one of the most delightful houses and sometimes open to the public.

Braintree and **Bocking** (6) are inextricable twins long fused by industry, through-routes and a market. Braintree stands at a junction of main Roman roads – from Colchester due west to Stortford and Ermine Street, and from London north, linking Halstead, Sudbury, Bury St Edmunds and Norwich in the Middle Ages. Shrines at Bury and Walsingham were very important medieval traffic-generators, and Braintree got grant of market 1190; hitherto merely a hamlet of Rayne. Bocking owned part of this north–south road (at Bradford Street end) and combined it with its own special assets, the weirs and mills of the Pant (upper Blackwater).

Both were doing well in the clothing industry by the middle of the 16th century, and later went in for bays and says with the help of Flemish emigrés. Later they were saved by Courtaulds (descended from Huguenots) with silk industry when woollens declined. George Courtauld moved his silk business from Pebmarsh to Braintree 1809. The famous Samuel Courtauld (1793–1881) added Halstead mill by 1826, Bocking mill by 1832. In 1846 he and colleagues were being given dinner by 1,600 workpeople in a tent outside his home, Folly House (now Foley House! rebuilt bigger in 1885) in the Bocking hamlet of *High Garrett*. Soon steam and gas-powered looms replaced the water-wheel, but the old mills remain at the heart of the factory buildings; business was being diverted from Bocking by the turn of the century. The railway had been brought 14 miles from Maldon by 1848, at a cost of £40,000 a mile. Main subsequent development in Braintree. Crittalls metal-window factory between the wars, foreshadowed whole prefab. housing industry: their *Social Club*, 1926, a period-piece.

To see effect of all this at a glance, stand at the corner of *Bank Street* and look down *High Street* to the south-west – comparing Robert Crane's marvellous painting of market-day in Braintree, 1826, with the present disheartening, disintegrating traffic-infested town. In Crane's picture, every building in the neighbourhood of the *Horn Inn* is in good trim, fulfilling itself, a scene dominated by people. One almost expects the bellow of "great John Digby" hollering his

Windmill at BOCKING

59

mackerel, loud enough to be heard, they reckoned, six miles away at Coggeshall. The Horn has lost more than its ironwork inn-sign. And look round to the left, in "Great Square", at the digni-fied decay of the *Constitutional Club*: Georgian front and remark-able Tudor interior. An alien, blank unfunctionalism has de-scended on the present "centre", east of Braintree church, itself defaced by a new vestry in 1953, and surrounded by well inten-tioned mistakes of the 1930s: Courtauld almshouses, looking like inter-war Dutch work – and the stony treeless fountain with boy and fishes, by John Hodge: modern Flanders rather than Essex. Meanwhile such a rich his-toric street as *Bradford Street*, comparable with the best medieval streets in East Anglia, is descend-ing from the seedy to the tumble-

down. Numbers 77 to 83, the former *Woolpack Inn* at corner of Woolpack Lane, for instance, would so well repay careful atten-tion. *Braintree church*'s exterior is mostly of the 1860s, but the basic framework and tower go back to the 13th century: the S.E. Guild chapel was built while Nicholas Udall was vicar (1537–44) with carved roof-bosses, also external recess apparently for fraternal feet-washing ceremonies. Inscrip-tion outside chancel to Dr Samuel Collins, principal physician to Peter the Great, Czar of Muscovy. Hawkins monument by Francis Grigs, 1645. In the N. chapel, a parchment roll names those who died of plague, 1684. The *White Hart* has had a nice white brick extension, 1966. *Bocking church* is much more rewarding. Superb south door covered in ironwork scrolls of *c.* 1260. Most of fabric

rebuilt in 15th century: roofs a little later. Brass. Used by "800 houseling people", 1548, when priest dependent on chantry priest's help. Deanery and Hall nearby. Best things now in rural Bocking: Dorewards Hall (one fine Elizabethan brick wing; ? rest never built), Lyons Hall, and other old farmsteads. Braintree and Bocking Civic Society hope to preserve *Bradford Street* if it can only hold out till by-pass built *c.* 1973 for through-traffic.

Braxted, Great (13). The church-yard forms a glade among the huge chestnuts, oaks and cedars of Braxted Park. The church is a noble building, despite odd late-Victorian arrangements to extend the small belfry from the east to the west side of the large tower. Tower has 12th-century base (see Roman brick quoins as in nave),

BOCKING: church and factory

60

The Essex landscape near BRAINTREE

heightened (see windows and arch) in 13th century. Chancel, like tower, 12th- and 13th-century. Chancel-arch rebuilt in the 19th century. The 15th-century S. porch roof has two crown-posts and carved stone corbels. Royal Arms of Elizabeth II, 1960, reveal the mortifying uncertainty of our age in simple matters of design. Du Cane family pews on high in Victorian vaulted transept. Du Canes bought the estate in 1751. Standing above a large lake, the house of *c.* 1670 was much altered 1752–6 to designs of Sir Robt. Taylor, junr. Surviving features include entrance-front and wings, glazed with octagonal panes. The garden-front and staircase are by John Johnson, 1804–6. The so-called "Hermitage" at the W. end of lake is an early 19th-

century ice-well that was formerly crowned by a summer-house. The well could be approached by boat from the house, and in it a man is said to have lived a hermit's life for a twelve-month. Noble view of house from here, coral-brick, with central projecting bay.

Braxted, Little (6). *Hall* with Tudor chimney stack, garden-wall and dovecote looks down over neat, idyllic weatherboarded and red brick watermill and across to the formidable great factory-buildings of Witham. Roberts family lived at Hall, *c.* 1480–1680: brass in church to William, auditor to Henry VII, himself an exacting accountant. Little apsidal *church* of *c.* 1120 remarkable as show-piece of its late-Victorian rector's talent for church decoration. Ernest Geldart was rector 1881–

1900. Several examples of his work as amateur architect and decorator may be seen in Essex (see Index). His handiwork here, 9 August 1881 to 5 October 1884 is amazing. Visions of Christ papered on to the walls, all in chocolate, crimson and pale gold, and full of fresh flowers. Grand-father-clock fixed into W. wall; home-made ironwork bookrest and three candlesticks fixed above font. Everything was transformed, and as a rare monument to the taste of that age it should be carefully recorded if not preserved.

Brentwood (8). A thoroughfare town along the great Roman Colchester–Chelmsford–London road, where the Ongar–Tilbury road crosses. A market was granted in 1227 at this obvious point and town presumably grew alongside. *Chapel* founded beside the road in 1220s and dedicated to St Thomas-a-Beckett: the mother-parish is South Weald. Site pleasantly hilly and still well wooded: this particular patch of woodland had been "brent" (burnt) by 1176, when the name first appears.

In the 1550s, the market came into the hands of Sir Anthony Browne, serjeant-at-law of Weald Hall, who founded the *Grammar School* and so provided the town with its educational advantages and also its most interesting group of buildings (beside the cross-roads): Browne's daughter laid the foundation stone 1568 on strip of waste land where in 1556 William Hunter, a boy-martyr, had been burnt.

New chapel built for the town in 1835, and St Thomas-a-Beckett's was converted into a National School. Railway arrived 1846. Victoria Road was at once laid out, 100 new houses and a large steam loom mill. By the 1880s a large new St Thomas's was needed: its tall slender spire and spikey spirelets provide a useful landmark in all the lower wooded country away to the south-east. National School now gone, and medieval St Thomas's is left as a carefully tended municipal ruin, disappointingly unpicturesque, with the Odeon Cinema rearing behind it one of those heavy cheese-coloured glazed-tile fronts of the '30s. The Palace Cinema is in business opposite. Outside, Brentwood's streets hold no delight. Old pubs survive from the horse-drawn world – White Hart and Chequers – but the great interest all now lies away from the motorized A12 and out in the wooded parishes all round. For a very enterprising recent U.D.C. housing scheme see Hernshaw, Herongate – (Kenneth Lindy & Partners).

Brightlingsea (14) means Brictric's island and is still often pronounced "Brykylsey" as it was spelt in 1513 when the *Peter and Paul*, belonging to John Beriffe, was among the ships hired to carry home

young Henry VIII and his army after the Battle of Spurs. Several Beriffes are commemorated in their (N.) chapel in the parish church; and their house "Jacobes" still stands in the High Street. In the Middle Ages Brightlingsea was connected with merchant shipping largely gone from the little port in our century, its place not quite adequately taken by the pleasure-sailing of our day.

Three thousand acres, the "island" is still bounded by the River Colne to the west and by marshes to the east, from Alresford Creek to Brightlingsea Creek. The marshes are still crossed by only one road, from Thorrington, climbing up to the church on its 50 ft. ridge, a mile away from the port which grew up beside Brightlingsea creek. There, down by the quay, with the winter sun purpling the brown mudflats at low tide, and the stillness broken only by the quarrels of flocking gulls, you can still grasp the meaning of this town, its physical membership of the old communities of Colne and Blackwater.

On the quay, apart from a too bulky *Anchor Hotel* and the yacht clubhouse, notice Aldous's boat-building yard where some of the first ketch-rigged barges ("boom-ies") were built, a century ago, and where the little 12-ton Colchester oyster-smacks were brought to perfection. Boat building here was hard hit in 1967 by the crisis in Nigeria, a main customer. In the High Street, *Jacobes*; timber framed with crown-post roof and picturesque Tudor-brick external stair-turret; Nos. 80–86 are made out of another timber framed late medieval hall-house. The general street-scene is of Georgian fronts, Victorian terraced cottages and older dwellings, all mixed up together, in a way reminiscent of the Slaughden end of Aldeburgh; it is best seen looking west from Hurst Green. The base of a Roman house was found in Wells Street. Another stood opposite the Roman fort at Wick Farm, Fing-ringhoe. *Church* has noblest flint and flushwork tower in Essex, 94 ft. high, a work of the 1490s,

the composition of its W. front the equal of any in East Anglia, and the whole completed by a fine parapet, unlike some of the best E. Anglian towers. South porch, too, has a fine freestone parapet; so, indeed, has S. vestry, c. 1518 and N. (Beriffe) chapel, c. 1521. Just west of S. doorway notice Roman bricks, showing this was S. wall of Norman church. Within, Beriffe brasses, and splendid monument to Nicholas Magers, a German who made a fortune in London insurance: signed by N. Read, 1779, and displaying a globe, with the W. coast of N. America detached as "the Isle of California". Since 1961, one light in a nave window has a picture of St Paul (? 17th century Flemish) salvaged from the London blitz. Since 1872, each parishioner "lost at sea" has been commemorated on a memorial tile on the nave wall.

Bromley, Great (14). Church stands beautifully, near the *Hall* which is now the Seven Rivers Cheshire Home for incurables, a plain early 19th-century house. *Church* a small masterpiece on the theme of Ardleigh, i.e. ironstone tower and flushwork porch, both of the 15th century. But here the flushwork includes the nave-clerestory as well. This runs only to seven lights, but it supports a superb double-hammerbeam roof within. Scale small but effect majestic.

Approach through elaborately carved S. doorway and original oak door with small figures of Adam and Eve over (cf. Ardleigh again) and do not miss the outside of the 15th-century *west* door, well carved. Interior floored with old yellow brick. South doorway leads into 14th-century S. arcade with capitals carved with beasts and oak foliage, and traces of original paint surviving. Through this, the glorious tall nave displays double hammerbeams that preserve much original painting in the three easternmost trusses, also many original carved figures. Handsome brass to Bromley

priest of 1432, with scroll from his lips saying "Mater mei, memento mei". Medieval stone figure now in niche at E. end of N. aisle: ? handbell ringer. 1941 notice still draws attention to hats of former bellringers going back to 1716: local custom to hang their hats high on inner wall of tower when they died, but none now visible. Crisp wall sculpture by J. Bacon, junr., in memory of Capt. Wm. Hanson, 20th Light Dragoons, of Bromley Hall, killed in action at Villa Franca near end of Peninsular War: tributes include one from Marshal Suchet.

Bromley, Little (11). Chestnuts and yews mark out the churchyard from broad, flat, treeless farmlands. Old red brick emerges at the top of the 15th-century tower, above dark, rusty-looking puddingstone. Gaps in cement-rendering show great lumps of puddingstone in the nave walls, which retain two Norman slit-windows. The timber-framed S. porch encloses painted Georgian royal arms: the S. door bears a prominent graffito: "R.S. 1640". A small Victorian organ in the ringing-chamber (four bells) keeps light from the big W. window out of the church. The 15th-century font is carved with engagingly rustic emblems of the Evangelists. East across the fields, the redbrick, square-built Georgian rectory shelters in a few trees.

Broomfield (6). Seventh-century Anglo-Saxon finds behind *Clobb's Row* in 1890s, linked with Sutton Hoo. Beside the nice narrow Green, the *church* displays its round tower and much red Roman brick among stone that is weathered a strong mustard yellow in nave walls: it's easy to see line of the Norman E. wall before the chancel was extended. Wall monument: Thos. Manwood of *Priors*, 1650, which is an emparked 16th-century farmhouse with exposed timber-framed front and two very tall chimneys. County Architect's delightful little *County Library* be-

LITTLE BROMLEY

side entrance to "Brooklands" a reminder that Broomfield is a suburb of Chelmsford.

Broxted (2), originally Brock's-head, apparently one of those places where in Saxon times a badger's head marked site of heathen sacrifice. *Church* on crest overlooks Chickney, both dominated already, in 1966, by snarl and roar of Stansted planes. Thin 13th-century lancets light cold white interior. Chancel would be better without organ, 15th-century N. aisle without crude modern tester. Monuments to Thos. Bush, 1791, "late of Westminster, who by diligent attention to business acquired an ample fortune", and W. P. (Pussy) Mellen, 1953, an American who stroked the Oxford VIII to victory in 1923, worked in the City of London, was a faithful member of the church choir, and gave *Church Hall* its well-served appearance. *Hill Pastures*, 1936, by Erno Goldfinger and Gerald Flower, converted into prospect house by present owner, D. H. Waterfield with Gerald Flower. Mr Waterfield's delectable garden and Chinese geese are occasionally open to the public.

Buckhurst Hill see Chigwell.

Bulmer (10). Church isolated, perhaps on site of Thunderlow, the hill of Thunor, a god of the early settlers. Impressive exterior, disappointing inside: nave with N. aisle and good Perp. tracery in S. windows. Fourteenth-century choir 45 ft. long, fine but bare-looking. Fifteenth-century font with wild man in panel, involved with a grape vine. Georgian pulpit with inlay. Tablet shows that Mr and Mrs Robert Andrews of Auberies, the subject of one of Gainsborough's sunniest, most halcyon pictures, lived on to be 79 (1806) and 48 respectively, and that they had nine children. At *Auberies*, the Burke family have lived since 1851 and the house now has an early 19th-century character, the hall and fine staircase lit by roof-lantern. The setting of Gainsborough's picture is scarcely changed, though the sap

now runs low in the oak-tree in the sandy patch on which the Andrews' posed: the ground still drops away idyllically to St Peter's, Sudbury, and the park is still arable on the right of the picture. Two ancient cedars house eight red squirrels in 1967.

Bulphan (8), now pronounced Bullv'n, originally the "burg-fen" of Tilbury. Whole church basically *c*. 1500, including stout timber belfry-frame, carved S. porch and traceried screen; screen said to be from Barking. An inscription suggests nave S. wall rebuilt 1687. Victorian timber-clad vestry. Tower tile-hung to commemorate Victoria's diamond jubilee.

Bumpstead, Helions (3) takes its name from its Domesday owner, a Breton called Tihell de Herion. *Boblow Hall* has at each end an Elizabethan red-brick chimney-stack pierced by an attic window: very lonely on ridge in open country, looks across to church on lower ridge. The *church* tower, red-brick, supporting a bell in a very rickety frame, is dated 1812 and part of a general restoration during incumbency of Rev. Thomas Mills. The nave was presumably given its barrel ceiling and clerestory at that time, and the S. aisle its new E. end with pointed windows. Whole interior lately (1967) cream washed: font, pews, arcade, walls, pulpit and adjacent organ. South aisle, cleared of pews, has attractive old brick floor: pamments in nave and chancel. Ugly monument, 1627, to Capt. Tallakarne, slain on disastrous Ile de Rhé expedition: recently daubed.

Bumpstead, Steeple (3). Visual riches spread over rolling farmland once well regarded for its cheeses; also clustered about the church, that stands above a ford. *Church*'s chancel and west tower are both early Norman: nave-aisles thrown out in early and later 15th century. Pleasant early 16th-century red brick in S. porch, clerestory, top of aisle wall and eastern end of upper tower. Within, the boss of the N. chancel door

CHAPPEL

is probably Irish work of the 8th century, with interlace, fishes and jewel-sockets. What is even more extraordinary is that it appears to be being kept polished as though it were any old door-knob. Extensive medieval graffiti include a complete Latin collect for St Erkenwald (possibly late 14th-century) on the E. face of the S. respond of the chancel-arch, and two fine dragons with fragment of music (S. arcade, 2nd pier from E). Aisle-roofs elaborately carved. Bendysh monuments (their house, *Bower Hall*, demolished 1926) include Elizabethan stone panels (divided by Corinthian pilasters) to John, 1585, and forebears of 1523 and 1486: small coffin plate to Sir Thomas, ambassador "from

Charles I" to Sultan Ebrahim Han Then of Turkey, 1647, whence he returned conveniently 1661: Sir Henry, 1717, like Miles Malleson reclining in a Restoration comedy, with infant perched on edge of gadrooned shelf, finely carved, and signed Thos. Stayner of London: Sir John and Dame Martha, with medallion portraits, *c.* 1740, signed J. Pickford and W. Atkinson. Large plain marble sarcophagus, 1834, to nonagenarian member of Gent family, owners for centuries of *Moyns Park*. Plaque says Edith Cavell sometimes worshipped here.

Church set amid old houses, notably *Parsonage Farm* S. of churchyard and *Post Office* across road to E. Cluster extends S. to

small Elizabethan village school-building; what were perhaps seven original timber window-arches run continuously on S.W. and S.E. sides. Schoolmaster was appointed by owner of *Moyns Park*, a grand moated house forming three sides of a quad: S.W. wing, facing into quad, early 16th-century, timber-framed with brick-nogging, much of the brickwork later but very picturesque: at right-angles, but facing outwards, handsome Elizabethan brick wing (stone-dressed) with three bay-windows semi-octagonal as at New Hall, Boreham, tall angular "Midland" gables, and very tall clustered chimney shafts. Of the other houses, *Latchleys* is moated, with Tudor brick bridge, moulded

66

ceiling beams; the pieces of 17th-century tapestry that hung in its most notable room are now in Saffron Walden Museum: *Brickhouse Farm* (1571 on chimneystack) has original bricknogging and shares open landscape with *Lowerhouse Farm*, timber-framed and oversailing: over the slopes towards Sturmer, *Great* and *Little Waltons* are marvellously unspoilt.

Bures, Mount (10). A triangular Belgic tomb, of about the time of Claudius's triumph, was found near the railway S.E. of the church, which stands in a neglected churchyard with neglected great Norman moated castle-mound on N. side. Roger of Poitou held the place in Domesday Book, and later the Sackvilles. Church may well have stood within castle-bailey, but no evidence of that: earthworks on slopes west of church are probably the site of a terraced garden belonging to Hall. Church itself marred by rebuilding of 1875, when it acquired new central tower with *Sussex* broach spire and transepts with quoins built of Roman brick, *looking* like genuine Norman quoins. West end of nave retains Norman and 14th-century features; 15th-century S. porch has carved spandrels and texture of red brick and flint.

Burnham-on-Crouch (16: *see also* Creeksea). Small town on long slope from riverside up to church, fifty feet above, with five miles of coastal marsh to the east that could feed 900 Norman sheep. *Dammer Wick, East Wick*, etc., represent early medieval dairy farms (Wick is Anglo-Saxon for dairy-farm and there is much evidence that mother-ewes provided the milk on these Essex saltings). Fourteenth-century market, disused long ago, presumably held in broad High Street near Charity Schools (1863) with Clock Tower (1877) dumpily reminiscent of the Queen whose jubilee it marks. Opposite, bricks of late Victorian "Standard Tea Warehouse" are moulded in flower-pattern. In those days people came by ferry from Wallasea, Foulness, and the

islands of the Roach archipelago for their provisions. The rivers were encrusted with oyster-beds, the creeks crowded with acres of slow-moving brown canvas of sailing barges. From 1565 the port appeared prominently on lists of Essex shipping. Now the main activity is symbolized by the Royal Corinthian Yacht Clubhouse, very up-to-date when new, 1931. Mid-1960s represented by "The Belvedere", a court of flats in buff and grey brick and the inevitable cliché of white weatherboarding between upper and lower windows: its name derives from the early 19th-century observatory put up by the Oyster Company.
Road climbs gradually from quay, crossing the Southminster branch railway, much as at Wivenhoe. Church, away out in farmyard, is long and low with stone-battlemented south aisles and S. porch in which four late medieval stone shields of arms are well preserved (? Fitzwalter). North porch early-Tudor brick, step-gabled. Interior an agreeable tunnel created by continuous nave and chancel arcades, nine bays and barrel-vaulted plaster ceiling broken only by three pairs of Victorian dormers. Pitch pine pews, with brass candelabra standing like tridents along the aisles.
Compact new school opposite, mostly glazed.

Burstead, Great (9: *see also* Billericay), still pleasantly rural. Stile in corner of churchyard takes an old footpath through on its way down to Barleylands. Timber-tipped spire newly shingled. Very rustic Annunciation in spandrels of N. doorway: medieval door with old stone steps descending to broad, light interior. Textures of masonry and carved oak: in S. aisle, big ancient dug-out chest, traceried 15th-century pews, clothes-pegs under S. window, Georgian wall-monuments, Kempe E. window. Zeppelin L.32 shot down in decisive engagement September 1916, crashed at Snail's Hall farm.
Burstead, Little (9) on S. slope of Broom Hill. Late medieval Essex belfry and shingled spire.

Tudor-brick windows in chancel. Walton family monuments.

Buttsbury (9). Ancient parish now merged with Stock and Ingatestone, its name indefensibly missing from 1-in. O.S. map. Church not far east of Ingatestone Hall, beside stream of Wid. Weatherboarded belfry and porch, and old doors with ironwork, some of it 13th-century. Interior delightfully light: brick floors: small symmetrical 14th-century aisles. With woodland for 500 swine and pasture for 100 sheep, Buttsbury appeared in Domesday Book as Cinga. Its medieval name was, incredibly, Ging-Joyberd-Laundry: present name derives from Botwulf's pear-tree, growing apparently *c*. 1220.

Canewdon (16). "The hill of Cana's people", rising 128 ft. above the Crouch marshes, provides an impressive site for the bold early 15th-century church-tower of grey ragstone that lights up like chalk in the sunshine. Itself 75 ft. high it is said to have served also as lighthouse. Big right-angled buttresses reflect the proportions of the four stages, of which the tall second stage breaks any regularity in the sloping offsets of the buttresses. Shadow-patterns add great interest to the structure, decorated by flintwork checkers and crosses only in the battlements. Porch similarly battlemented.
Arms of Henry V obliterated in central panel over W. door. Oak doors original, and medieval timbers support ringers' chamber. Massive tie-beams and king-posts in nave roof, renewed 1638: red pamment floor. Carved oak pulpit as for a Wren city church: vicar George Walker, also canon of St Paul's, built vicarage here 1758, much altered. Small Georgian Gothick organ. Village cage and stocks, 1775, at the east end of the churchyard. *Hall* 1807, silvery white brick, recessed round arches, moated.
Model village 1960, well designed housing of grey pantiles and Victoria plum brickwork: grouping too rigidly formal for "village". Informal appearance of *Anchor*

CHAPPEL: viaduct

pub, with old roofs at three levels, a hint ignored. *Lambourne Hall*, 15th/16th century, rears red mansard roof-line down towards marshes and *Lion Wharf*.

Canfield, Great (5). Strong sense of Norman Romanesque village below Roman road, large boscy motte with bailey-earthworks of de Vere's castle, in detail one of the best preserved sites of its kind in England and well repaying careful inspection: presumably a subsidiary of Castle Hedingham. Nearby, the *Hall* farm, and the substantial four-square *church*. The Norman S. doorway (in a good 15th-century stone porch) has remarkably exotic capital: two ibises pecking at an oriental head. Pevsner easily persuades us, the eccentric carving in the tympanum represents the Sun.
Impressive interior. Great semi-circular chancel-arch (carved Saxon graveslab used as abacus of *south* respond: R.C. erroneously says north). Through that, triple round-headed reredos, with central madonna and child gracefully delineated in 13th-century red paint. Expressive marble (by Wm. Stanton?) of Sir Wm. Wiseman, 1684 and first wife who died at 23 in 1662. Wiseman brass, 1558.
Canfield, Little (5) straddles Stane Street. To the north of it, the most interesting building is the most inaccessible: a romantic Georgian Romanesque folly called *Stone Lodge*, in a wooded hollow beside the derelict airfield of Little Easton. Appearing already on Chapman and André's map of

1777, it was presumably a cottage ornée of the Maynards in Easton Park. In 1965 it was recovered from dereliction, but unluckily having to submit to the indignity of an added wing in conventional suburban style with diamond-leaded panes. The *facade-principale* is of old brick, with "Romanesque" rounded arched doorway of three orders, three round-headed niches above, and on either side a circular turret rising from the ground in two stages to a conical roof, slated. Each of the two side walls of the building contains a 14th-century stone mullioned window, presumably removed from the parish *church*. This has stone mullions of identical pattern, Victorian copies, perhaps replacing Georgian windows when the church was given its present grand Midland Gothic stone tower and the chancel its new S. and E. walls and decorations by rector-architect, Rev. C. L. Smith, *c.* 1847, under the supervision of Wm. Ollett, junr.

Canvey Island (9) already in Domesday Book partitioned among lords of eight mainland parishes for purposes of sheep-grazing, the boundaries lasting down to our day. In 1607 Camden said it pastured 4,000 sheep, of very delicate flavour. He saw youths, with small stools fastened to their buttocks, milking the ewes and making cheeses in sheds. The whole island is lower than the level of spring tides. In 1622, the main owners agreed with Joos

Croppenburgh that he should have one third of the lands in consideration for his successful reclamation of 3,600 acres. After his day these "third acre" lands were still devoted to the upkeep of sea-walls, and a small distinct Dutch community was still here in the early 20th century.
It is a sensational and evocative descent to the island from Southend highway, past "Roman fortlet" and modern "castle" watertower and Round Hill, where the River Thames swings into view beyond Benfleet Creek. Just over the creek, looking east, one sees Hadleigh castle silhouetted above its low cliff as Constable saw it in one of his smaller pictures now in the Paul Mellon collection. Driving south over the island is exactly, and appropriately, like a drive across Holland, at least till you hit bungalow-dom.
Two charming small colour-washed octagonal thatched cottages survive from Croppenburgh's day, one dated 1618 and now a museum, the other 1621. St Nicholas church, 1960, concrete, is modern "Dutch", roof-line unbroken from ridge to ground. Fifty-four Canvey Islanders were killed in World War II. The Memorial Hall was officially opened on the afternoon of 31 January 1953: the M.P. opening it said it would remind us we are never so great as in adversity. That night the island was submerged. Fifty-eight dead, including eight children. "You should have seen that sea beating into our house in the dark."

CHELMSFORD. The cathedral from the south-east

Much industrial geometry at Deadman's Point.

Chadwell St Mary (8). Originally "cold-well". Extensive ancient chalk-workings ("Dane Holes") here, as at Little Thurrock (q.v.). Small Norman tympanum set in Norman walls above later medieval N. doorway of church. West end of nave rebuilt with 15th-century tower, now dangerously moth-eaten. Early baroque "Discovery of Moses". New public library opposite, well-designed as usual in Essex. Acres of recent housing. *Bennett Lodge* shows good use of traditional materials.

Chappel (10) lies in the broad valley ("pant") of the River Colne, and was originally called Pontesbright. Takes present name as chapelry of Gt. Tey. This it was from at least 1285: apparently it became a parish in 1433. Rightly renowned for the *railway viaduct*, 1847, of thirty arches, noble as anything the Romans themselves contributed to a neighbourhood still profiting by their roads. Houses of high enchantment cluster near little *church* with white-boarded very pointed spire, and enjoy view of Wakes Colne water-mill and church. Georgian S. porch and Royal Arms (1742).

Chelmsford (6). A thoroughfare town, the county town since at least the 13th century, fairly centrally placed on the great Roman way between London and Colchester. Over 50,000 inhabitants, and fast multiplying. Named Caesaromagus by the Romans, the only British town with imperial prefix: apparently a bath-building (of septaria bonded with brick) was uncovered just S.W. of Moulsham Bridge, 1849. The Roman name was conceivably transferred to the river (as Colonia to the river Colne), and back again by the Saxons who settled beside their fords over Chelmer and its confluent here, the River Can. The Can was difficult, and traffic apparently went round by Writtle till *c.* 1100, when the bishop of London, whose town this was, provided the first bridge over it. Present

69

CHELMSFORD. *Shire Hall, 1789–91, by John Johnson*

stone bridge by County Surveyor John Johnson, 1787, combines carriage of traffic with shapeliness: those were the days. Chelmsford prospered on the county's business and the vast through-traffic of cattle and other provisions for London. A watercourse from Burgess Well flowed as an open stream down High Street from a conduit where Chief Justice Tindal now sits, brazen (by E. H. Baily, 1850), among the red and white NO ENTRY traffic-signs.

The bishop got a grant of market here in 1199. John Walker's map of the bishop's manor, 1591, in the Essex Record Office (now one of the town's principal magnets), gives a clear house-by-house bird's-eye view of the market-place stretching south from the churchyard along High Street to

Moulsham Bridge, with the close-built street continuing over the river into *Moulsham* as it still does: buildings down the wedge of the market-place already beginning to form Tindal Street. Chelmer and Blackwater Navigation brought water traffic from coast at Maldon, 1797, with locks and wharves in *Springfield*, much of which was incorporated in the borough. Extensive Napoleonic War barracks and camps (all gone) brought as many as 8,000 troops here. The town was kept to its original shape by surrounding entailed lands of the Mild-mays: their great house in Moulsham demolished *c.* 1816, and entail cut in 1839: New London Road and New Bridge Street at once provided an alternative crossing of the Can, and developed a new suburb. Eastern Counties

Railway opened 1843, crossing W. side of town on a viaduct of 18 brick arches; from it, a double staircase descends to Duke Street. Chelmsford now looks its best from the train; a trimly land-scaped park south of the station, and a well-watered natural golf-course. Its streets, except near the cathedral churchyard (St Mary's became the cathedral of Essex in 1914), no longer seem like those of a county town: decent bustle has given way to desperate motor-traffic much engendered by access of light industries: Marconi, English Electric Valve Co., Hoff-mann's Quality Bearings, etc., whose works one sees from the railway. The streets look better after dark, for even where the outlines remain good, the textures have mostly been spoilt. Exceptions: the cathedral and churchyard, parts of Tindal Street and a fragment of Duke Street, Nos. 72–3, for instance, with twin doorcases, and the Quaker Meeting, now a gym. Tindal Street has qualities of Petty Cury at Cambridge, and is so far less spoilt: Dolphin, Spotted Dog and White Hart are all good, also ironmonger and gunsmith. After the White Hart, an awful gap is inadequately screened next to the newly scrubbed impressive yellow brick Victorian Corn Exchange. John Johnson's Shire Hall is very noble with three fine panels in relief (done in Coade stone by the elder Jn. Bacon): the silvery-grey brick rear of the building (in churchyard) is like very neat flintwork. It adds greatly to the dignity and atmosphere of the "cathedral close". So do two eminent tombs, and two houses in New Street: "Maynetrees" with low Doric portico, and "Guy Harlings", named after a 15th-century brewer, and now the Diocesan Office.

From the south-west, the cathedral shows good touches of red brick in the aisle-end, and the top panels of the porch contrast well with the flushwork and predominantly silvery colour of surrounding brick and stone. Thin rigid needle-spire and lantern, 1749, on 15th-century W. tower, which bears the de Vere mullet and the Bourchier knot in spandrels. A vault was being opened between two S. aisle pillars in January, 1800, and that night the whole late-15th-century nave collapsed. By 1802 it had been rebuilt by the excellent John Johnson. South aisle piers replaced on 15th-century model, but in Coade stone, handsome. Pretty carved and ribbed ceiling by Johnson, lately too prettily painted in pastel shades. Johnson's first idea, to use "Naples or Patent yellow water-colour", would have been seemlier, as well as authentic. Various monuments include a rich sarcophagus, almost oriental in shape, of Thos. and Alice Mildmay, capped by a sort of fluted ogee with Ionic capital and a ball. Memorial to Jn. Pocock Tindal killed at 17 by a cannon-

ball in the moment of Duncan's victory at Camperdown. Beneath it, with central upright skeleton, see the Rudd family, 1615, she in large hat. Earl Fitzwalter (Mildmay), 1756, and Mary Marsh, 1757, both have beautiful urns: his very large, and signed by Jas. Lovell. Outside, Friday market stalls have now ceded most of the open, very un-urban former Market Place to hundreds of parked cars: cars also on the adjoining Bell site. Beside Johnson's stone bridge the area named Barrack Square, from Napoleonic experience, looks more desolate than any military parade-ground (1967). Waste land and shabby buildings dominated by elephantine block in ominously white stone. Over the bridge the W. side of *Moulsham Street* has a battered ancient roof line. St John's Victorian parish church is kept locked "on advice of the police".

In 1899, the first radio factory in the world started production in *Hall Street*: Marconi's. This company has an unbeatable pioneering record, equipping the first ship, lightship, lifeboat and lighthouse that ever carried wireless, as well as the first land wireless-station. Before the B.B.C. was set up, the first programmes in Britain were broadcast from Marconi stations in Writtle and London. A Local Industries Room is a feature of the attractive small *Chelmsford and Essex Museum* established in Oaklands Park, out along Moulsham Street beyond the College of Further Education. Collections include archaeology and natural history as well as the usual by-gones. One of the best single exhibitions is a room full of Castle Hedingham ware. The pictures are mostly antiquarian, including only a couple of good modern paintings. Surely this Museum and Gallery, crammed into a modest suburban house of the 1860s, could with great benefit to Chelmsford and Essex expand into Hylands Park (see Writtle). Farther out, near A12 roundabout, *Moulsham Mill* preserves Georgian dignity beside elaborate gasworks.

Springfield, half in Chelmsford, half out, contains county gaol, 1822 (Thos. Hopper) and 1848, formidable with rusticated entrance and Tuscan detail. Outside the Borough, the *church*, firmly locked, with Norman work in its nave, and its 13th-century font superbly carved with foliage, stands near the Green and three large Georgian houses. *Springfield Place*, immediately E. of the church, is especially striking: its brick front with grand stone doorcase and fan-shaped attic windows in the wings, masks an earlier interior with tall 17th-century chimneys.

Widford, being swallowed by Chelmsford. Small Georgian red brick *Hall* with noble cedar. *Church* rebuilt in 1862 on the site of the old one and at the expense of Arthur Pryor (of Hylands, Writtle): Kentish rag, freestone spire. Massive low stone pyramid in churchyard, to Sarah, Viscountess Falkland, 1776, by Edward Pearce from design by G. Gibson. Fruity Victorian E. window and other Victorian and Edwardian glass.

Chesterford, Great (2). A quiet unmetalled lane runs from Stump Cross on A11, down to Ickleton ford through the River Cam and marks the shire boundary. Chalky fields slope up eastwards. Village nestles in the valley, with remains of Belgic settlement, Roman fort and later Roman town all lying underground N. of village. Town walls quarried away for road-making. Dull over-restored church, but stone tablet outside S. door bears unduly severe Elizabethan inscription: "How dreadful is this place (Genesis, 28)". Sixteenth-century roof timbers of S. aisle richly carved, a chantry-chapel, endowed by Wm. and Katherine Holden. Beside the churchyard, a green-washed medieval house with corner-post is pargeted 1672. *Crown and Thistle* with noble chimney-shafts is pargeted with frieze, apparently 1825 copy of 17th-century work. Boring new housing in Jacksons Lane. **Chesterford, Little** (2). Travellers on A11 admire embowered group of Manor house and church just east of the road. A tarred old pigeon-house stands north of the very remarkable *Manor house*, which presents two gables to the south. The E. wing, with stone walls three feet thick, is the early 13th-century house, with offices below and hall above reached by an outside stair. Early in the 14th century, the house was given a timber-framed extension and converted into a hall-house with screens passage on the conventional later medieval tripartite plan; except that an aisle was created on the S. side, and two fine posts of this still rise from floor to roof. The solar wing at the west end is perhaps a 15th-century development, with immense floorboards. The last major contribution was Elizabethan, the horizontal division of the great hall, and creation of bed-chamber on the first floor, one with a nice frieze-cornice of the period.

Thirteenth-century *church* with a round-headed Perp. window added on N. side of chancel. Perp. screen. Very good sample of early 19th-century timber benches in choir and nave. Scant memorials of inhabitants of the Manor house. Brass of 1462. Neglected monument shows James Walsingham, who died *aet.* 82 in 1728, as a young man reclining with a book (book now broken). Erected by his sister, and signed by the sculptor Henry Cheere.

Chesterford Park is the Edwardian Jacobean seat of Fisons Pest Control.

Chickney (2). The church is approached from the east through picturesque old farm buildings of the Hall, itself redesigned 1935 with a dispirited curved "Dutch" gable at the south end. A pyramidal roof caps the 14th-century church tower. Rest of fabric East Saxon and very erratic in plan. Interior tremendously atmospheric and unspoilt, with brick floors, rustic crownpost roof, rich 14th-century font. Early 19th-century altar-rails before *stone altar*. Handsome plain Georgian pulpit. *Sibleys Farm*, with medieval timber frame and Elizabethan newel

stair, has a dove-house in the front garden: nice tiles and plaster. Doves now nest beside the medieval barn.

Chignall (6), two old parishes joined, 1888. Chignall *St James's* church attractively grouped above small terrace of clapboard cottages. Tudor brick S. windows. Interior boring. Old part of Hall nicely plastered, goes back to 1552, the work of "John Masan" according to rough inscription. At Chignall *Smealy* the little church makes an impression from having tower, nave, chancel and vestry of diapered Tudor brickwork. Very convincing broad N. aisle facsimile added 1847, with 2-bay brick arcade. Aisle plastered: rest of interior stripped; original Tudor screen and S. door. Very unconvincing timber-framed house west of the church. Away to the east, *Broomwood*, an essay in traditional "Essex" by F. Rowntree for the Essex antiquary Miller Christy, is now the home of Lord Ironside.

Chigwell (7) is best approached along Roding Lane, off B170 from Buckhurst Hill. You then arrive calmly at the church through an avenue of chestnuts and limes. Copper spire and clapboard belfry. The externals are 19th-century, S. wall stucco, and the old church was doubled over the site of the former N. aisle in 1886. So it's a surprise to be confronted by the tall Norman S. doorway, and to find the impressive timber-frame of a 15th-century Essex tower within. Roof of former nave crowded with decorative funeral hatchments. High-backed pulpit and décor of Victorian chancel, Bodley's work. Rich "adoration" in N. window by Kempe. The chancel arch was rebuilt in 1886 in a form that suggests that the original may have been a triple 14th-century arcade of the same type as Stebbing's. The splendid and famous brass of Archbishop Harsnett, 1631, is absurdly set on the wall in a corner too dark, and anyway too high, to be seen.

Old King's Head, opposite church, has "Dickens Hall" in 1901 wing,

but the 17th-century front with five irregular gables above two storeys, each jettied, remains impressive, and two old weatherboarded cottages to the west have been incorporated. The fine panelling, fireplace and piers of the first-floor restaurant have been coated in an unseemly toffee colour. Famous for pigeon-pie in Dickens' day, the place features as the Maypole in *Barnaby Rudge*. South of the church, *Chigwell Hall*, Norman Shaw, 1876, is now used by the Metropolitan Police. North of the church, the village-street atmosphere of an earlier age survives – the Grammar School Archbishop Harsnett founded, with its original school-room, and the pleasant sash-windowed house added at right-angles by the headmaster, Peter Burford, in 1776, now with large rear extension of 1871. Then almshouses, houses, cottages and shops in various pleasant styles with white fences to road.

Farther along, *Grange Farm* is a Camping and Sports Centre run by Chigwell U.D.C. North of it, *Tailours* is one of the prosperous Georgian houses that distinguish the place. At the corner, by the nursery-garden, is the melancholy ruin of *Rolls Park*, the seat of Captain Eliab Harvey, one of Nelson's band of brothers. The Georgian stables have been converted to a bungalow. The house *c.* 1600 with several extensions, including a room of beautiful rococo plastered walls, is mostly open to the sky. Two garden seats are alleged to be of timber from Harvey's fighting *Temeraire*. *Woolston Hall*, built by the Scott family *c.* 1600 and improved by them over the next two centuries, has particularly fine early Georgian wrought iron gates. *Turnours*, with early 17th century features, is fronted by extraordinary Victorian moulded brick.

Buckhurst Hill divided from the mother parish by the green finger of the Roding valley, is now acres of commuters' houses rising to a ridge of the ancient Waltham Forest, ridge marked by ragstone spire of St John's (1875) and ragstone Congregational tower.

CLACTON Pier and fishermen

Ninety acres of Forest still at Lords Bushes.

Chigwell Row runs E. for a mile and a half from Grange Hill Station on the new Central Line loop. The road was originally laid out along the northern edge of Hainault Forest at the expense of Admiral Sir Edward Hughes (1717–94), whose engagements with the French are depicted in six pictures by Dominic Serres in Ipswich Town Hall and whose Chigwell house, *Luxborough*, was pulled down soon after his death. By 1844 Chigwell Row had "many handsome mansions with beautiful pleasure-grounds", mostly occupied by London merchants. Chigwell Row Races, the first Tuesday in August, the course was "thronged with genteel company". All that is being replaced now by modern housing and flats, denser, but not all unattractive. For instance, Stanley Keen has designed blocks of flats at High View in good ochre-coloured brick.

Loughton has formed part of Chigwell U.D. since 1933, but see separately.

Childerditch (8) one of a group of ancient parishes planned in north–south oblongs to share southern flat-lands and steep slopes in the north. As a result of recent local-government reshaping, Childerditch is not even named on 1964 edn. of 1-in. O.S. map. Anyway, it is named by Edward Thomas:

"If I should ever by chance
grow rich
I'll buy Codham, Cockridden
and Childerditch."

(Cockridden's nearby in E. Horndon, Codham in Gt. Warley.) Church, high up, rebuilt 1869, with carved Tudor font given by Jhon and Ceceli Throsscher.

Chrishall (1). In wide, high undulating country of great open fields Chrishall occupies a long narrow strip, $4\frac{1}{2}$ miles from Roughway Wood in the south (458 ft. up, probably the highest point in Essex!) to the north where the Grange's curved brick gables, of *c.* 1700, look down the slopes to Cambridge. The village clusters round the former Green. The *church* appears boldly on its ridge beside Park Wood, which has on its south side a moated earthwork, 40 ft. in diameter, with a broken rampart round the *outer* rim. The church tower, of *c.* 1300, rises from N. and S. aisles of *c.* 1400. Brasses include good effigies of Sir John de la Pole and wife, Joan de Cobham, *c.* 1375, hand in hand.

Clacton (Great Clacton, Clacton-on-Sea and Little Clacton) (14). Clactonian man, living between two glacial periods perhaps 400,000 years ago, made some of the earliest flint tools, giving their name to a whole "culture". Almost more curious, a yew-spear has survived as well.

Great Clacton, a medieval market-village, had nothing but three Napoleonic Martello Towers at "Clacton Cliffs" as late as 1862, with an Inspector of Towers, battery-keeper and three guns "ready for mounting"! Clacton-on-Sea emerged in the '70s: Promotion "Sale-plan" 1871, Royal Hotel with 1st-floor balcony along front, 1872. Next year the pier. The Prom, bolstered by Kentish ragstone, was all done between March and September 1889, by Clacton-on-Sea Commissioners. The Pier Pavilion was added in the '90s (by Kinipple and Jaffrey), marked now by a series of glossy turrets that altogether fail to suggest the Pavilion's name; the "Blue Lagoon". Additions of the 1930s include a Scenic Railway: at low tide one sees a forest of

LITTLE COGGESHALL: Watermill

stilts supporting an agreeable complex of sea-side shapes. And fishermen continue to haul their nets up on to shallow sand-and-shingle beach alongside.

A graceful concrete pedestrian bridge crosses the approach to the pier. Some older sea-front buildings (e.g. Ramsey Court) are themselves fronted by rows of "neo" Dutch gables, their stiff shape peculiar to the place. At right angles to the sea, Albany Gardens is grouped round a pleasant long pinetum, Lancaster Gardens round a long strip of firs. "Moot Hall", reconstructed from a medieval barn at Hawstead, Suffolk, with brick-nogging, persists in looking out of place, despite the determined reference to Aldeburgh Moot Hall. Crossley House, grown with euonymus, is a distinguished large

sea-side house of two low storeys and curly bargeboards. To the south, Marine Parade curves round a Martello Tower emplacement. Beyond, the recent building, with lovely views of the sea, is deplorably un-seaside in design. Then Butlin's two great wheels; the Martello Tower on the golf course, which ends with the huddled shackery of Jaywick.

Great Clacton. The Maltings, St John's House and the Queen's Head preserve the bones of the 18th-century village just south of the great church. The *church* (Norman, with 14th-century chancel, 15th-century tower) is imposing in size and for its interior sense of space. The outside is of camel-coloured septaria with hard red brick Victorian quoins and window-arches replacing the Norman (Roman) brickwork: a stone

frieze curves over the tall S. doorway. At close quarters one sees the mortar-joints of the septaria walls still stuck with bits of flint: this "galleting" protected the mortar, was not meant to "key" an overall plaster-coat. The interior is white plastered. Big round chancel-arch. Again, too-red bricks from 1865 over-restoration. Well carved font.

Little Clacton. Church, plastered, with cream weatherboard belfry, in pleasant old-fashioned churchyard, with none of the architectural pretensions of Gt. Clacton, has much more charm for the traveller and, presumably, for the parishioner. Rustic medieval S. porch. Square late-Norman Purbeck font. Brick floors. Nice modern low box pews. Large organ and Victorian Commandments at W. end. Flourishing

Royal arms, 1726, painted and framed. Two small Victorian grisaille crucifixion scenes in nave window, like sepia transparencies.

Clavering (2), pronounced Clavering, and meaning clover field. The English apparently managed their politics before the Norman Conquest without building castles, except here and in Herefordshire and at Dover. The castle here was not much of an exception, for its builder, Robert Fitz Wimarc, a Frenchman (Breton) who anticipated the Conquest, served both Edward the Confessor and William the Conqueror as Sheriff of Essex. There may be substance in the dramatic legend that the Confessor was present at the dedication of the church here, gave his ring to a beggar, and had it returned to him (by two pilgrims back from the Holy Land) with the news that in six months he would die "and join St John".

North of the church, impressive moats of the *castle* survive in a crook of upper Stort, which was perhaps given these great banks to feed a mill-pond as well as moats. In 1768, stone walls existed "not long since". Village shaped round castle-site. Two especially attractive contrasting houses in the short lane running down to the church beside a great pink-flowered chestnut. One, with a rather grand Queen Anne brick front of red stretchers and black headers, earlier plastered rear and 17th-century wall-paintings, nevertheless has a small shop built into side.

The *church* is remarkable in being all of a piece, 15th-century, and very East Anglian in atmosphere and detail. Tower, clerestory, aisles and porch are embattled to repel the assaults of the Devil. Inside, the low pitched roofs are defended by large carved angels, still at their posts though they have lost their wings: very notable and good oak bosses in south aisle. Some original glass is in the windows, but jumbled. Original traceried screen, too, slightly dilapidate, with painted outlines of saints in three panels. Legless early 13th-century knight in Pur-

beck marble; brasses; large ledger-slabs (Bansons of Brent Green); small marble to Rev. John Smith, pastor, 1616; and three busts of Barlee family, one of them, 1747, very calm in black and white marble.

Codham *see* Gt. Warley and Wethersfield.

Coggeshall, Great (6). Evidence of Roman occupation has been found both at *Highlands*, a tall house of *c*. 1600 with Georgian front, ½ mile W. of the medieval town, and at the S.W. corner of churchyard. From the usual agricultural beginnings, the town used its natural advantages to become one of the half-dozen leading Essex cloth-making towns of the later Middle Ages. A stream flowed down Church Street into the upper Blackwater, which runs behind all the houses along the south side of Stane Street and which turned a fulling mill at Stock Street as late as 1777. The will of Thomas Peaycocke, 1580, whose brass effigy survives in the church, gives an idea of the bustle of Elizabethan Coggeshall: he left money to "thirty of the poorest journeymen Fullers" in the town. This Thomas lived next door (now the *Fleece Inn*) to the famous house *Paycocks* built by (presumably) his great-uncle Thomas, who died 1518. Heavily restored in the 20th century by the Noel Buxtons, who succeeded the Paycocks here in the 17th century, it remains one of the best examples in England of leading clothier's house at that trade's most prosperous moment. Now owned by National Trust. The red brick-nogging has been renewed in the front, but there are magnificently carved timbers, inside and out. Authentic small secular figure either side of the cartway at east end of front.

No less than 97 secular buildings listed by the Royal Commission, which does not include some of the most attractive Georgian and later buildings that greet you at the Colchester end of East Street. Market Hill leads off to the north. Here Stoneham Street leads left

past attractive hexagonal clap-boarded clock-tower and watch-bell (? 17th century) which seems to have survived the demolition of the market-cross in 1787 and been restored in honour of Victoria's golden jubilee. Terrible wirescape. Church Street goes to the right, with many old buildings, the best of them the *Woolpack Inn* at the end on the left just before the church. It has a 15th-century 2-storey central hall, with crown-post roof. Before this, on the same side, Vain Lane (? taking its name from the 1736 text on the corner-house: "Except the Lord build the house"), leads to house with good Restoration carving (fireplaces) in Back Lane.

Church tower and nave were practically destroyed by a bomb from a lone German raider on 16 September 1940: lovely slender S. arcade and clerestory (and chancel) survived. All now repaired and rebuilt under Mr S. Dykes Bower, who has taken the opportunity to abolish the clutter of Victorian pews and restored the sense of space from floor to roof-timbers that one associates with cool white-washed Protestant Dutch interiors: appropriately, for this was a Puritan centre.

East of the town, *Houchins Farm*, *c*. 1600, a familiar top-heavy sight to travellers along Stane Street, is three storeys high, with each upper storey exuberantly oversailing. Back in town where Market Hill meets Stane Street, new timbered shops are ominously ill-adjusted to the old building-line. Opposite, a triangular site flanked by *The Gravel* is the site of the Tudor shambles. There is an old established isinglass business. Tambour lace was made here from the early 19th century. Where The Gravel joins Bridge Street, Short Bridge marks the boundary with –

Coggeshall, Little (6) approached over Long Bridge, a rebuilding of 1705 incorporating many of the early medieval bricks that are perhaps the most remarkable feature of Little Coggeshall Abbey. *Rood House*, built on the north-east side of bridge, may commemorate a crucifix cast down "in the highway by Coxhall" in 1532. South-west of the bridge two large sub-urban houses have lately been built, while the superb medieval barn (abbey grange) continues neglected.

Founded by Stephen in 1140, *the abbey* soon became Cistercian, and like all Cistercian ruins these beside Blackwater, with a nearby water-mill, are utterly idyllic. The outlying gate-chapel has a font, and may have competed with Great Coggeshall church. An abbot secured a market and fair for the town, and presumably Cistercian sheep-grazing underlay the town's textile enterprise. The abbey church is gone, but the Abbot's lodging survives, con-nected by a corridor to the 1581 house of a husband of a Paycock. To the south, the abbey's small guest house was built *c.* 1190 with bricks specially made for the job, among the earliest that are cer-tainly known to have been made after Roman times.

Colchester (13) advertises itself as a town of rose-growing, oyster-eating boiler-makers, also as "Britain's Oldest Recorded Town". This carefully-worded greeting at all the approaches can give no idea of the extraordinary visual pleasure, the immense sense of historic continuity into the present that is peculiar to the very lively character of the place. The High Street, now an abysmal one-way torrent of motor-traffic, runs along the spine of a major hill-top town of the Roman Empire. The actual surface of the Roman road beneath can be seen in profile in the basement-bar of the George Hotel. The steep ascents to High Street by East Hill and by North Hill (from the railway station and main-road by-pass at the level of the Colne river below) had ob-vious defensive value. But no one can be entirely prepared for the sight of the majestic Norman castle in its open grounds beside the High Street, at the head of East Hill. Only the keep survives, and that severely reduced in height: it was the largest keep ever built in Europe. In plan it is half as big again as the White Tower, in London. And it was

founded upon the vaults of the great temple of Claudius's victory in A.D. 43.

These vaults may (and should) be seen, for the castle and the adjacent Georgian town-house, Hollytrees, now form the town-museum. The collections of Roman finds housed on the first floor of the keep, imaginatively presented and linked with the topography of the streets and adjoining countryside, bring one as nearly as possible into touch with the Roman *colonia*.

The invading Romans naturally headed for this place in 43, be-cause from Camulodunum, the widely fortified Iron Age settle-ment on the lower slopes to the west, Cunobelin (Shakespeare's Cymbeline) had ruled the whole of south-east Britain during the last two decades of Christ's life and the following decade. The 1-inch Ordnance Survey map shows clearly long lines of earthen ramparts and dykes that still run fairly continuously from Colne river in the north to Roman river in the south, protecting the whole W. side of Camulodunum (it means "fortress of Camulos", Celtic god of war). Hut-sites were found when the by-pass was building in the 1930s, near the Sheepen Farm, in the area of Technical College and Sussex Road. Out at Gosbeck's Farm, Shrub End, they had a great temple, where a remarkable figure of Mercury emerged, and where a timber D-shaped theatre is being excavated in 1967. In Lexden, a suburb now purged by motor-traffic, a tumulus still visible in Fitzwalter Road yielded in 1924 gravegoods so rich that they might conceivably have been those of Cunobelin himself.

After the conquest, the Romans soon found London made a better capital than Colchester. In 49/50 they created the town on the hill-top as their first *colonia*, a sort of military depot and settlement for ex-servicemen, uncannily antici-pating part of its modern role. Tacitus wrote of its theatre, Senate House, public statues and a great temple. This was presum-ably the shrine to Claudius's vic-

tory. Its mortar can hardly have hardened when, in Nero's day, the Iceni of N.W. Suffolk and S.W. Norfolk attacked under their Queen Boudicca, besieged the temple two days, killed the op-pressive Romans and destroyed the town.

Boudicca having been dealt with, the Colonia rose again. Great surrounding walls were added, probably in the late 2nd century. They still mark the outline of the old town. Within them the street-pattern, too, survives, though it lies buried under trim municipal turf N. of the castle-keep, and though the High Street originally continued due W. through the Balkerne Gate and made for London. Sometime at the end of the Roman occupation the Bal-kerne Gate was "closed to through-traffic". The London road was deflected to the Head Gate (the name already in 1086 given to the south gate, reflecting its importance). But the Balkerne Gate itself survives, a little old pub perched on one side, as romantic a ruin in its way as, say, the Porta di Nola at Pompeii; best seen from the E. side, though more complete effect of whole great gate preserved on W. side. The name Colonia, too, survives, in that of the River Colne, and so in "Colchester", the Saxon word for "fortress on the Colne".

The historian of Colchester, draw-ing proper attention to the stone and bronze sphinxes, the cen-turion's monument and cavalry officer's tombstone (both found in Beverley Road), the Colchester Mercury and the Colchester Vase (showing gladiators and hunts-men), adds that the most ordinary objects from Roman Colchester in the Castle Museum are made impressive by their numbers: "The cases of lamps, toys, brooches, cooking-pots, beakers and even coffins suggest a well-stocked de-partment store strangely trans-ported in time." (Colchester has, perhaps naturally, been fortunate in its historians: Morant in the 18th cent., J. H. Round in the 19th, Geoffrey Martin in our own.)

A Saxon borough was established before the Norman conquest. It embraced Lexden, Berechurch, Greenstead and Mile End. Early in the 10th century, Edward the Elder had the town walls repaired. Late in the 11th, towards end of his reign, William the Conqueror ordered the building of a vast stone keep, on the lines of the White Tower but bigger – presumably as a bastion to daunt E. Anglia, whose two capitals, Norwich and Ipswich, had been largely reduced to ruins at the time of Domesday Book. Colchester, by contrast, flourished to the point of being occasionally referred to as "civitas" – city. It probably had about 450 houses throughout the critical years from 1066 to 1086. No less than 276 Colchester people are actually named in Domesday Book,

p. 78
*COLCHESTER:
St Botolph's Priory,
the nave*

p. 79
*COLCHESTER:
William the
Conqueror's Keep
The dome is Georgian*

among them 7 priests; Leofleda, a woman, was possibly the wealthiest of the townsfolk. The names are mostly English, and, as Round wrote, "lingered long among the fields and copses after fashion had banished them" from the font. Seven priests conceivably imply 7 churches. St Peter's was named. Trinity was certainly already built.

After Domesday, Eudo the Dapifer (the king's steward) was entrusted with the castle. In 1096 he founded St John's abbey just S. of the town. About 1110, not to be outdone, priests of the nearby small community of St Botolph sent three of their number abroad; they came back with "St Augustine's rule", to re-found St Botolph's as the first English house of regular Augustinian canons. Meanwhile Eudo built, or rebuilt, St Helen's chapel, W. of the castle (Maidenburgh Street). From Richard I the town acquired its first charter of self-government, 1189.

By 1300, St Peter's church had acquired the splendid ironwork of its S. door, wrought apparently by Thomas of Leighton Buzzard, who made the grille for Queen Eleanor's tomb at Westminster. By then, Colchester cloth had made a name for itself: town set on modern career of industry. Castle already sunk to function of county gaol. Friars came in 13th century – Grey (Franciscan) to East Hill, Crouched (taking name from Cross, or Crutch and giving it to Crouch Street) to W. of town at corner of Maldon Road. By the 15th century there were sixteen parish churches – as there were in the 18th century when Chapman and André drew their beautiful map of the town: eight within the walls, four without,

COLCHESTER: St John's Abbey gatehouse

and four in the four villages of the borough.

The medieval cloth-industry decayed in Henry VIII's reign. In Colchester it got great infusion of new life under Elizabeth I. About 500 Flemish refugees (known as "Dutch") were settled here by 1573, skilled in making of "New Draperies" – bays and says. Dutch company disbanded 1728, but their "Dutch Bay Hall" was replaced by a Corn Exchange (the present Essex & Suffolk Fire Office) only in 1820. One result of this beneficial incursion has been the labelling of an area of Stockwell Street "the Dutch quarter"; another, the modern popular fallacy attributing to "Flemish weavers" the whole local cloth industry, going back to the 13th century, with mills and wealth and timber-framed houses. Another result was the strengthening of local Puritanism and nonconformity. Several large late-Stuart and early-Georgian houses still give a strong flavour of the centre of Colchester. By the 1760s they were owned by the Tory Creffeild-Gray family, later by the Round family (notably Hollytrees) and by the Whig Rebows (Headgate and Wivenhoe) – all of them inheriting money and blood of leading 17th-century Flemish family called Tayspill. The Minories, an attractive house above East Hill, was remodelled as late as 1776 by Thomas Boggis, successful baymaker.

Civil War and plague made heavy marks on Colchester. Town Parliamentarian, but ironically, in 1648, a Royalist army of 3,000 heading N. had among its leaders Sir Charles Lucas, whose family home had been at St John's Abbey since soon after Dissolution. Fairfax's army caught them resting in town, encircled and besieged them for 10 summer weeks, surrounding town's defences with rings of batteries and siege-works, battering and starving them to

COLCHESTER: East Stockwell Street　　　*COLCHESTER: West Stockwell Street* ☞

COLCHESTER: Mile End, from North Hill

submission. St John's House was wrecked, and the vault of the abbey-gatehouse is still scarred; St Botolph's famous Romanesque priory-front was fractured, and its church, parochial since Reformation, was now left in ruin. "Siege House" at East Bridge owes its scratches to Royalist fire from the town, but Greenstead church, centre of a Parliamentarian fort, owes prominent wound on *north* side of tower presumably to counter-attack against sortie carrying Royalists briefly out on to this ridge. In the W., St Mary's church, a Royalist watchtower and strongpoint, was shattered. Along S. side of town, Scheregate and the adjacent houses are all that survive from before the siege. The mound in St John's abbey

grounds is said to mark an even grimmer visitation. Apparently, over 4,000 townspeople died of the plague in 1665–6. No wonder several open spaces still characterized the map of Colchester in 1825. "Native" oysters have always been partial to estuaries and creeks flowing over cold "London clay" (Harwich to Margate). Colchester got control of the Colne fishery after the 14th century: modern methods of oyster-culture probably go back to the early 18th century, organized dredger-men to the early 19th. Oyster-ceremonies and feasts for the mayor and corporation go back at least to 1667; the more lavish beanos with distinguished visitors started about 1845. Railway arrived from London in 1843.

With engineering established (Davey, Paxman and Co. began in Culver Street in 1865, moved to the Hythe, "Standard Ironworks", in 1872) and with a permanent military garrison (1856), the population doubled from 17 to 34 thousand in the half-century 1841–91. (It has not quite doubled again since 1891.) Cant's famous nurseries were established in St John's Street in 1766. From a gift of French roses, 1853, Ben Cant developed hybrid perpetual and tea roses that have brought the town as much réclame as her oysters. He moved rosary to Mile End, 1879; defecting nephew Frank to Braiswick 1875. The great thing about Colchester's 19th-century commercial and industrial expansion is that it did

82

not involve the destruction or even blighting of large parts of old town. Paxman's moved away from the centre. Even the ancient Grammar School moved out (to Lexden Road). Roman Road and Castle Road are good central residential developments of the 1850s, but most new housing spread outside, especially to S., and the heart of the town remained habitable as well as serviceable, with commercial and public buildings. University of Essex began in 1961: *see* Wivenhoe.

Out on the *Mersea Road*, beyond the abbey wall, evergreens give the Victorian cemetery an uncannily Roman look on a hot, sunny day. *Roman wall:* well worth following right round town, about 1¾ miles' walk. If that is too long, bits to visit are *Balkerne Gate* (just west of Head Street and Jumbo, the ponderous folly erected as water-tower 1882, the year a Barnum and Baily elephant of that name was in the news): the long stretches beside Priory Street and Vineyard Street (exposed by clearance for car-parks: as lately as 1965 some very urban "rookeries" backed on to the wall on the Eld Lane side, visible from Vineyard Street): much septaria in the walls as well as flint and red brick and white valerian: bastions in this

stretch thought to be 14th-century additions: one is topped by a Georgian brick summerhouse: E. end of St James's churchyard on East Hill (the East Gate was just below this): and finally the long low stretch below the castle park, along the N. side. Looking from here towards the castle keep, notice the graceful bandstand on a slight eminence: immediately beneath it, lies a dividing wall between two Roman courtyard-houses: a built-up Roman street ran past present bandstand entrance.

Castle-keep started as single storey, its battlements and whitish Barnack-stone dressings still embedded in wall-surfaces when they later advanced to four storeys. Its total grimness hard to imagine since it was reduced to two in 1680s. Quoins of upper ranges marked by Roman brick, glinting red. Upper walls themselves are a warm clay-colour from predominant local stone, septaria. Large bow projects at S. end of E. front: provided apse for chapel up on 2nd-floor level. Chapel probably had arcade and ambulatory as in White Tower. Prominent turret W. of entrance contains main staircase under red Georgian roof. Outer works of castle mostly gone, though bailey imposed kink in

straight Roman line of High Street.

St Botolph's Priory. Magnificent fragment of W. front, of grimy rubble, sand-coloured freestone, and red re-used Roman brick, fashioned into triple portals (the N. one almost gone) surmounted by two horizontal tiers of interlaced arcading; the brick marvellously adapted to Romanesque use, recapturing a true echo of Rome. These tiers in turn surmounted by (surviving half of) the earliest large round window in England. Two storeys of round-arch nave ruins, again quoined and dressed in red brick, are frequented by pigeons: seen from the north, they resemble some aqueduct in Rome. Later medieval window-tracery suggests use of N. aisle by parish. From Dissolution to disastrous bombardment of 1648 this was the principal town church.

St John's Abbey. Very grand 15th-century gatehouse, dressed in sophisticated flint-flushwork, survived Dissolution and 1648 bombardment. Even now has rural setting at upper corner of a Green, with small brick cottage, 1823 Gothick, standing deferentially below. A tall central gateway is combined with features of a broad church-porch and an angle-buttressed church-tower.

Streets. East Hill (and High Street east of the castle) includes several handsome houses: *Hollytrees*, housing the Museum's post-medieval exhibits and Essex Archaeological Society's fine working library; *The Minories*, art-gallery, ideal setting for Georgian furniture and pictures (including work by Constable, who knew, and drew, the town), very attractive Georgian Gothick summerhouse-folly in garden beside main Bus Park; *the Gatehouse*, refronted and plastered *c.* 1680, next to Hollytrees, and much good Georgian work down the hill; 17 is timber-framed with medieval door; the road broadens on W. side of river to East Bay, with *Bay Cottage* and Y.H.A. Hostel beside a Green; East Street across river, a medieval suburb, includes *Siege House*, the *Welcome Sailor*

COLCHESTER: Garrison chapel, 1856

Bourne Mill, COLCHESTER

with remarkable roof, and picturesque large timber-framed *Rose and Crown*.

High Street. Impressively broad, it contained the medieval market, also church of St Runwald till 1878 traffic-clearance. (St Nicholas's lost through disuse, 1955, and replaced by Co-op.) High Street Victorian in feeling, with one good three-storeyed medieval timber-framed survivor, the *Red Lion*. The dominant building is the *Town Hall* (1899–1902, designed by Sir John Belcher) on the site of a Norman building destroyed in 1843; its fine neo-baroque corner-tower, Victoria Tower, dominates even Jumbo, and holds the figure of St Helena aloft to see over surrounding Essex and half-way to Jerusalem, which she faces. Tip of her cross 162 feet above the pavement. This tower was the gift of Alderman

James Paxman, who successfully exhibited engines in London international exhibition, 1872. The main façade bears statues of mixed company: Archbishop Harsnett, who left the town his books and was opposed to all Puritanism; and Boudicca, who reduced the town to ashes that can still be found under Jacklin's café, and Curry's shop, just across road from town hall. Nearby, on the N.W. corner of the street, the *Fire Office* brings the taste of Regency London to town: designed in 1820 by David Laing, it has a Doric colonnade of cast-iron. Round the corner, *North Hill*: like East Hill, it has tremendous character, very Georgian, beginning with the red-brick tower of St Peter's. Good details on both sides running down to cattle market, river (footpath to Middle Mill), and small medieval

suburb ("middleborough"). Just east of town hall, *East and West Stockwell Streets*, two delightful narrow streets sloping down north from High Street, with medieval timber-framed and Georgian brick houses, lively witness to town council's policy of restoring and maintaining old houses. Beyond lies open country, Kingswood Heath. The rural view of Stockwell from back of Cullingford's printing works is truly astonishing: pantiled farm buildings and un-urban trees a few steps from the High Street and the Red Lion. *Scheregate and Trinity Street*, on S. side of old town, should not be missed. Scheregate is an ancient postern (subsidiary) gateway, a pedestrian passage, with steps, through the wall: owes its picturesqueness to the medieval timber-framed house built over it, and to the congeries of old houses

84

at its approaches: medieval corner-post at corner of St John's Street (and a neat row of recent shops, 1967), 17th-century plasterwork and roofs, and above all, the pedestrian bustle proper to towns that keep motor-traffic in perspective. Across St John's Street, notice the "carpenter's Gothick" of Scheregate Hotel, especially its windows. In Trinity Street, immediately west of the church, the beautiful Georgian brick house on site of one where John Wilbye (great madrigalist, 1574–1638) lived in the household of Countess Rivers. Immediately south, "Tymperleys", a large late-medieval house, was the home of the scientist who founded the study of electro-magnetism, William Gilberd (1540–1603: try to see his epitaph in Trinity church): house seen from Trinity Street through a gateway of handsome Georgian red brick.

Churches.
All Saints, opposite castle, 14th-century W. tower. Now a slightly dispiriting Natural History Museum. *St Botolph.* "1837 Romanesque" in lifeless white brick, so clumsily lumped alongside the great priory-church that one could wish it away. Nor does a life-size allegory of Hope, 1854, redeem it. *Holy Trinity*, disused 1952 but not secularized. Work of repair stopped in August 1965 for want of decision about use. Visitors are now (early 1968) greeted by a porch-floor deep in bird-lime and by locked doors. Unable to see the elegant S. aisle arcade and the monuments, we can still enjoy externals and setting. Tall Saxon tower with rich Roman red-brick dressings, including Romanesque flushwork arcading below belfry, well seen on S. and E. sides: W. wall has triangular-headed doorway, a purely Saxon shape. Date perhaps *c.* 1000. West wall of nave even earlier than tower. Fifteenth-century mazer (hard-wood) bowl, now in Castle Museum. *St Giles's*, now a depot of St John's Ambulance, originally intended for laymen attached to St John's abbey. Early Tudor brick N. chapel and S. porch. Elizabethan "Dutch"

used it. Here lie the shot Royalist siege-leaders, Lucas and Lisle, in N. chapel. Nave-arcade and W. gallery of 1819. *St Helen's Chapel*, in Maidenburgh Street, is now a Museum-store. Fabric 13th-century, earlier foundations under N. wall, presumed Norman (? or Roman). *St James the Great*'s black flintwork E. wall, parapeted, rises incautiously above reduced Roman wall on East Hill: part of the grand rebuilding of chancel and chancel-chapels *c.* 1500: fine effect inside, and effect of whole building splendid from by-pass below. Norman S.W. corner of nave, the rest of which developed later. Clerestory and aisle windows 1871, pleasantly tree-shaded. Monument showing Arthur Winsley informally dressed in 1727 cost him £250. His almshouses, off Old Heath Road, he gave for "twelve ancient men that have lived well and fallen into decay". *St James the Less* (R.C.), Priory Street, 1837 by J. J. Scoles, contemporary with St Botolph's, inevitably "Norman". *St John's Ipswich Road*, 1862, early work of Arthur Blomfield. *St Martin's*, since 1958 a hall for plays and concerts. In 1968 picturesque but neglected, behind chestnut trees down W. Stockwell Street. It has a ruined late-Norman tower. The limit of the original narrow Norman N. aisle is marked by brick quoins in the W. wall of the early Perp. aisles which curiously do not *quite* swallow early Perp. transepts. Much red Roman brick, and timber-framing on N. side, create very homely texture. This church decayed after the 17th century. Dec. (early 14th-century) chancel, crossed by splendid timber archbraced tie-beam with traceried spandrels reaching to central boss from which crown-post rises with four-way struts. *St Mary Magdalen* (Magdalen Street, on road to Hythe) began as chapel to Norman leper-hospital, final rebuilding 1853. *St Mary's-at-the-Walls*, beside the town's west wall, where "St Mary's Steps" lead through Roman and medieval postern. Of the medieval church, the stump of the attractive stone tower alone

survived 1648. Tower raised 1729, re-topped 1911. Rest of the church rebuilt in 1714 at the expense of Sir Isaac Rebow, but this was replaced in 1872 by another of Sir A. Blomfield's designs: harsh red brick. Voluptuous capitals on nave piers of antique slenderness. Chancel décor rich, 1925, designed by George R. Phillips, paintings by F. A. Jackson. Rebow memorial records Tayspill parentage, shows Rebow averting gaze from Blomfield's nave. The town school stood in this churchyard down to the 16th century. Morant describes the laying-out of lime-walks here in his day, "the best about the whole town . . . resorted to by people of the best fashion". Limes (pollarded) still cross churchyard. Alas, beautiful St Mary's House, with Constable associations, still (1968) unoccupied, neglected. *St Peter's* Georgian brick tower nobly set above North Hill, this building epitomizes Colchester's history. Already well endowed in Domesday Book, and retaining a splendid ironwork door of *c.* 1300, its brass and stone memorials record prosperous parishioners of the 16th and 17th centuries. Slab in N. aisle commemorates Sir Wm. Campian, a young Royalist from Kent, killed in 1648 "upon a sally out of the town" that shut the Head Gate in Fairfax's face. The central tower, faulted in European earthquake 1692, was replaced by one at the W. end in 1758. Next summer in this church "the Oratorio of The Messiah was performed before a very numerous and polite Audience . . . without Accidents or the least Disorder". With its fine pulpit, of *c.* 1700, and its great balconies running forward above the aisles, St Peter's still holds echoes of those triumphant choruses.

Hythe and *Old Heath* (originally Old Hythe: "hythe" means haven) are not among the four separate medieval villages. St-Leonard's-at-the-Hythe is one of the medieval suburban parishes, and Old Heath, the Saxon haven, belonged to St Giles. *St Leonard's* looks well from river. The surviving old buildings around it have a rather

desperate look. The church's S. porch, with chamber over, contains a door of medieval timber and ironwork. Gloomy interior. Tower suffered in Essex earthquake, 1884: great buttresses cross the middle of the S. aisle. Road to Old Heath crosses the bourne. *Bourne Mill* is a marvellous Elizabethan fantasy fishing-lodge built by the Lucases of St John's Abbey: on the site of a medieval mill, it reverted to milling in the 19th century (see weatherboarded hoist-loft), and was indeed one of the last finishing mills for Colchester bays. Cannock Mill lower down the bourne is in working order.

Villages in the Borough
Berechurch, or West Donyland. Near army camp, red-brick *church* of *c.* 1500, much rebuilt, stands secluded in park. Panelled doors like Southwold's. North chapel, with hammerbeam roof, marble floor and ironwork screen has Audley cartouches painted on hammerbeams and wallposts, and several Audley monuments, including an engaging likeness of Sir Henry, semi-recumbent, 1648, done in marble in his lifetime. Mrs White couchant and resurgent in marble by J. Edwards, 1858.
Greenstead Hall derelict 1967. The *church* stood at the centre of a Parliamentarian fort during the siege of 1648, see dent in N. wall of small Tudor-brick tower. Hazelmere Junior and Infants School, Bromley Road, is a very trim building of the mid-1960s.
Lexden, a fashionable 19th-century garden suburb, set with evergreen trees amid Romano–British ramparts and dykes, is still strongly attractive. Victorian Italianate Hall. Stuccoed church, set up in group beside Sun Inn, has 1821 nave, 1892 chancel, Kempe glass. Fine old cottages on brink of by-pass.
Mile End. The medieval parish known as Myland grew out of a large belt of Royal Forest, King's Wood, linked under Forest Law

WAKES COLNE watermill

with the castle. It lay across slopes N. of town, between West Bergholt and Ardleigh. Some woods survive near Myland Hall, but rose-nurseries are now more thought of. Foundations of the medieval church lie behind the 1842 rectory, half a mile S. of the 1854 "early English" church with broach spire, by Hakewill.

Colne, Earls (10). The de Veres were the earls. They founded a Benedictine *Priory* here *c.* 1100 and were buried in its church, the grand outlines of which are known from excavation. Some of their tombs survived in the house until removed to Bures (Suffolk) in 1935. Present house Victorian with Georgian Gothick features, beside an ornamental lake, is (1966) home of Sir Reuben Hunt, whose *Atlas Ironworks* (founded 1825) and works-houses in red and white brick of all periods from 1875, dominate the opposite end of village. Large gloomy *church* adorned by W. tower mostly of Tudor brick with spectacular parapet of flint and freestone (flushwork) studded with the mullet (star) badge of the de Veres and with their arms in bold relief. (Above the parapet a gilt ironwork crown for weathervane.) Monuments to Harlakendon, Eldred, Wale and Cressener families; the Eldred monuments brought from the ruins of Little Birch. Roubiliac carved a very theatrical little Mercury on John Wale's, 1761. Apparently Wale did much to wreck the priory-site. There was already a collegiate minster here *c.* 1040. The church's dedication to St Andrew may go back to the 7th century.
Colne Engaine (10) (emphasis on last syllable). *Colne Park* is very agreeable, the white-brick house now reduced to its original (1775) pretty, clean-cut proportions with Ionic details, amid evergreen trees and a column of 1791 by Soane. (House and gate-lodge are themselves reminiscent of Soane's work.) *Church* tower of smouldering red Tudor brick (with de Vere mullet on E. face), on earlier base. Porch, too, Tudor brick. Tablet to Philip Hills, F.R.S., F.S.A.,

1768–1830, Morant's grandson, "late of Colne Park". Memorial window by Alan Younger, 1961.
Colne, Wakes (10). Church has interesting Norman fabric and well-designed weatherboarded belfry, the base of which was enhanced by Gothic screen-work in 1920 for a war-memorial. Walls under the chancel-arch were meant to support a central tower. The E. wall is bedizened with late-Victorian painted angels. The Hall, early Victorian white-brick, is now a Spastics Centre. Watermill.
Colne, White (10). *Colneford House*, Pound's Green, is covered with magnificent pargeting, dated 1685, and initialled $\frac{\text{T.}}{\text{G. E.}}$ The church was transformed in 1869 by C. J. Moxon, but Roman-brick quoins still smoulder red. A bright interior is transfused by the amber and ruby from Ward and Hughes' east window of 1884. Pulpit Caroline rather than Jacobean, with three flamboyant carved figures applied later. The Jacobean Puritan "flock" alleged their vicar, Mr Addam, "seldom preacheth, then unprofitablie", and readeth the psalms "unreverendlie, with his hat on his head, gaping and yaueninge as if he were half a sleepe".

Copford (13), where Stane Street crosses Roman River. A small settlement, including Copford Place, stands north of Stane Street, but most lies to the south: Copford Green, with a thatched "Dutch" barn, and then the Hall and the Church, which are of the greatest interest. The Hall has a dignified red Georgian brick front (Mr Brian Harrison, M.P. for Maldon), and overgrown cedars: this was a manor of the bishops of London to Elizabeth I's time, and one of her bishops, Bonner, is accredited with planting the verdant oak-walk to church. The church gives few external hints of its extraordinary interior, decorated with a very complete scheme of Romanesque wall-paintings, probably done in the 1140s when the church was built with an (extremely rare) barrel vault. Vault replaced by timber structure c. 1400, but its springers still spring from nave and chancel walls. One arch of the S. aisle, late 13th-century, has its bricks exposed: some are Roman but those in the inner orders are contemporary, products of very early revival of brick-making in this neighbourhood (cf. Coggeshall, and in Suffolk, Wenham and Polstead). The paintings, uncovered in 1690 and again in 1865, have been very heavily restored, but their design remains deeply impressive, especially in the dome of the apse: Christ enthroned inside the complete circle of a rainbow held aloft by angels. The great arch spanning the entrance to the apse displays the signs of the Zodiac.

Easthorpe, see separate entry.

Corringham (9). The tremendously impressive great square early-Norman bell-tower stands south of a very pretty group of old houses and cottages, mostly weatherboarded. The bell-tower has blank arcading and a pyramidal roof, and is set in even earlier nave- and chancel-walls: see the stratified stone courses of the S. side. A small grim face looks over the nave from the keystone of the tower-arch. An early 14th-century wooden screen crosses the N. aisle. A good modern copy between nave and chancel is described as original by Pevsner. Much new housing, related to –

Coryton (9) itself named after the brothers Cory, Victorian oil refiners, it includes Shell Haven, already so named in charts of Henry VIII's reign, and Thames Haven. In 1872, ships were forbidden to carry oil products up river from this point, and the first store-houses were built in 1876. The railway already ran through to Stanford-le-Hope, with a branch from Mucking to Thames Haven. Since 1953 Mobil has built an astonishing air-lift Thermofor catalytic cracking unit, about 380 ft. high. (Apparently gasoline is improved by cracking oils in the presence of a catalyst.) A well-designed recent addition to

site is the Welders and Fitters Shop. The whole place has the vertical look of Cape Kennedy. Shell's refinery, started at Shell Haven in 1916, is today one of the biggest in this country.

Crays Hill *see* Ramsden.

Creeksea (16) (sometimes Cricksea, or Crixeth) means "hyth" or landing-place, in the creek. Above *White House*, formerly the Ferry House, the well-wooded park of *Creeksea Place* shelters a popular caravan-camp and all that survives (much of the N. wing) of a large Elizabethan house, dated 1569 on a downpipe. In 1965 the camp-owner hopes to restore this fine range of building as a clubhouse. One room of particularly good Elizabethan panelling is preserved on the first floor. Two parallel wings running south were pulled down c. 1740. A late-Victorian or Edwardian wing, on the site of original (main) E. front, bears the motto, "Punget sed placet", and also a vast magnolia melancholia. The Elizabethan builder, Arthur Harris, married "well" a Waldegrave of Bures: their descendants affected the spelling Herris, as seen on their great-grandson's brass, 1631, in *church*, a rebuilding of 1878. Nearby, the *Hall* front is of pleasant Georgian red brick, the rear part an earlier black-and-white timbered building with its original newel stair.

Cressing (6) is the site of a 12th-century preceptory of Knights Templars, who were replaced, early in the 14th century, by Knights Hospitallers, well endowed with lands here and in Witham and Rivenhall. They were attacked by peasants in the revolt of June 1381, who bore off armour and valuables and destroyed records. Some measure of the wealth of these Hospitallers is still very evident in two surviving wonderful barns: the barley barn is weatherboarded, the wheat barn brick-nogged, and both from their structure have been confidently dated earlier than 1330: radio-carbon tests allow the age of the

timber in the barley barn to be early 11th-century! Whole oak trees were used as main posts. The preceptory itself was entirely replaced by the Tudor house of the Smiths. In Pepys' day Cressing Temple provided Rotherhithe shipwrights with hundreds of oaks and ashes. A large oak "horkey" bough hangs in the roof-ridge of the wheat barn from a Harvest Home of how long ago? The parish church, a chapel of Witham in the 12th century, contains masonry of that date and the odour of incense. Anne Smith's monument, 1607, repainted, shows an infant granddaughter trussed in a shroud.

Crockleford *see* Ardleigh.

Danbury (6). A wooded peak, of 346 ft., raises aloft the tall thin 15th-century shingled spire, a landmark between Maldon and Chelmsford. The village is disrupted by Maldon–Chelmsford road traffic, but within the peripheral sprawl lie the pond, the village stores, and, after a gradual climb, a Tudor house (*Frettons*) and a small square green, north of the church. Here, at the summit, church and rectory stand with a large heart-shaped earthwork, best seen by following the footpath through the S.W. corner of the churchyard. From the name, originally Daningbury, some sort of fortified Danish settlement is conjectured, but the site awaits systematic examination. Meanwhile the magnificent southern slopes, perfect for lateral prospect-terracing, are in the 1960s being carved up into vertical roads with housing facing inwards!

The spire stands on an earlier bold tower of rough texture. Very broad bare church inside, with wide nave aisles, though the nave is only three bays long. In the N. aisle: stone recesses with two strikingly carved 13th-century oak effigies of knights, possibly St Cleres. A similar recess with slightly later figure is incorporated

Great Graces, LITTLE BADDOW, near Danbury boundary

in the Victorian S. aisle. The S.E. corner of the church, blasted off by a bomb in May 1941, contains a beautifully carved Italian alabaster Annunciation commemorating (1892) the first Bishop of St Albans residing at *Danbury Palace*. This is a large castellated red brick "Elizabethan" house of 1836, by the versatile Thos. Hopper, near the site of a Mildmay house. Danbury Park is open to the public with beechy walks, lake and views. Danbury Common, gold with gorse, National Trust, lies on the road to Bicknacre Priory (Woodham Ferrers). On slopes to the north, Lingwood Common, is also National Trust property. New Riffhams, white brick, of *c*. 1815, is nobly set above lake and park.

Debden (2). Idyllic, on a back road from Walden to Thaxted, the "deep dene" was landscaped into a park with lake and bridge and waterfall, possibly by Repton: its possibilities were first exploited by its Norman owner, Ranulf Peverel, who planted it with vines. The vineyards have gone, but a wood is still called Peverels. The *house*, Grecianized by Henry Holland, was pulled down in 1935. The church is now the chief excitement at the heart of Debden, but scattered about the parish are several lovable farmhouses: *Pamphilions, Broctons, Swaynes Hall* and *Mole Hall* in timber and plaster; *Amberden Hall* (a Domesday manor), *New Amberden* and *Thistley Hall* in good red brick. *Brick House* is in fact a nice mix-

ture of timber, plaster and brick. The Old Rectory, now *Debden Manor*, was built in 1796 of white brick made on the site. *Mole Hall* now lives up to its name and is a "Nature Reserve", a small zoo based on the moated pink-washed Elizabethan farmhouse.

The *church*, basically of *c*. 1220 (see the round columns of the S. aisle, with very flat leaf-carving), had a central tower. The S. porch and a splendid chest are of the 14th century. Otherwise the whole character of the church is Georgian Gothick, very original. The tower fell in 1698 and 1717, and the chancel was first rebuilt 1733. The nave was thoroughly repaired, re-roofed and given its bold battlements in 1786. The font, also of this date, by Henry

Holland's cousin Richard, is extraordinarily sharp and delicate work in artificial stone – Coade's *Lithodipyra*: niches contain minutely detailed figures of Faith, Hope, Justice, etc. A steeple of 1786, by the "late ingenious Mr Essex" of Cambridge, was replaced by yet another in 1930, very Essex in its way. In 1792, the chancel, rebuilt after the design by John Carter the antiquary and musician, broadens out eastwards into a sort of octagon, with ribbed plaster vault, connected to the nave by an ante-chapel with timbered pendent arcading.

The Chiswell family, very prosperous London booksellers and publishers, were seated here from 1715. One of them left the estate in 1772 to his sister's son, Richard Muilman, who landscaped and Gothicized it. He put up very pretty monuments to his parents Peter and Mary (see also Castle Hedingham), by a leading Bath statuary; himself took the name Chiswell, and lies under a prodigious tomb-chest, presumably Carter's design.

Dedham (11). The village still clusters about its noble church tower in the bottom of the broad shallow Stour valley, wide open to the sky and in appearance much as it was when the boy Constable walked down daily to school here through the fields and water meadows from his home in East Bergholt on the ridge of the Suffolk slope. The phrase Dedham Vale is almost synonymous with "Constable's country", itself already used in Constable's hearing as he left by coach for London one day in 1832. The village appears in the middle distance of many of his most magic landscapes envisaged from Langham on the Essex side, perhaps best of all from Bergholt, as at the start

of those daily boyhood walks, the gleaming ribbon of water winding below, marked occasionally by a sail, occasionally by barges drawn by horses that could leap.

Constable's most famous "close-up" of Dedham shows the water-mill his father bought with proceeds of successful business down-stream at Flatford. This mill provides the key to Dedham's own development. A year after Constable's birth it still served as both a corn and fulling mill, though by then the making of bay-cloths was "greatly upon the decline". Dedham's modern character as residential village with Assembly, Balls and such-like was well established.

Dedham runs two or three miles downstream from the A12 which provides its (Roman) W. boundary. East boundary along Shir-brook, where now prettily weather-boarded mill (established between 1066 and 1086) is familiar to rail-travellers on main London–Ipswich line which shares the little gully. Village street-plan grew up in relation to Hall Farm which once stood just E. of church, and to the famous mill whose fulling enabled the cloth-making to thrive. The Tuesday market was held north of the churchyard, from the Sun Inn along to the Marlborough Head at corner of Mill Lane. The history of the place is vividly expressed in one of the best churches in Essex and one of the most attractive village-streets in England.

As in the Suffolk clothing towns, Dedham's climax of prosperity

DEDHAM

came in the time of Henry VII, the 1490s and 1500s. The church is all of this time and basically one fine design, though the fabric is externally poor and all stuccoed except the magnificent flintwork tower. Nave, S. aisle and chancel finished by 1500; N. aisle and richly carved N. door (much defaced) from High Street added to commemorate the leading clothiers, Webbes and Gurdons. Low-pitched timber roofs, supported on stone shafts exactly on the pattern of Long Melford, form a perfect simple canopy over all. Good Victorian glass by Kempe in the chancel windows. Polygonal corner-buttresses distinguish the noble W. tower, link it in design with Redenhall, Norfolk. There is a way through the tower to the south churchyard by a stone-vaulted passage, richly panelled; Tudor roses and portcullises dominant as at King's College Chapel, and with the Webbes' merchant's-mark in the soffits. Compare their tomb-chest in the N. aisle. The tower was nearly finished in 1510: Stephen Dunton left £100 for battlements 1519. The old brick tower-gallery-stair at the W. end of the nave has its stone parapet continued across tower in 19th-century timber facsimile. Springers of unfinishing fan-vaulting in the ringers' chamber are now reached on the E. side through nice neo-Georgian doorcase, gilded and with fanlight (Raymond Erith, 1963).

Dedham was one of the Stour Valley power-stations of advanced Protestantism. A lectureship was

DEDHAM

founded here in the 1570s to preach on Sundays and Tuesdays, when market day began at 8 in a crowded church. Edmund Chapman, first lecturer, died in 1602: last line of his epitaph in the chancel shows he preferred to be buried outside in the churchyard, "the shepherd asleep among his lambs". John Rogers, lecturer 1605–36, is depicted in the chancel (a bust painted an unpleasant stone colour) preaching one of his famous Tuesday sermons which drew people on foot and in coaches from miles around. Easy to see how "Dedham" is among the early settlements in Massachusetts. After 1648, cloth-making declined, and the market came to depend on the lecture. Both vicar and lecturer were debarred in 1662. The lectureship was reorganized in the 1690s and associated with the grammar school, which moved into the lead in the 18th century under Dr Grimwood, the father of Constable's discerning headmaster.

The grammar school (now two private houses) stands east of church; good brick building, part dated 1732, with an empty niche for Dr Grimwood.

Dedham repays long explorations, but its character is seen at a glance on leaving church: medieval timber-framed houses, pub

on left with tall carriage-way through to rear, grocer's shop in middle with smart Georgian bow-window and brick façade, and on right "Shermans", an elaborate early Georgian façade with red and yellow gauged brickwork masking an old timbered rear. Sherman is the name of the prosperous cloth-family who lived at Southfields, a remarkable quadrangular timber-framed house (stripped, alas, of its old protective lime-plaster), beside its own abundant brook, approached by the footpath leading S. between chemist's shop and old grammar school. Among other relics of High Street do not overlook whole row opposite grammar school and series of delightful old shopfronts: at the west end of the street, Great House is a dignified neo-Georgian design by Raymond Erith.

Dengie (13), g pronounced hard, seems to mean "island of Dene's people": gives name to whole peninsula between Blackwater and Crouch. In an 8th-century charter, it is already described as a "regio", including Danbury. The *church* has the familiar texture of septaria, flint and a local yellowish brick dated as early as the 14th century (cf. Wenham, Suffolk).

Doddinghurst (5) has an untidy assortment of modern dwellings. A curiously long (17 ft.) early Tudor porch leads into a church of such gloom that the remarkable life-size timber rood, carved and coloured, is hardly visible. Possibly German 16th-century work, it is the gift of an early 20th-century rector. The vertically-boarded belfry on cross-strutted posts is of great structural interest, possibly put up in the early 13th-century and also now in the dark.

Donyland, East (13) includes Row-hedge, with attractive old fishermen's quayside, neglected. A derelict Georgian house at the corner of Dark House Lane has a handsome doorcase. Ferry to Wivenhoe. Middlewick firing-ranges of Colchester garrison are liable to close the road from Row-hedge to Roman Hill Farm. East Donyland church was rebuilt in 1838 (Wm. Mason of Ipswich) "in imitation of" the chapter house of York Minster: in white brick and some materials of the old church on a distant site. The slate roof, like the top of a great dovehouse, is an odd landmark for miles. A monument shows

GOOD EASTER: "*pole—scape*"

94

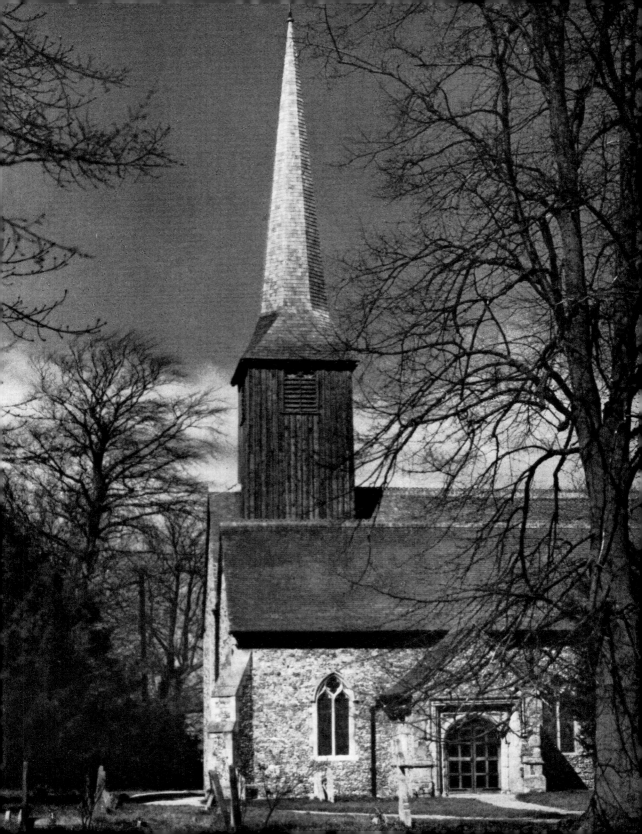

LITTLE EASTON: Bourchier and Maynard tombs

Elizabeth Marshall, 1613, sitting with one foot propped up on a skull, very unladylike. It has a beguiling inscription by the vicar, a contemporary of Sir Nathaniel the Curate. The red brick 1700ish Hall takes part in a pastoral scene with a herd of silky cattle.

Donyland, West, alias **Berechurch** *see* Colchester.

Dovercourt *see* Harwich.

Downham (9). From the church a great view extends south-west across the upper Crouch to Basildon. The *church* is a rebuilding of 1871; the nave grey Kentish rag, and the chancel a nice mixture of flint and rusty ironstone conglomerate. Fifteenth-century timber S. porch with restored tracery. Monuments. Downham *Hall*, L-shaped Georgian house with brick dovecote. Fine house of

Cromwellian major-general submerged beneath Hanningfield Reservoir.

Duddenhoe *see* Elmdon.

Dunmow (5) ("hill-meadow") extends on both sides of the Chelmer valley, hills rising from 150 ft. only to 300: a small town grew up where the Chelmer-valley road (Chelmsford–Walden)

96

crosses Roman Stane Street, and where a Roman road joins from the Rodings in the south.

Great Dunmow, had a grant of market in the 13th century and has all the qualities of a thoroughfare town, strung out along main roads. Nothing spectacular, but seemly house and shop-fronts, many of them Georgian, and the whole appearance much enhanced in 1966 by the removal of electric wires from the streets. The best things lie down Star Hill, past Doctor's Pond (in which the first Lifeboat was tried out, in 1785), The Downs (a kind of Town Green), and beyond North Street to Clock House on "the Causeway" near Church End. *Clock House, c.* 1600, with a picturesque brick front of a little later, topped by curved gables, was the parental home of Sir George Beaumont (1753–1827), amateur painter and patron, of Coleorton, Leicestershire (see Rossi's monument in church: also Horsnaile's to earlier Beaumonts). The house owes its name to a turret on the roof with an old clock and bell said to be inscribed Bryan Eldridge, 1651. *Newton Hall Park* lies beyond. Other good houses include *Shingle Hall* (originally "shingled") and *Brands*, to the south. The *church*, with a good 15th-century W. tower capped by small corner turrets, stands in a poor group of cottages. Fine early 14th-century S. doorway and E. window. Late 15th-century timbered gallery in S. aisle, reached from porch (? early example of squire's pew). The 16th-century church-warden's account book, in beautifully tooled leather, is now in Essex Record Office.

Little Dunmow. Widely known for its ancient memorial ceremony of presenting a *Flitch of bacon* to any married couple ready to swear they had never in the previous twelve-months regretted their marriage. This is believed to be a Norman or Breton custom introduced by the Fitz Walters. It was revived by Harrison Ainsworth in 1855, and transferred to Great Dunmow. The happy husband was carried in a chair kept in the church.

It is a remarkable church, with a Victorian ornamental roof-ridge, and a bell-cote like a chimney, and the entire appearance of bleak Nonconformist chapel until one is close enough to notice the elaborate and beautiful window-tracery. This is the surviving S. chancel chapel, or Lady chapel, of an Augustinian priory church that must have been magnificent. Ironically it owes its present depressing interior to the Victorian revival of ritualism! An 1837 engraving shows a homely brick-floored interior, with box pews, double-decker pulpit and sounding-board, and all that the Victorian High Anglicans deplored as trappings of the Nonconformist preaching-house! The N. wall piers have been dated *c.* 1200. Five glorious S. windows are probably of the 1360s, and beautifully carved effigies of Walter Fitz Walter and wife, alabaster, of a century later. A marble female on a pedestal with a portrait medallion by Thos. Adye, 1753, mourns Sir Jas. Halley.

Priory Place has been found to contain remains of a timber aisled-hall, possibly part of the medieval guest house.

Dunton *see* Basildon.

Easter, Good (5) rhymes with Chester and means Godith's sheep-fold ("estr"). It signals you from afar with a tall needle of a shingled spire on a vertically-boarded belfry. Pevsner demonstrates in detail how one sees that both nave and chancel are of the 13th century, the chancel replacing a Norman one. Very clean and spruce. A chalybeate spring flows in the parish.

Easter, High (5) stands rather higher than its neighbours. The church-walls rise among village houses, timber-framed buildings that have been spoilt by re-plastering with too much cement, weathering green and dirty. Contrast them with the overcoat of proper old lime-plaster on the *Cock and Bell*. It is a square, battlemented flint *church* tower. Red Roman brick makes the

beautiful texture of the Norman chancel, much of it laid in herring-bone pattern. Tudor porch. Fine clerestory, very red Tudor brick, rises sheer above nave walls, its windows designed to light handsome grooved and traceried oak girders, queen-posts, bosses and spandrels. There are masons' marks of *c.* 1400 on the N. arcade. The organ occupies a third of the chancel.

Easthorpe (13) now joined with Copford. It has a small Norman *church*, with remains of apse and several windows; of the 13th century, the E. wall holds three beautiful lancets, also there is a painting of the Resurrection in a window-splay; it is all full of daylight, and set beside a quiet Roman road with the 15th-century *Hall*, a great moat and a cottage.

Easton, Great (2). Remains of a motte-and-bailey castle beside the road, east of the large, rather lifeless church. A remarkable 15th-century house, with original traceried bargeboards, stands quarter of a mile to the west. *Blamster's* (Blancmoustier's in 1280) has a spectacular pear-tree beside the A130. Girls' school, founded in 1759, now in a Victorian building.

Easton, Little (5), *Easton Lodge*, almost completely demolished, is at the edge of a disused airfield: a handsome red-brick rectory (*c.* 1755) still stands in the ancient park of the Bourchier earls of Essex (*c.* 1365–1540) and the Maynards (1590–1938). Last of the Maynards, Daisy, Countess of Warwick, would have made it a Labour College if the General Strike had not drained T.U.C. funds. (It had been mostly rebuilt by Thos. Hopper after a fire of 1847.) She was Edward VII's mistress. As the handsome bust of her in *church* acknowledges:
"— Her Angel Face
As the great eye of Heaven
    shyned bright,
And made a sunshine in the
    Shady Place."
A bronze plaque nearby says Ellen Terry loved to worship here.

Lord Warwick, rector's warden forty years, is noticed on the farther wall.

The nave retains a dramatic Romanesque painting of a prophet, seated, c. 1150; also a 15th-century series depicting the Passion in an Italian way. The S. chapel is steep-roofed, like Thaxted's and Finchingfield's (and matched by a N. vestry, 1881). It is railed off by earlier lodge gates for Maynard tombs: well carved recumbent figures of Sir Henry, Dame Susan in hood, and ten kneeling children, 1610; Lady Frances, reclining, 1613; on W. wall 1st Lord Maynard, 1585–1640, and wife, possibly by the fine sculptor Edward Pearce c. 1690; their grandson Banastre and his eleven children are magnificently commemorated opposite by the Danish sculptor Charles Stanly, 1746. A Bourchier tomb-chest with brasses, 1483, brought from Beeleigh Abbey, is rudely divided by Maynard railings. A Bourchier tomb of c. 1400 N. of the chancel, with shields of arms, bears a miniature Knight of c. 1250. Beside the church the very shapely sprawl of the 17th-century *Manor House*; its garden often open to the public. Stocks and whipping-post in cottage garden. Half a mile north-east, *Butcher's Pasture* is the scene of the bustling village activity that was engraved in Wright's *Essex*, 1835, with pub and wooden bridge and ford.

Eastwood *see* Southend.

Elmdon (2). The quiet village centre stands at three-ways on a hillside: the thatched pub, *The Carrier*, and the (re)pargeted and weatherboarded *King's Head*, both nestle close to the church. *Elmdonbury*, still higher, has a few new-modelled houses grouped round great medieval moats: a moated mound in an adjoining wood presumably represents the castle of Roger de Sumari. A pargeted, barge-boarded old farmhouse called *Farthing Green* lies just below church. The large *church*, behind a screen of limes, is largely a careful Victorian re-building of the old walls, so that the external mellow grey of flint is well preserved. The tower is still a substantially 15th-century fabric, with renewed W. window. Interior dark. 15th- and 16th-century brasses. Small panels of 17th-century glass brought from Wenden Lofts.

Duddenhoe End is a world of deep hedgerows with a lingering sense of the life of the great surrounding open-fields from the days before enclosure. Church infinitely rustic, like a barn, thatched, and beside a thatched cottage, and itself entirely of timber – with simple oak piers and tie-beams, a few oak mullions, the whole standing on a brick plinth and covered with weatherboarding. Inside, the atmosphere is created by plain scrubbed pine pews bearing slender turned-pine candle-sticks, each with a single brass holder. Interior oriented on the small sanctuary with curly altar-rails in the middle of the long E. side. Perhaps the building *was* originally a barn?

Elmstead (14). The tall late-medieval *Hall*, plastered and pink-washed, stands with the *church* remote among fields. The church, cement-coated, has a truncated tower with pyramidal tiled roof, and a promisingly "domestic" dormer in the nave roof.

Of the half-dozen most agreeable church interiors in Essex this is probably the best. A simple Georgian wooden stair leads from the porch up to a W. gallery. From the porch there are two steps down to the brick floor of nave, which is beautifully kept and with all its old box pews of panelled unvarnished pine. Handsome 2-decker pulpit and sounding-board with sun and star inlaid. South aisle-chapel with low windows and time-ravaged recumbent timber effigy, apparently of Sir Roger de Tany who died 1301, perhaps a little before the main rebuilding of the church. The Norman N. doorway is framed by Roman brick, its Norman door now preserved inside. Contemporary glass in the low S. windows has been brought from the E. window (much reduced: see outside, where two angels mark width of original). Lovely empty chancel, with rails on three sides of altar. Commandment boards on E. wall: also painted wooden epitaphs to Thos. Martin, "Rector of Alesford and Vicker of Elemsted", d. 29th January 1672, and his son who died eight years earlier: touching doggerel. Piscina and sedilia. Royal Arms of 1749 and charmingly painted Georgian texts: "This is none other than the House of God". Iron hat-rack.

Elmstead Market acquired 1253 by a de Tany presumably took place on the green where the Georgian brick front of *Tudor House* provides a nice contrast with the straggling main-road development. A market is also said to have been held here during 17th-century outbreaks of plague in Colchester.

Elsenham (2). Walls of nave and chancel pleasantly coloured by a mixture of red bricks and the yellow mortar binding the flintwork: they are Norman, early 12th-century, from which period the most notable remains are the round Romanesque chancel-arch and tall S. doorway. Thin barley-sugar columns of the doorway, and responds of the chancel arch (appearing through plaster), are all four grooved with irregular zigzags. The small capitals of the doorway are carved with symbols possibly the sun and moon: a tympanum is built-up of several stones chipped with a pattern of little saltire-crosses or stars. This Norman carving is in fact axe-work, before stone chiselling came in. The oak door itself is medieval. The church was given to the Conqueror's abbey in Caen, in 1070, by the Norman owner of one of the two estates recorded here in Domesday Book, which shows this as very thickly wooded, even by Essex standards: Elsenham and Takeley had between them enough woodland to feed 3,500 swine. Today the *Hall* stands in a well wooded park, and at *Elsenham Place* some of the vertical timber framing of the internal walls is unusually close-set. *Tye Green* is

ELMSTEAD: Wooden effigy and old glass

a beautiful old rural hamlet, at the very brink of Stansted's existing airfield. All in jeopardy.

Epping (4) means "the people on the upland", which explains why the ancient church of Epping lies in rural "Epping Upland" among the original scattered farms, moated and timber-framed. Farms spread south as the forest was cleared, and the main-road town developed with a market. It was boosted by a new road south-west to Loughton Street in the 17th century, forerunner of the present A11. Previously the London road went west via Waltham Abbey or south via Abridge. Epping's own High Street follows the line of one of the ancient "purlieu banks" that marked the edge of Waltham Forest (now known as Epping Forest, though still mostly lying in Waltham Holy Cross). Parts of the bank survive on Bell Common and probably under the E. side of the High Street, whose houses stand higher than those on the west. As A11 crosses Bell Common, *Copped Hall* stands romantically on the skyline above the wooded park to the west, at first sight complete, but on close inspection still gutted from fire of 1917: a white brick design by John Sanderson, 1751–6, refronted *c.* 1895 with superb masonry by C. E. Kempe, who also designed the splendid remaining Renaissance garden pavilion and nearby *Wood House* modelled on the great pargeted house in Ipswich Buttermarket. *Coopersale House*, cheerful above a small lake, has lost a painted ceiling that showed William III casting out Popery and was recorded by the Royal Commission in 1921.

Beside the A11 at the south end of the town, *Epping Place*, of *c.* 1700, with a handsome staircase, served as an inn 1758–*c.*1844; and *Winchelsea House* was built as an annexe. There were twenty-six inns in Epping *c.* 1800, but in the 1840s the railway spoilt business till a branch came here in 1865 and, later, motor-traffic developed. A red brick water-tower with Gothick detail, 1872, is the most prominent building in town. Bodley and Garner's *church* on a main corner-site, 1889, has a tower of 1908, virtually detached: the interior is lofty and light, with arcades rising right out of the paving, all unencumbered by pews. The glass in the E. window and the S. aisle's W. window is the work of Kempe. The tower presents a noble appearance as you enter the town from the north. Here, east of Church Hill, a large new neo-Georgian development 1966, Theydon Grove, 2-storey with dormers, single and in terraces, was offered at prices from £9,500. The yellow brick Georgian W. front of the old *Cock Inn* has been given a neat dark-blue brick and glass N. front and renamed *Epping Forest Motel*, 1962. Another hotel and two restaurants adjacent. Third hotel in Station Road. On the west side of High Street, the International Stores is on the site of the original grocery where Henry Doubleday was born and died, 1808–75. He established the fact that the oxlip, that grows best in Essex, is a distinct species; he studied the haw-finch among the hornbeams of the Forest; he grew marvellous strawberries; in 1859 he published his great *List of British Lepidoptera*. He also acted as Treasurer of the local Turnpike Trust and Poor Law Union.

Epping Upland. The *church* is entirely roughcast except the Elizabethan brick tower with little roof over stairturret. The interior is a

EPPING UPLAND

100

FAIRSTEAD: detail of wall painting over chancel arch

long tunnel, 109 ft., but only 21 ft. wide, waggon vaulted and ceiled, the chancel ceiling elaborately painted in a recent restoration, the only distinction between nave and chancel. Homely clock clanks away every 2 seconds. There is a brass to Thos. Palmer, "Professor of that illustrious and flourishing science of the Common Law", 1621, who lived at *Gills*, a house of *c*. 1560, moated. Fifteenth-century inscriptions are curiously carved in oak and now in the base of the tower: "Praye for the sowlys of Wylyam Holwey & Jone and George Lucas and Margorye". A fragment opposite commemorates Wylyam Connier & Benet his wyfe.

Fairstead (6) in open farmlands – lanes, elms, rolling cornfields. Small Norman nave and chancel. Embedded Norman quoins of Roman brick in the N. wall show the starting-point of the chancel's extension in the 13th century, when lancet windows were put in and the sturdy great W. tower added, with its small W. doorway. Of four bells, one is by Peter de Weston, *c*. 1340. A suitably bold spire, of perhaps *c*. 1600, is a noble landmark. The astonishing interior is beautifully cream-washed around the medieval wall paintings. Best series, the Passion above the plain Norman chancel-arch: at the summit, Christ on a rather short-legged horse riding past a tree (? into Jerusalem); below, twelve figures at table, a thirteenth (? Judas) kneeling, a

Last Supper; to the right, a possible mocking and scourging; bottom left, a lively person in broad-brimmed hat perhaps giving Christ the crown of thorns.
The nave has a high round W. window (pre-tower), several consecration crosses in red paint, and a great iron-bound dugout chest (thought to be 13th-century); also a late medieval ribbed canopy in the wall for a former N. altar. The baptism was registered, in 1568, of a son of Tusser the great farming-improver, appropriately near the much later model farm at Terling. There is a black-letter injunction on the S. wall to pray for "the excellent prince" James I. A curious and successful effect in the well-lit chancel is the way the splays of the lancets have been plastered so as to leave the stone quoins recessed. The middle lancet in the E. wall is set above a trefoil-headed recess, presumably made for original reredos: now filled with a coloured wood-carving of shepherds, angels and star (? early 20th-century), which is strikingly effective. Solid oak panelling in N. porch.

Fambridge, North (9/16), "fen-bridge"; the name goes back to the 11th century, and presumably refers to a ferry over the Crouch. *South Fambridge*, across the river, is now part of Ashingdon (q.v.). North Fambridge has two cottages beside the ferry, but is mostly well above the river, on idyllic slopes, echoing with curlews and doves; one of Essex's

"Best-kept" villages. Georgian brick church. In it, a modern painting of aged saint and child is signed A. Gay.

Farnham (2). Scattered. Over-sailing farmhouse and thatched group at Hazelend. The *church*, of 1859, with a gold mosaic reredos, of 1885, and a medieval glass figure of St Basil, stands beside the well-wooded park of Hasso-bury. Here Robert Gosling replaced the old farmhouse by a grim grey-stone "medieval" pile in 1868. Descendant lives at large buff-brick old rectory. Nearby, *Walkers Farmhouse* is as rewarding as Royal Commission found it exactly fifty years ago; Elizabethan, with specially interesting panelled solar-with-chamber-over at the S. end, each with an old powder-closet omitted by the R.C.

Faulkbourne (6), pronounced Fawborn, with a famous red brick castellated house of the 15th century nestling down beside the "falcon's stream". It began the 15th century as a timber-framed house, took on a more defensive appearance after 1439, for Sir John Montgomery, a leading soldier in France. His son, Sir Thomas, showed all the political agility of the Howards, taking part in the governments of Edward IV, Richard III and Henry VII, but dying in 1494 without surviving offspring. Like his contemporaries, Lord Cromwell who built Tattershall Castle, and Sir Roger de Fiennes who built

FOBBING: the tower above the marshes

Herstmonceux, Sir John was probably recreating something that had impressed him in France. (This may also explain the church's dedication to St Germain, though we have no evidence of the date of dedication.) His N. front faces the valley, with a charming small 2-storey bay window near the middle and a "donjon" at the E. corner, with skilful brickwork in the spiral stair. The hall was single-storey from the start. Over it an oriel of perhaps Sir Thomas' day, was added, possibly for a visit by Henry VII. There are very striking brick corbel-tables under all the battlements, which are more reminiscent of Hadleigh Deanery in Suffolk than any-

where else in England, but that was built *c.* 1495. The Bullock family added a large timber staircase in the 17th century, and there is much later addition.
Church Norman, its E. wall 13th-century. In the W. wall the upper window is original. Monuments include a 13th-century knight in alarming flat-topped helmet; Hannah Bullock, seated in 1759, by Scheemakers, and John Bullock, 1809, with life-size Greek lady standing unsigned. John Constable's sister saw a Vandyke here, in 1825, for which £900 had been offered.

Feering (13) lies across the A12 like Kelvedon, from which it is

divided by the Blackwater and for which it supplies a small suburb, transformed by opening of the recent by-pass. From Rye Mill, just N. of A12, the homely grey church-tower stands on a slight rise in the main cluster of the village. Upstream, between Feering Place and Feeringbury, the site of a fulling-mill is now marked only by masonry in river-bank. The *church*, beside the gabled old Rectory where John Constable used to stay, displays a S. nave wall, windows and porch all of glorious early-Tudor brick, rich red, with silver and black diapering, all battlemented and with the usual fine corbel-table like a crotcheted fringe. Porch finely

FINCHINGFIELD

vaulted, with merchant's mark in boss. Constable drew it in the summer of 1814. North aisle altar now has the Risen Christ he painted for Manningtree in 1822, brought here by the present rector in 1965. Beautifully cleaned and re-framed, it shows a corporeal Christ floating up from the place of skulls in the gold glow of Constable's strong faith. It now has for companions a Nottingham alabaster Virgin and Child, *c.* 1400, from Colne Priory and a Florentine silver crucifix of *c.* 1700. The pulpit contains 17th-century carved scenes from the Crucifixion. The chancel has well carved poppy-heads and a tablet to Constable's old friend Walter

Wren Driffield, fifty years resident curate here, who died at 86 in 1828. He had baptised the painter; his own infant daughter died at 6 months.

Felsted (6), a large parish of interesting old farmhouses and cottages scattered about no less than nine Greens, and with the central village setting of a well-known boys' boarding school. The British Sugar Corporation's early factory provides a very ugly lump on the landscape.

The *church*, part of a remarkable group at the centre, is approached from the south through a lych-gate formed by the timber-framed original School-house (already

built at the time of Lord Rich's 1564 foundation). This properly retains all its plaster coat, and in the lych-gate two windows have their original shutters. The church-tower of the 1140s, with W. doorway and round nave-arch, contains clockwork by John Ford-ham of Gt. Dunmow, dated 1701, and is crowned by an open cupola on octagonal timber pyramid of about the same date. There is a S. doorway of the 1180s (re-set) and an impressive S. arcade of the same time, with two round piers, leaf-capitals and very early pointed arches. The chief magnet now is Epiphanius Evesham's beautiful sculpture in marble and alabaster tomb, done years after his death, of Richard, 1st baron Rich of Leighs Priory. He died in 1566: the monument was erected in 1621 by the 3rd baron's will. Lord Chancellor two years under Edward VI, this 1st baron was a blatant opportunist, consecutively betrayer of the Catholics, Thomas More and Bishop Fisher, and then persecutor of the Essex Protestants, notably those of Bocking. His tomb-chest bears incised black panels showing him on horseback with mace-bearer, and on his hearse beneath a canopy. His almost living effigy on top of the tomb-chest shows a most civilian Lord Chancellor, surrounded by very fine allegorical panels in which he is optimistically accom-

panied by Hope, Charity, etc.: the Lord Rich-in-Virtue nobody knew in his lifetime. In Mary's reign he naturally founded in this church a chantry with dirges for the dead; in Elizabeth's they were scrapped, and the endowments went to found a grammar school. Opposite the church, the *Swan*, timber-framed and oversailing, has been stripped of its plaster coat. Across the Chelmsford road from the Swan, a famous bressummer is lettered "George Boote made this house 1596". Boote was builder and carpenter, also churchwarden: at school he repaired the tables and (often!) the orchard fence. Viewed from the chestnut tree east of the church,

Boote's house and the old schoolhouse have identically tall narrow gable-ends: building-fashions changed slowly. East of the church a stout red brick house, *Ingram's Close* (five bays, the middle three projecting) were rebuilt for the school 1799–1801 by the architect John Johnson. Then, well back from the road, comes the daunting conventional range of the 1860s, Felsted's "Arnoldian" period, when the school was virtually refounded under the headship of W. S. Grignon. *Grignon Hall* stands farther east, at right angles, a pleasant red brick building with curved gable – "1931 traditional". A white brick *Congregational Chapel* is a reminder of the extramural life of the village.

Many interesting buildings are scattered about in the rest of parish, from *Quakers Mount*, a thatched cottage with parge-work (wheat sheaf, fishes and windmill) probably on the site of a Quaker burial-ground near *Bannister Green*, to the small *Gate House Farm* near *Gransmore Green*, with its remarkable 14th-century tie-beam structure, like that at Campsey Ash priory, in Suffolk; it took its name from a feature of the quadrangular lay-out of the farm buildings, still partly preserved and partly moated.

Finchingfield (3), six miles by four of rich farmland includes most of "Wethersfield" air base as well as its own justly celebrated village grouped above and around the pond and Green formed at a stream and road crossing. The beauty derives entirely from the grouping, on the slopes down to the pond from east and west, of a variety of cottages with tiled roofs and plastered walls, surmounted by the great square Norman west tower of the church, standing a little behind the cottages on the south-east side, and itself topped by a box cupola and vane; more discreet than the spire that blew off in 1702. Above the Green to the west, opposite the church, the barge-boarded gables of *Hill House* make the most respectable impression; dropping away from it, before a screen of

Congregational chapel, FORDHAM

FINGRINGHOE

elms, the north side of the Green
starts with the neat white brick
roof-pediment of the Congrega-
tionalists, the austere Gothick red
brick of the Victorian School, and
the one timber-framed house from
which the plaster overcoat has
been wrenched.

The pond is formed in the gulley
of a tributary stream of the Pant.
Just east of it a road leads north
to Steeple Bumpstead, and a
gleaming white post windmill
comes into view. It and the church
dominate the view of the humped-
up village as you approach from
the north. Here many of the well
preserved 18th-century thatched
cottages and 19th-century slate-
roofed cottages bear the mark of
the Ruggles-Brise family who
have lived at Spain's Hall since
the 18th century.

The range of the timber-framed
Guildhall, c. 1500, now almshouses, provides a lych-gate
through to church. A large Victorian red brick tower-buttress
spoils the view of the Guildhall
from the south-east path. The
(south) chantry chapel has a tall

"domestic" roof like those at Ashdon and Thaxted. In the Norman
W. doorway, a boldly projecting
human head is carved on either
side of a goat's head. Fine detail
on the carved 14th-century S.
door. Inside the tower, notice
blank arcading. Clerestoried nave
and chancel. Looking west from
the elaborate screen, one sees big
Royal Arms of 1660 above the
round tower-arch that frames the
font. Scratched in a ledge of
the S. aisle window is a diagram of
9 Men's Morris. In the S. chantry
chapel stands the Purbeck tomb-
chest of John Berners and wife,
1523, beautifully decorated, with
traces of colour still, and fine
brasses. Tablet with swags to
William Kempe, of Spain's Hall,
patron of Stephen Marshall the
formidable Puritan, who hoped to
reform the bishops. Pretty urn for
John Marshall, 1760. Medallion
bust of Thos. Marriott, 1766,
carved when he was 74 by W.
Tyler: Anne Marriott by Sir
Richard Westmacott, 1811. Series
of modern monuments to the public service of the Ruggles-Brises,

including Sir Evelyn, 1857–1935,
the founder of Borstal.

Their house, *Spain's Hall*, is a
large, mullioned, red brick predominantly Elizabethan house,
with curved gables and tall chimneys, screened by tall elms. At
Cornish Hall End a brick church
was built in 1841 to take outlying
parishioners.

Fingringhoe (13) occupies slopes
that overlook the Colne estuary
and marshes in the east and south,
the Roman River with disused
tide-mill below to the north-west.
Vestiges of Claudian quay were
found beside the Colne. Gravel
quarriers own a quay looking
across to Wivenhoe's water-front.
The village street straggles agreeably from the red brick *Grange,
c.* 1790, with a parapet and nice
doorcase, near Langenhoe, and
the *Old Rectory* with handsome
stuccoed (and pinned) front, past
the *Whalebone Inn* and a spectacular spreading oak, to the
church and *Hall*.

The church is irresistibly beautiful,
outside and in, for its colour,

105

FRINTON, The Homestead by C. F. Voysey, 1905

shape and, above all, texture. The square-topped tower is striped horizontally in narrow bands of silver-grey flint and limestone, coloured with red brick in louvres and stair-turret and safeguarded by the crosses of iron ties. Warm red roof. Glorious S. porch of glittering flush-set flints, tall battlemented parapet in checkered flushwork enhanced by a few skilful patches of checkered brickwork, side windows blocked to look like attractive Gothick dummy-windows, and in the spandrels above the outer doorway a superbly spirited Michael brandishes sword and shield out at an equally game dragon. The S. door is beautiful in the same way; over the centuries, much of its delicate 14th-century tracery has gone, but how suggestive the remains are! The interior retains its dappled dazzling medieval plaster with several patches of painting – on the south arcade the Virgin, Christ as Man of Sorrows, Michael with a seated woman: St Christopher in his usual place. The main attraction is the sculptured figure of "George Frere late of London Marchant", 1655, hand on skull, eye on eternity. The Stuart Royal arms were presented in 1763.

The *Hall*, red brick, was built perhaps for Frere. The N. front is slightly stiff with three large trefoil gables of exactly equal size; interior delectable.

Fobbing (9). The Lion Inn and tall church tower (silver-grey ragstone) hold the hill overlooking the marshes and Shell Haven, both of them conspicuous to Thames sailors in Lower Hope Reach, especially when the trees are bare. There is a blocked Saxon window through the N. wall of the church. The broad 14th-cen-

tury S. aisle has a separate roof gable. The large timber S. porch probably dates from 1551, when the church was in such "great ruin" that the Privy Council allowed them to sell £30 worth of goods towards repairs. (Main roofing may also be middle Tudor.) A spandrel of the porch has a lively carving of a figure suspiciously like Neptune, while someone nearby feeds a sea-serpent. Clear light interior with a view from the S. door across the simple Tudor pews of the S. aisle to the Georgian pulpit N. of the chancel arch. Early memorial tablet, *c.* 1340, to Thomas de Craweden.

Prosbus Hall stands north-west of church: a Georgian checkered brick front and early Stuart chimney stack. The Victorian *vicarage* of beautiful Victoria-plum brick is diapered in black. To the north, *Wheelers House* is Wealden shape, beautifully white-weatherboarded. *Fishers Farm Cottages*, a similar shape, thatched, have insensitively devised modern cottages alongside.

Ford End *see* Waltham, Great.

Fordham (10). *See also* Aldham. The 14th-century church, flint with some Roman brick, has bands of brick in the late medieval rebuilding of aisle-walls, and much brick repair to the tower which lost its lofty wooden spire in 1796. The church now crouches more cautiously on the edge of its high plateau. Notice a late medieval merchant's mark in the stonework of the S. doorway. Broad light nave with aisle. Georgian altar-rails and a marble monument of 1719 showing men-of-war in low relief and a bust of John Pulley who died at Port Mahone, aged 26, having been Captain of H.M.S. *Launceston* "several years".
Plastered timber-framed late medieval *Hall*, with the date 1586 on interior plasterwork, and much 17th-century alteration. It stands well grouped with the church and *Oak House* (formerly almshouses) and the *Three Horse-shoes*. The Congregational *Chapel* (endowed with minister and singing-teacher for the Countess of Huntingdon's Connexion, 1789) lies at the North end of the village, beyond acres of deplorably unrural new housing.

Foulness (16) seems preferable to Stansted for the site of London's third airport. It is intolerable that its rich soil should be sealed off in "defence" projects practicable elsewhere: it originally provided pasture for six "mainland" parishes. A chapel was founded on the Ness in 1408. A parish-church was provided in 1850. It was in use in 1965, "with resident padre", according to the guard at Landwick Police Lodge, Wakering, the frontier post. The *Mappin Sands* are passable at low water along the very ancient *Broomway* – marked by hundreds of poles looking like garden-brooms.

Foxearth (3) in a pleasant valley, tributary of the Stour, sounds like early hunting country, and there is a *Huntsman's Farm*. Moated *Hall*, with roof-structure of open 2-storey hall. Another house pink-washed between Hall and church started with 2-storey hall and had chimney and good fire-places inserted early in the 16th century. *Weston Hall* is an Elizabethan building near the site of its medieval predecessor. A medieval chapel stood on the nearby Green. *Constable's Farm* has a well carved bressumer with a merchant's mark, initials I.I., and date 1601. Grim church tower is of 1862 and most of the rest is lavish work of 1885. Ss. Barbara, Helena, Mary Magdalen, Dorothy, Apollonia (very sovereign against toothache), B.V.M., Christ, Alban, Walstan, Felix, Edmund and Augustine the Doctor are all painted and harshly over-restored on the early Tudor base of the screen. *Old rectory* has a handsome brick Georgian front.

Frating (14) means "gluttons" in Anglo-Saxon: what for is not clear: woods, cornfields and orchards now. The church, with a patch of early Norman herring-bone brick and a rich texture of iron conglomerate, has a porch with unusually solid knotty oak spandrels. Much Victoriana, including tower parapet of brick-and-flint stripes like Ardleigh's. The north chapel, with marble and alabaster altar-tomb, 1603, has a solid oak roof of the 17th century.

Frinton (14) is endowed with an attractive low cliff and a glorious sweep of sea. Alas, when he decided to develop a resort here in the 1890s, Sir Richard P. Cooker had apparently not seen Southwold with its similar position, also its houses built round lovely open greens. We must be content with the sloping cliff, sand, wooden groynes and a view to Walton Pier, the whole now dominated by two skyscraping blocks of flats, of eight storeys and twelve storeys,

not well massed, and more suited to London than the shores of the North Sea.
Nothing else in Frinton is up to standard of *The Homestead*, Voysey's model middle-class villa of 1905, on the way down to the tennis-courts, at the Holland Road corner of Second Avenue: the corner sets the pattern for the house, L-shaped, with kitchen leading through butler's pantry and entrance-hall to dining and drawing-rooms: 9-in. brick walls, rough-cast, projecting eaves with straight rainwater troughs running past upper windows, and Westmorland slate roofs. Every last detail was devised by Voysey, including shoe-scrapers, and, within, original needlework bell-pulls with traceried brass ends. Voysey's signature is the heart-shaped iron boss for the letter-box on the front door, and the heart-shaped key-holes on all the magnificent oak cupboards. Maurice Baring's purple-brick house next door, with Edward VIII–Mrs Simpson associations, is now flats. *Frinton Court*, the 12-storey block of flats rises on a cruciform plan, hardly out of consideration for the almost miniature *church* whose view of the sea it replaces. An early-Tudor church-porch of smouldering red brick was added to a tiny 14th-century nave of septaria. This was expanded east into a Victorian sanctuary, and west by 20th-century extension. Since World War II, the E. window has acquired beautiful William Morris glass, designed by Burne-Jones: an Annunciation in three lower scenes, with rich green and gold robes, is marred in summer by the green of a fine chestnut-tree outside: above, St Peter celebrates communion. Near the porch, Capt. James Bushell was buried, "famous as fishing for wrecks" and drowned in the early Great Tide of 1736. *St Mary Magdalene*, next to the Georgian Council House in Old Road, by Sir Charles Nicholson, 1929, gains gaiety of texture from the mixture of septaria with the flint and red horizontal brick.

Fryerning *see* Ingatestone.

Fyfield (5). The *Hall*, with tilting chimney, stands in a green paddock across the road from the church. The chimney, dated 1700 on a plaster panel, is misleading: this part of the house was built as a simple open aisled hall, and has been attributed by experts to the late 13th century.

The central tower of the church is topped by a squat pyramidal spire. The outside is spoilt by cement roughcast: stone casket with handsome urn stands in the churchyard at the W. end. Inside, there are warm red pamment floors in nave and choir (under central tower). Heavy restoration, but 14th-century chancel windows and sedilia are still rich with carved ballflower, and with heads at the lintel-stops. Anthony Walker, D.D., rector 1662–92, endowed a schoolmaster, "that Atheism, Ignorance, Profaneness and Sin may be rooted out of the parish, as much as may be". Rueful afterthought.

At *Clatterford End*, Fyfield County Secondary Boarding School (co-ed) combines 1885 "Queen Anne" (curved gabled) brick building of old West Ham boarding school with pleasant 1960s work. Amid shallow fields, *Lampetts*, basically an aisled hall of the 14th century, is roughcast, but its barn has an attractive length of tiled roof. *Pennyfeathers*, with an old chimney, is clapboarded and handsomely sheltered by elms.

Galleywood *see* Baddow, Great.

Garret, High *see* Braintree.

Gestingthorpe (3). The "Village of Gyrstlingas" was already recorded *c.* 1000, and nearly a thousand years earlier there was a Roman settlement in the valley ½ mile east of the church. There is Roman brick in the E. wall of the church; plum-red brick is a Tudor adornment of the church, especially its beautifully designed W. tower, and is also part of the distinction of *Over Hall*, opposite. Over Hall was built early in the 17th century for a Sible Hedingham clothier (Elliston), and brick-cased *c.* 1735, presumably for the

last of the Ellistons, who is commemorated in church in marble by Thomas Scott the Younger, 1741: there is a fine staircase and plastered drawing-room of about this date.

The old village brick-field closed down early this century. So did the pottery, down at Pot Kiln Chase, after about three centuries; some of its ware are to be seen in Hollytrees Museum, Colchester, and the Fitzwilliam, Cambridge.

Moat Farm is timber-framed, of the 15th century with a 17th-century pigeon house; both are beautiful examples of white-washed plaster-work. About 1498, the romantically castellated *church* tower and stair turret were built of brick, leading through a tall broad tower-arch to the nave with a loft and a delicate double hammerbeam roof of the same time: the names of Petir Barnard, Thomas Loveda and their wives are inscribed in north and south wall-plates; presumably donors (see Introduction). The ringers' chamber, seen in section, is part of an 1898 restoration (A. Blomfield Jackson). Georgian Moses and Aaron (? by Robert Cardinall like those of St Peter, Sudbury) now appear rather startlingly cleaned. The chancel is almost over-spotless through the successfully reconstructed medieval screen (1907). John Sparrow, 1626, is commemorated in an alabaster arch hung with trophies. A gleaming brass plate in the nave recalls Captain Oates, the "very gallant gentleman" who walked outside to death in the Antarctic to try to save the rest of Scott's expedition in 1912, and whose safe return here from the Boer War had been the occasion for recasting one of the old church bells. In the churchyard, a finely carved headstone of *c.* 1790.

Goldhanger (13). The "slope where marsh-marigolds hung" before Norman times, the main delight now is its creek on the Blackwater and the walk from Decoy Point over to Osea Island (see Totham). In the village the *Chequers* is a place for tales of wild-fowling and

the old barging days. A wheel-turned village pump is still in use at the corner of Head Street and Church Street. The church's building history can be read largely in the E. wall with its Roman-brick quoins, mixed chocolate pudding-stone, buff septaria and grey flints: Norman chancel and nave: S. aisle late 14th-century (see S. doorway), S. chapel and W. tower 15th-century. South chapel and aisle must have become ruined: the arcade and upper walls are now Victorian.

Gosfield (3). A large park is edged by a long lake and the church in the south, the village in the east, with Samuel Courtauld's Victorian timber-framed houses. *Highgates Cottages* has been made out of a remarkable old farmhouse. A vast haphazard bungaloid growth is spreading through park and village.

Thomas Rolf, serjeant-at-law, built chancel and nave *c.* 1435: he appears in his robes in brass on a Purbeck altar-tomb with a Latin inscription saying what a flower he was among lawyers. What kind of flower is not specified here, but evidently he was a pretty poisonous plant cultivated in the earl of Oxford's garden. The tower was added *c.* 1500. The N. chapel was built and the chancel widened on the S. side *c.* 1560, in red brick except for flintwork round the E. window. These extensions were presumably to accommodate the tombs of Sir Hugh Rich and Sir John Wentworth, also of Purbeck marble, with brass inscriptions that are gradually being stripped. The white-washed interior of the N. chapel makes a delightful impression since its restoration in 1953. An extraordinary (locked) Georgian family chapel and squire's pew west of the N. chapel contains Rysbrack's splendid monument to John Knight and his wife, with an urn between them, 1733.

The *Hall*, a great quadrangle, now M.H.A., is open to the public on Wednesdays and Thursdays, 2–5, May–September. It is basically Tudor, but exactly when and by whom built remains baffling. Probably by one of the Wentworths, a cadet branch of those at Nettlestead, Suffolk. Pevsner, Morant and others suggest "mid" 16th century, but the Tudor W. front (with main entrance) remains curiously early-looking and defensible: no windows on the ground floor (which has the long gallery above). The E. front with great hall was remodelled by John Knight (Rysbrack's sitter). Later Georgian remodelling by Earl Nugent (who also devised the lake) and by the Marquis of Buckingham who with Lady Buckingham started *c.* 1790 the straw-plait industry that substantially helped the poor of these parts. "The first hats produced were of a coarse and unsightly appearance" but the Buckinghams pushed sales by wearing them "in sight of the whole village".

Grays *see* Thurrock.

Greenstead near Colchester *see* Colchester.

Greensted-juxta-Ongar (5). St. Andrew's famous little nave has low walls of vertical oak trees, blackened by time (and treatment?), cleft down the middle, with the cleft flat surface forming the inner wall, the rounded circumference of the trunks facing out. Down their sides they are grooved and tongued together. In 1848 a thorough restoration supplied a brick plinth and new sills and altered the W. wall. Timbers of N. and S. walls are original, varying from 7 to over 17 inches in diameter, and Dendro-magnetic tests give a date of *c.* 850 for some of them. St Edmund's body may have rested here in 1013 on its removal from Bury to London to be out of reach of the Vikings.

The chancel is of rich red Tudor brick with a reeling doorway: digging has shown two earlier timber chancels. The nave is lit by dormers in the roof. The inner wall surface was stripped of plaster in 1848, and the joints covered by fillets: this gives the slightly panelled effect. The ancient oak

surface bears rough marks of the adze for keying-in the medieval plaster. The small late-medieval tower is weatherboarded, with a pretty Gothick window of 1848 and broad spire lately shingled. Craven Ord (1756–1832), antiquary and collector of brass-rubbings, is himself buried north of the church.

The red brick creeper-grown *Hall* adjacent was mainly built by the Cleeves in the 1690s, and much remodelled in 1875.

Hadleigh (9). The small Norman *church*, complete with round chancel-arch, and apse, crouches now amid a swirl of Southend's suburban traffic. In a window-splay is a lively, almost contemporary, picture of "Beate Tomas" of Canterbury. To the north, some of the great woods have mercifully been kept that once almost insulated Hadleigh on N. and W. sides.

Ruins of the *castle* built for Edward III in the 1360s are intelligible only with the aid of a plan: one long side of the elliptic curtain-wall has subsided into the Thames estuary, as it had when John Constable made his pencil sketch in 1814. Fifteen years later, in the Spring after his wife's death, the great painting now in the Mellon Collection emerged: ruins in the foreground, the sky full of tears. Far out in the estuary the waves are gleaming and shining. A beam of light escapes through the cloud. The full-scale study in oils is at the National Gallery. Here the Ministry of Works is tidying up the ruins. A majestic sense of space and of the Thames remains.

Hadstock (2). The road from Walden climbs steadily to 370 ft. on Hadstock airfield (disused), which has long views east to Castle Camps. Then it drops sharply into the village. An entirely unsophisticated village-green is at the centre. *Hall* on the east side, *church* to the south.

St Botolph's *church* is basically a late Saxon cruciform building, in great need of help. In 1966 elder was growing from tops of but-

tresses. A bell of 1739 lay outside the W. door, which has very early ironwork. Walls of nave and N. transept are Saxon and so, astonishingly, is the iron-bound N. door, leading through a crude semicircular arch like the start of a tunnel. There are Saxon nave windows, double splayed, at clerestory height. Within, although the S. transept was rebuilt in the 14th century, and the arch into it was rebuilt in the 13th century, the supports of this arch are Saxon and very impressive. The carving on the abacuses is crude, nearer honeysuckle than acanthus-leaf, but cf. the rudimentary modern carving of names on the oak memorial reredos in the S. transept chapel. There is a beautiful little 13th-century S. doorway. The tower is 15th-century, the chancel 19th.

There is a memorable view north from the church over the unspoilt village to *Hill Farm*, which retains its hall-screen at the W. end. It and the end cottage on Walden road belong to the Cambridgeshire Cottage Improvement Society.

Hainault Forest *see* Chigwell and Introduction.

Hallingbury, Great (5). The Houblons' opulent Georgian house has gone from the park. The shingled spire of the church is prominent in the Stortford hinterland. The church is heavily Victorian, but its main feature is the broad semi-circular early-Norman chancel arch, built entirely of Roman brick into E. wall of nave, which Victorians have pierced with tracery to give more view of the sanctuary from the nave. The *Hall* has a pretty red-brick early 19th-century front, an earlier rear.

Hallingbury, Little (5). Contains *Wallbury Camp*, that gives Hallingbury its "-bury": it is an early Iron Age settlement in a superb natural defensive position overhanging Spelbrook Lock (British Waterways) on the Stort Navigation. Strengthened by a double rampart as at Erbury (Clare, Suffolk), and Pitchbury (Horkesley). Now known as "Wallbury

Dells" and developing very dingly. The *church* has a Norman doorway of Roman bricks, within a traceried 14th-century timber S. porch. Pond. Low Georgian brick *maltings* and *Old Rectory*. *Gaston House*, 5-bay 3-storey Georgian red brick.

Halstead (3), a thoroughfare town. High Street drops steeply from Chipping Hill, up by the church and the fragment of a prominent "smock" windmill, where the market ("Cheeping") was established by 1251, down to the Colne Valley below, where Courtaulds established a branch of their silk manufactory in 1826, in what remains the most handsome building in the town. A great horizontal white-painted weatherboarded mill-building, it straddles the stream like some ancient bridge on to which warehouses have been crowded, or like the side of a great stranded liner. "The Causeway" leading to it has excellent gabled, terraced houses on the right, good factory building opposite, across the stream, and a charming "works clocking-in" house at the end, a cross between a bandstand and a gazebo. Their housing on Maplestead Road replaces good old timber houses but affects Jane Austen names: Sense, Sensibility, etc.

There are now two civil parishes – Halstead "Urban" and Halstead "Rural". In Halstead Urban the broad, climbing High Street is worth a look: 36 is a lively essay in mid-Victorian polychrome brickwork; Georgian red brick at 22–24; the White Hart opposite, with traceried Victorian bargeboards; 27 has an Ionic doorcase, pilasters and a Georgian brick house at right angles. 26 has a good Georgian first-floor front and jettied side that hints at its age: it is the house of the chantry-priests founded in 1412 by Bartholomew, Lord Bourchier.

The Bourchiers, one of the most powerful English families in the 14th and 15th centuries, lived at Stanstead Hall in Halstead "Rural". *St Andrew's Church* at the top of the High Street is largely the product of a £5,000

restoration of 1851–2: its tower was entirely rebuilt, for about the fourth time, in 1850. But what survives from before 1850 is largely from the time of Lord Chancellor Robert Bourchier, who fought alongside the Black Prince at Crécy, and was buried here in 1349, probably one of the innumerable victims of the Black Death. His scheme to convert this into a collegiate church was probably another victim of the Black Death. The Bourchier tombs are rather jumbled. His now *seems* to bear the effigies of his father (d. 1328) and mother (through whom Stanstead Hall came to them), his own effigy gone? His son John, Governor of Flanders and K.G., lies more intact with wife under canopy, *c.* 1400, but grandson Bartholomew, founder of that chantry of 1412, has his brass and that of his two wives barbarously covered by seating. Meanwhile a vast marble inscription perpetuates the will of Elizabeth Holmes (1706–83) "the surviving representative of a pious, industrious and at length opulent family". In the Holmes' tomb outside the S. porch, John Morley is buried, presumably the builder of Bluebridge House, with lovely ironwork and brickwork of 1714 on the road E. to Stanstead Hall. Bluebridge's summerhouse, which had a ceiling painted by Thornhill, seems to have been destroyed by a bomb in World War II.

There are two notable early Victorian churches by G. Gilbert Scott: *Holy Trinity*, 1843–4, a truly noble essay in "E.E." and managed in flint with white brick quoins: his first tower fell in 1844 and was replaced at once by this tremendous object. Next year he built *St James*, with a beautiful shingled spire, at *Greenstead Green* in Halstead Rural, and pronounced "Grinsted", the gift of Mrs Gee of Earls Colne, who gave £3,000 of the £5,000 that Holy Trinity cost. The late Victorian chapel in Fremlin's Brewery contains some fine fittings from a Wren church (All Hallows, Gt Thames Street). The Colne Valley railway reached Halstead in 1860. The last Bourchier Earl of Essex

was thrown from a horse in 1540. *Stanstead Hall*, at present providing four "flats", is the surviving S. wing of a large quadrangular red brick house built probably by his successor as Earl of Essex, Lord Parr. A 1553 survey showed a large chapel forming the N. side of the court. Medieval fragments survive, and a complete moat, some of it faced with masonry. The E. gable, its "shaped" trefoil top rebuilt, is flanked by turrets. The S.W. wing is relatively modern. *Gladfen Hall* is a pleasant timber-framed Elizabethan house above Bourne Brook.

Hanningfield, East (6) is now centred on the *Tye*, an entirely delightful small green, with *Rails Farm* at the S. end, and some industry; the well-kept church of 1885 is half-way along. The medieval church, a mile away to the south, was burnt out after Christmas 1883; its site is now inaccessible behind the Hall.

Hanningfield, South (9). The churchyard now finds itself pleasantly close to Hanningfield Water, the large reservoir formed from Sandon Brook, lying like a calm lowland loch. The late-medieval belfry, much restored, is reared on four great posts in the W. end of the nave with two arched braces. Delicately painted vine-scrolls and a fragment of medieval glass in the S. window.

Hanningfield, West (6). Housing for the Hanningfield Water Joint Managing Committee was well sited beside the water, 1955. Attic rooms at *Clovile Hall* were painted with arabesques and arms of Skynner impaling Fulke and Bowyer, 1615. A nearby clapboard cottage has "R F 1747" in E parge-work. *Elms Farm*, formerly Clockfoot, still has 16th/17th century outlines: the W. bay of its S. wing was lost in the 19th century. The *church* (Ss. Mary and Edward) is remarkable for its timber W. tower, one of the famous Essex series. Here charm and oddity are combined with

Courtauld's Mill, HALSTEAD

110

virtuosity of structure. An early date has been argued (13th-century), but this tower stands midway along the W. wall of the combined nave and S. aisle, which was not added to nave before *c.* 1330. The tower is held steady by a buttressing of tall ground-floor extensions on all four sides: shaped arched braces on the upper floor meet in a central wooden boss – carved into a smug face with decayed nose. The whole belfry-tower is cased in clapboard, with (blocked) Georgian Gothick windows in the S. extension and the odd shingled bow projecting from the W. wall of the bellchamber. The church's interior is very unsophisticated. Nave roof: tie beams with tall crown-posts and struts like umbrellas inside-out. A late-Stuart communion-rail is at the raised entrance to the choir. There are also a vast medieval chest, a few scraps of medieval glass, Georgian Commandments and royal arms, and early 19th-century Charity boards.

Harlow (5). A little medieval clothing-town with extinct market just east of the London–Newmarket road (A11) and a celebrated cattle-fair on the Common till the last century, gives its name to a New Town, created since 1947, in stages fully chronicled, on the site of four very rural parishes just west of A11 – *Latton, Netteswell, Great* and *Little Parndon.*

Creating a New Town is a most exciting activity in any age, irresistible to watch. Harlow took twenty years to achieve its new identity, and will continue to mature for at least two more decades. To test its self-sufficiency and its influence among neighbours the best time for a first visit is market-day (Tuesday, Friday, Saturday), best of all a fine Saturday morning in summer. *Stone Cross* market-square lies at the heart of the town-centre, *The High,* its name extravagant even by Essex standards (the ground has risen from 100 ft. at Town Station to a bit over 200 ft. here), but high enough to give central

buildings focal emphasis. The first feeling is wonder: we have reached this town-centre without quite grasping that we have driven "through" the town, parked the car easily in the open at ground level, and walked straight into a centre free from traffic nuisance, yet full of bustle. The market is delightful, like Norwich's or Leicester's, but on a more agreeable scale with gay awnings, and modern bronze sculpture that is already as much at home as an antique column in a Roman market (Ralph Brown's "Meat Porters" and F. E. McWilliam's "Portrait Figure"); and stalls full of country green-groceries and fishing rods as well as the inevitable rolls of lino. Here is the clue. In the bleak days after the 2nd World War, Sir Frederick Gibberd conceived, and has now seen reaching full growth, not just some characterless New Town for the absorption of London "over-spill", but a New Country Town. Gibberd's master-plan is simple: industrial firms on the line of rail and river and the proposed motorway, along the N. side of the town, with a second site in the north-west to avoid any dominant concentration of industry in one place. Housing in four main "clusters", each made up of three or four "neighbourhoods", and each neighbourhood composed of a number of "housing areas". Each "housing area" is the work of a different firm of architects, so that there is variety between the areas, and within the area the horrid confusion is avoided of everyone's house being different from everyone else's. Three "clusters" have their own shopping centres: the fourth is related to The High. Gibberd compares his road system to a river system. The original springs and trickles are the groups of houses in the heart of the neighbourhood: moving away from them, roads widen and intersections become fewer as traffic grows in volume: main town roads, like park-chases, run through natural landscape that divides the four clusters, which are (as far as possible) built on higher ground.

What to see. The latest edition of the official Harlow Guide (3*s.* 6*d.,* bookshop in Broad Walk, off Stone Cross market) has a useful map. Pevsner's *Essex* is good on Harlow, but the map is printed without "legend". Excitement enough in "seeing how it all works". I suggest looking first at The High, then at N.E. cluster, since it was built first and is most "mature"; then at S.W. cluster, since it is still building, and with some of its new high-density building (19·5 dwellings to the acre at Bishopsfield: most town authorities still think they have done well with 10 per acre) seems to mark some modification in Gibberd's original ideas and certainly represents experiments of great interest for the future of all towns in Britain. Then readers of this Guide will want to know what survives of the old parishes on the site.

The High. Stone Cross market is unexciting architecturally, though Lyons Buttery provides a useful first-floor open-air observation platform. Broad Walk has advantages and limitations of all such shopping ways. It leads to the excellent new library building one finds now in so many Essex towns (H. Conolly), and librarians well charged with first-hand information on the current developments in the New Town. (Public Information Office in Adams House – named after the Corporation's first General Manager.) Dominant building at The High, appropriately Gibberd's Town Hall, cruciform with eleven-storey tower block on S. arm; recessed upper storeys topped by splendid observation room, with delicate arcade over, an amusingly Italianate coiffure from which purists recoil. St Paul's church (C. of E., Humphrys & Hurst), standing more in the open than it will ultimately, is the most graceful building at The High, cruciform, with walls like lace (effect of clear glass, thin concrete columns and tracery, rich golden sandy-coloured brick), and almost dazzlingly light interior in which John Piper's mystic figures, in mosaic, materialize from an almost black background. To the

HARLOW: Stone Cross

south, the terraced garden with canal, on a good scale, is still a shade flat.

N.E. Cluster. Before driving here from "The High", it is worth going along Fifth Avenue, towards the Town Station, with the Park on the right, to see the remarkable Sports Hall (Gibberd) on the left. It is better equipped than anything provided in towns three times bigger than Harlow, and helping to make this a regional centre for sport. The N.E. Cluster (Mark Hall North, Mark Hall South, and Netteswell; all based on centre called The Stow), is all as rural as any country town and most villages, in the sense that landscape enfolds the housing, is never banished by it, even in close-built streets like The Chantry, Mark Hall North, where

old Latton church (see below) asserts its "village" presence. Mark Hall North, the first to be built, was criticized for not being "urban enough", and one of the interests here is to spot successive attempts at denser housing without resorting to tower-blocks of which Gibberd designed a famous example (The Lawn) here. Also see, at Mark Hall North, Our Lady of Fatima (R.C. church, full of very striking, indeed strident, stained glass by three monks of Buckfast Abbey: the interior has remarkable "atmosphere"), Barbara Hepworth's sculpture "Contrapuntal Forms", and Sylvia Crowe's children's wild play-area. The best single building is probably the Mark Hall Secondary School (1954, Richard Sheppard & Partners). It is, however, just

east of A11, drawing attention to the way that highway divides Old Town from New Town: the highway itself has been diverted westwards, so as no longer to slice both Old Town and Potter Street in two.

S.W. Cluster, reached by Southern Way. The cluster's centre is Staple Tye, all contained in one building, and here the emphasis is on urbanity. The three housing estates to see are Old Orchard, Shaw-bridge and Bishopsfield (with Charters Cross). Old Orchard (Clifford Culpin & Partners) is the winning design in competition sponsored by R.I.B.A. and "Ideal Home" magazine: very attractive, in silvery grey brick (cf. Warley) combining a degree of elegance with a density of 15 dwellings per acre (too many urban authorities

are content with 10 per acre). At Shawbridge, Eric Lyons's uncompromising black brick cubes and wedges form terraces that have an urban London look and achieve 18 per acre. With Bishopsfield, Michael Neylan won 1st Prize in international competition sponsored by Harlow Corporation in 1961. 19·5 dwellings per acre! Concourse of underground service-roads and garages at crown of hill, flats above this and then L-shaped single-storey "patio" houses descending the hill like a section of the Colosseum, with access from truly urban brick alleys. Show-house well worth seeing. Ingenious and greatly preferable to suburbia. On a big scale it would present the aspect of some old Italian hill-top town. *Old Harlow*. In 1967 undergoing major surgery: the Dunmow/Hatfield Broad Oak road is being brought in on a new route that will cut Churchgate Street off from Mulberry Green, but will enable High Street to be devoted to pedestrians only, and recapture some of the character that motoring destroyed. (At right-angles, London Road has already lost its through-traffic to the new A11.) High Street, mostly Georgian in character, runs east to *Mulberry Green*, also Georgian, with the *Green Man*, Elizabethan and 17th-century: north of Mulberry Green is the Norman chapel (now a barn) of *Harlowbury*: east of Mulberry Green, Churchgate Street with very picturesque oversailing pub, the *Queen's Head*, more Georgian building, and the *Churchgate Hotel* much altered from former Chantry. The *church*, cruciform, and over-Victorianized, contains several brasses. *Potter Street. Baptist chapel* 1756, with good doorway, and light interior. St Mary Magdalene, Harlow Common, 1888–98, was rebuilt by Rev. Henry Elwell, vicar 33 years, whose likeness is carved above the clock on the S. side of the tower (good brief *Guide*). Remains of the fine 14th-century crossing of *Latton Priory* church,

embodied in a barn, now come into the ecclesiastical parish of Harlow Common, though nearly a mile south of the New Town boundary.

Latton church, nevertheless, is very much part of the New Town (see Mark Hall North). It has a timber-framed S. porch with red brick walls. The Tudor stone S. doorway and nailed door are let into a Norman S. doorway dressed with brick (see also small Norman S. window). Another round-headed brick doorway presumably provided early Tudor access to the rood-loft. There is now a recent rood of distressing design. The 15th-century N. chapel has an iron grille through to the sanctuary and original painting on the arch over, also on the wall above Sir Peter Arderne's tomb. This is set into a remarkable triple arch of the 15th century, with foliated caps and frieze of foliage combined with Arderne initials. Altham monument 1583, falsely coloured with a kind of fluorescent blue.

Netteswell. The old *Hall* and *House* contrived to stay in the new "Netteswell" neighbourhood (near the Swimming Bath): the parish *church* is south of Second Avenue in Tye Green neighbourhood: pleasant red-tiled roof, and dark timber belfry with small broach spire: equally fine roof of barn alongside: all looking out of place amid some very dull housing.

Great Parndon. In this S.W. cluster, *High House*, Kingsmoor Road, and *1 & 2 Peldon Road*, white weatherboarded, are good representatives of the past amid all the works of the present. The *church*, beside a large chestnut tree prolific with conkers, stands framed against the concrete palace of B.P. offices (J. M. Wilson, H. C. Mason & Partners). The church is 15th-century, with an Edwardian N. transept, and a S. transept that is Georgian or earlier (Pevsner and R.C. adrift). Stained glass includes two 15th-century faces (one in tears) and the name of John Celley, esquier, benefactor in 1588.

Little Parndon church, a Victorian

rebuilding with apse, contains a tablet to a 17th-century Speaker of the House of Commons, Turnour. The golf-course to the west has been very attractively laid out by Henry Cotton.

Harwich and Dovercourt (12). Famous as a port of passage to mainland Europe, Harwich is little visited, for North Sea passengers sail from Parkeston, 2 miles west; and, though the train-ferry pier was built at Harwich itself (1924), that affords no way of sightseeing in the town. Medieval Harwich, once walled with the local septaria, and gated, and with a castle-bastion at the N.E. corner, was packed on to a thin peninsula, only 95 acres, jutting up into the confluent estuaries of Orwell and Stour that splash and lap round it and provide it with a great natural anchorage to north and west, sheltered as it is from the east by Landguard Point, Suffolk. From this tight urban mass, two distinct shapes emerge as one approaches by water: the slender nonagonal lighthouse tower (1818) and the capacious pale-yellow brick church of St Nicholas (1821) with stone dressings and respectable spire. What survives from the Middle Ages is situation, a sense of seafarers. The narrow grid-pattern of streets and passages, storehouses and old pubs, boarded-up cinema and new Trinity House offices, bears the marks of slump and revival that seem as remorselessly part of Harwich's long life as the rise and fall of the tide.

Dovercourt, to landward, already named in the 10th century, means "water-court", embodying the ancient Celtic "dubro" as at Dover in Kent. From Dovercourt's mother-church, St Nicholas's in Harwich was born by *c.* 1210. (Its spire rose above a pleasant wooden octagon.) The name Herwyz seems to have been born

p. 116
HARWICH:
Low Light and High Light
p. 117
HARWICH:
Trinity House buoy store

about the same time. The town was chartered in 1319; in June 1340 it watched the great marshalling of Edward III's fleet for Sluys. Twelve years later it was walled. In 1528, when Wolsey asked for septaria from Beacon Cliff to build his colleges, he was told "it lieth as a foreland to defend" the town. This explains Harwich's survival on a coast that destroyed Dunwich. The removal of millions of tons of septaria for Roman cement-facing of Nash's London resulted in immediate erosion till a great breakwater was built to the south-east, over 1,500 ft. and faced with Kentish rag, in 1843. Recurrent fortification, of 1539, is reflected in a wall painting in 14 King's Head Street: it shows a Harwich man about to touch off a cannon. The Royal dockyard, begun in 1657, was already doomed, by constriction of site, to be supplanted by Sheerness: shipbuilding and victualling fluctuated with national crises, and after 1713 Harwich declined almost to status of private yard. Late 17th, early 18th-century prosperity still apparent. Opposite the *Angel* and *Globe* pubs, notice, on the present "containerization" quay, the bell ordered by Admiralty for the Old Naval Shipyard, 1666. See, also, the old crane from here, operated by two human tread-wheels and apparently costing £392 in 1667. *Monuments in church* include inscription to Sir Wm. Clarke, "secretary-at-war to the most serene King Charles II", who lost both leg and life in the great Four Days Battle along this coast, 1666. *Portraits in the guildhall* include that of the most serene King. Perambulate the four main parallel streets, starting on the E. side with Kings Quay Street. North end with *Angel* and *Globe*, weatherboarded and gabled, just right. Beyond, the recent remodelling combines good Georgian redbrick and plastered fronts with new red-brick blocks quite well in character: then the close-built old housing is marred by the shell of the Palace cinema, somehow still haunted by the roar of the throttled engines of "Hell's An-

gels". King's Head Street, untroubled by traffic, is narrow at the N. end, with notable old buildings, expecially 13 which oversails at first *and* second floors, and 14, with carved bressummer, and with wall painting already mentioned and plaster mural of charging Tudor Knight; 16, Georgian red brick; 21, oversailing, bears iron plaque proclaiming it the house of Capt. Christopher Jones, master of the Mayflower: S. end of street rebuilt on good urban scale. In Church Street notice the *Guildhall*, with panelled Gothick doorway, bearing portcullis, the borough's arms, and above, a notice saying rebuilt at the expense of the Corporation, 1769. Main character of West Street Georgian, including almshouses. The waterfront, looking N. to Shotley peninsula, is dominated by the *Town Hall*, built much too big as the Great Eastern Hotel, 1864. Beside it, the *Pier Hotel*, with 1st-floor ironwork balcony and 3rd floor belvedere, was a more realistic and delightful response to the arrival of the railway, 1854. *High Lighthouse* housed carrier-pigeons till the days of the electric telegraph. It now stands in a rather seedy area, where ornamental gardens and a bowling green stood *c.* 1709 – outside the former South Gate.

Dovercourt aspired as a sea-side resort: Undercliff Walk had been built over a mile along the seashore by 1858, costing the local M.P. nearly £10,000. The seafront remains Dovercourt's best feature, its two most distinctive buildings the small six-legged iron movable lighthouses, literally "leading lights", built in response to the growth of Landguard spit opposite, but disused since 1917. Nearby, eight timbered houses were given by the people of Norway to rehouse victims of the great tide of January 1953. The north end of the cliff is still dominated by World War concrete emplacements and lookouts that should be removed or embodied in holiday-attractions. New Secondary Modern School, 1957, with prefab. tiles like diapers. Distinguished factory-build-

ing for Standard Yeast by Ove Arup & Partners. *All Saints-and-St Augustine*, in Upper Dovercourt, covered with roughcast and harsh red tiles, displays interesting 14th-century window-tracery, and a 14th-century bell. Interior impressively murky. Through the gloom one perceives two massive nave tie-beams, a 14th-century grey panelled font, an iron-bound poorbox of 1589, and brightly enamelled Royal Arms suspended from the great rood-beam that is carved and with console brackets dated 1615 (cf. Ramsey). Chancel walls lean out. Large nave S. window is full of poor glass of 1898, but occupies so much space at eyelevel it exerts fascination: The Six Works of Mercy. The window in the tower commemorates Dovercourt's works of mercy after the futile Walcheren Expedition of 1809. This lurid glass was given by a grateful German ally.

Hatfield Broad Oak (5), sometimes still known as Hatfield Regis from its having been royal forest, reaches 5 miles south from Stane Street. In its N.W. corner, some hundreds of acres of oak and hornbeam forest, with great rides and agreeable picnic-places are preserved by the National Trust. One tree, "the Doodle oak", is growing out of another that stopped leafing in 1858 after about 850 years of growth. A lake was created in 1760 by Jacob Houblon (see Hallingbury) with the aid of local unemployed. On its shore, the *Shell House* had its shell-covered room added in 1759, the designs by Laetitia Houblon. It now serves tea and light refreshment.

The *church*, with stately W. tower, is the surviving nave of a Benedictine priory-church founded by de Vere in 1135 as a cell of St Melaine's abbey, Rennes. Sturdy shafted piers buttressing the east wall were built as the western base of the former central tower. East of this, the monastic church has vanished: it had been lavishly rebuilt *c.* 1310 by a Hatfield man whose benefactions to the monks included a shop in the village. The nave (except the N. wall) was

HATFIELD BROAD OAK

rebuilt in the later 14th century, the aisle moulded and with carved heads. The interior regales its visitors to the sight of low box-pews expertly carved in oak *c.* 1850; a great glittering chandelier of real presence; a panelled tie-beam roof (formerly hammer-beam: see sole surviving kneeling angel); George III's royal arms, still properly above E. end of nave; the earlier-Georgian panel-ling and railing of the chancel, exceptionally fine, is apparently by John Woodward, a craftsman employed in the chapel of Trinity, Cambridge. Central position in chancel occupied by a recumbent, rather shattered stone effigy, evi-dently Robert de Vere, 3rd Earl (died 1221), though it was made late in that century. The N. wall is articulate with a range of old monuments beneath windows set high above the vanished cloister.

They include Barringtons of Bar-rington Hall and Selwins of Down Hall. The stuccoed library at the S.E. corner of the church was built in the early 19th century to house the fine collection of an early 18th-century vicar, George Sterling, in whose day Matthew Prior lived at Down Hall. A 15th-century sacristy and priest's cham-ber lie behind the early Georgian panelling at the end of the N. Chapel.

Cottages round the S. side of the church create a little the effect of the cloister formerly on the N. side. The village street contains a new infants' school (1966) with low timbered dome, supported by its own tension; also Georgian and Victorian brick housing, the *Cock Inn* with elaborate iron sign-bracket, and old gabled timber-framed houses, mostly at *Cage End* (the W. end) where the village

pump remains, and the lock-up once stood, and where the village ends abruptly in furrowed fields. *Barrington Hall*, in the park north of the church, externally a Vic-torian "Jacobean" house, never-theless contains a magnificent very early Georgian core: the hall is especially noble, with wall-paint-ings and two great carved fire-places. In 1771, "A Gentleman" noted that the saloon chimney-piece, "of white marble, curiously carved and polished, alone cost £700". Other rooms were begun in this splendid manner, but by 1771 the whole building was "much neglected".

Three miles south, *Down Hall*, now *Downham*, is a girls' boarding school. Rebuilt in concrete by the youngest Cockerell (F. P.) in the 1870s, and decorated with sgraf-fito to look like a Florentine palace, its grounds include walks lined by elderly hornbeams that in their youth may have bemused Matthew Prior.

Two new flinty churches were provided in 1859: one at *Bush End*, the E. edge of "Hatfield Forest" (N.T.), the other at *Hatfield Heath*, a large Green.

Hatfield Peverel (6). The A12 was deflected in the middle 1960s, but the village centre is uninteresting. On Maldon Road, notice Martha Lovibond's terrace of attractive almshouses, single-storey, with Gothick windows and weatherboard porches, 1820. As at Hatfield Broad Oak, the *church* is the nave of a former priory-church; this one was founded by a Peverel as a cell of St Alban's. It is approached through the pleasant park of *The Priory*, a white-brick house of 1776 owned by the Mariannhill Mission. The Norman W. doorway is set in a plain W. wall mainly of yellow septaria and flint, beneath a large Perp. window of glass by the Victorian glazier Kempe. White's *Directory*, 1863, mentioned two W. turrets with small spires, now gone. It is a bare, rather dull interior. The E. windows are formed in the semicircular crossing arch of the once large monastic church. Jumbles of early glass, mostly foreign, brought in, presumably when the ancient 6-gabled *Priory House* was demolished in the 18th century. Tall stone figure of man, *c.* 1300, with heart in hands, lying on N. windowsill badly eroded. Hatfield Place, built 1791–5, is one of John Johnson's more distinguished Essex houses, disfigured by a Victorian porch.

Hawkwell (9) is contiguous with the Hockley and a contrast, for most of its bungalows, pre-1939, have a less cheerful air than Hockley's. The weatherboarded broach spire above the belfry of the church projects a sharp white spike into the sky.

Hedingham, Castle (3). The de Veres acquired Hedingham at the Conquest. By 1086 they had a vineyard here. Fifty years later, on a promontory commanding the ancient Colne valley-route they erected the famous square baronial keep whose two corner-turrets, 100 ft. high, still seem to watch over all the lands around. Less well known, but scarcely less distinguished, the late Norman church they built after perhaps another fifty years nestles below in the sleepy village for whom they acquired market-rights from King John. The market has long been forgotten, but its triangular site (base in James Street: apex at E. end of churchyard) explains the shape of the village centre. The two best houses are out along Queen Street: a splendid red brick Georgian *rectory* (6 bays, 3 storeys on garden front), and, adjacent, *Trinity Hall*, early Georgian with dormers and a white plastered front. The name of the small hamlet of *Nunnery Street*, beside the Colne, is virtually all that survives of the nunnery founded by the de Veres in the late 12th century (a pink farm-house is near the site). From it, Sandy Lane winds two attractive miles to *Kirby Hall*, a small Elizabethan house acquired by Peter Muilman, who contributed to the publication of *A New and Complete History of Essex by a Gentleman*, 1769–72, and whose nephew's portrait with two young friends by Gainsborough in the '50s reminds us that Sudbury lies just over the hill.

The Castle (open to the public on Tuesdays, Thursdays and Saturdays, 2–6 p.m. May–September, and Bank Holidays 10–6). As you climb up to it along Castle Lane from the village you cannot escape the sense of approaching one of the great French *donjons* of Normandy or the Loire. In this part of England, only the royal keep at Orford is grander. Hedingham's great keep, of flint rubble, faced with Barnack stone and retaining a great deal of its original internal plaster, is reckoned among the best preserved tower-keeps in England. It stands on a natural promontory, an "inner bailey" divided off from the lower part of the promontory (the "outer bailey") by a simple deep ditch, crossed now by an impressive early Tudor bridge, almost the only surviving sign that the castle was occupied by the later de Vere earls of Oxford. This bridge may have been built for the reception of Henry VII here in 1498. Most of the castle was pulled down by the spendthrift Elizabethan 17th earl. It was sold to one Ashurst, whose monument in church says he built the present Georgian house from the ruins in 1719. *Plan of keep:* outside-stair to first floor, thereafter the staircase climbs up in the N.W. angle; the walls, 11 ft. thick, contain small chambers. There are round-headed fireplaces with Norman zigzag ornament (cf. Colchester) in the main first-floor room and the great second-floor Hall.

The church is at first sight early Tudor, with a good red-brick W. tower, S. porch and clerestory. The clerestory bears the de Vere mullet (star-emblem) that was in the ascendant under the 13th earl, who fought for Henry VII at Bosworth, and doubtless paid for this work. (An inscription on the W. face of the tower says it was "*renovated* in 1616" by Robert Archer, master-builder.) Inside, too, the fine hammerbeam roof is early Tudor (thought to be by Thomas Loveday; cf. Gestingthorpe and see Introduction). But everything else, the main fabric of nave and chancel is magnificent work of the late Norman period: so late that the chancel arch, though decorated with Norman zigzags, runs up to a point. Of a piece with this Norman work, do not miss the vast and splendid original S. door with ironwork, nor, on the path across the churchyard, the carved 12th-century stone cross, removed at the Reformation to prop up the cellar of the old Falcon Inn on the N. side of the market-place, and restored in 1921 as a war memorial. The principal monument in church is to John, 15th earl, 1539 (hitherto they were all buried at their priory at Earls Colne): black marble with polished top, probably by Cornelius Harman who carved the Audley monument at Saffron Walden: four daughters kneel at the foot, Elizabeth, Anne,

Frauncis and Ursela, with the motto: Verite vient.

Hedingham, Sible (3). Much folded, with fields and Greens at the edge of the Colne valley, the valley road itself lately and deplorably swamped by overmuch housing. As usual, a good simple modern library by the County Architect. *Swan Street* is interesting to the south of its junction with *Alderfoot Street*, which has Georgian bows at No. 15 and a weatherboarded water-mill at the end. *Southey Green House* is a prosperous building of the 15th century with exposed timber-frame and 16th-century additions. *Rectory* of very prosperous Georgian red brick, *c.* 1714. An attractive small Georgian farmhouse stands in the churchyard.

The *church* is mostly of the 1330s, the inside faint from much purging, but the early Tudor S. porch has oak roof-timbers well carved with the Bourchier knot, the de Vere mullet and an angel; and the two W. bays of the S. aisle roof are very elaborately carved, also early Tudor. The early Tudor rebuilding of the W. tower incorporated a roundel with carved hawk over the W. window, in proud commemoration of Sir John Hawkwood whose fine cenotaph inside has a big ogee arch decorated with hawks and other beasts. Son of a Hedingham tanner, he was at Poitiers with the Black Prince, then joined freelance "Late Comers" and formed his own freelance brigade, the White Band: this was so successful that when the Venetian Republic was threatened by Austria in 1376, they tried to secure Hawkwood's service as the most famous captain of his age; but his price was thought too high for Venice, and Venice was in its heyday! He served Florence so well against Milan in 1392 that, since his death in 1394, he has been steadily regarded as a chief defender of Florentine liberties. Uccello's huge trompe-l'oeil painting on the N. wall of Florence's cathedral, done in 1436, shows him mounted as proudly as Marcus Aurelius on the Capitol, or as Colleoni beside the Zanipolo in Venice.

Hempstead (2/3), village in brook bottom, church above, with Harvey monuments. The tower fell in 1882 and was rebuilt with old materials 1933–61 and money from William Harvey Memorial Fund. The spandrels over the S. doorway are wooden. Nave clean Victorianized, but the N. (Harvey) chapel retains old red pamments and white plaster as the setting for its collection of marbles. The most remarkable is the bust of Wm. Harvey, 1578–1657, the discoverer of the circulation of blood, admirably carved by Edward Marshall. Harvey's bones were brought up from the family vault in 1883 to lie in a great white sarcophagus provided by the Royal College of Physicians. Nearby wall monuments commemorate Eliab Harvey (d. 1661), a London Merchant, and Admiral Eliab Harvey, commander of the *Temeraire* at Trafalgar. The admiral was a son of Wm. Harvey (of Winchlow Hall at Hempstead and Rolls at Chigwell) whose monument here, with sensitively carved portrait medallions is prominently signed by its designer and sculptor Roubiliac. A tablet says the Admiral's eldest son fell honourably at Burgos, 1812, aged 22. A large monument to Wm. Harvey of Roehampton, Surrey, 1719, is unsigned. Seventeenth-century lead coffins in the Harvey vault are said to bear modelled faces. Brasses. The moat of old Winchlow Hall is now occupied only by a small cottage.

Henham (2). The Green is built round with pleasant cottages of several periods and well planted with clumps and a screen of limes: Essex's "best-kept village" in 1966. A long moat-like pond runs along the N. edge of the Green. A close-built jumble of housing has developed in 1965–6 to the south. Why could the developer not have learnt about siting from the rest of village? The *church* has an elaborate medieval screen, ill-kept; the font carvings are well preserved. A monument to Samuel Feake, 1790, by W. Vere displays an urn sculpted with a man-of-war: he was a nabob in Clive's India.

Henny, Great (10). The *church* has a beautifully shaped broach spire on an old flint tower, and is set high in landscape idyllically like Gainsborough's "Auberies". A brass says of George Golding, 1617: "Foes count him feirce, He had a tender hart". Constable descended from Goldings of these parts. There are very rustic coloured figures with musical instruments at the base of wall-posts of the late medieval roof.

Henny, Little (10). Small church long vanished. The Ryes, Regency, is emparked on a ridge.

Herongate *see* Horndon, East.

Heybridge *see* Maldon.

High Beach *see* Waltham Abbey.

High Wood *see* Writtle.

Hockley (9). Westwards along "Main Road" and northwards towards the parish church, a bright, salubrious garden-suburb has spread, mostly in the 1960s. *Hockley Spa*, based on salubrious spring-water 1838, was unsuccessful. The pump-room, of 1842, was taken over by the Baptists by 1862, and now stands forlorn beside the commuters' drab walk to the railway-station.

The *church* occupies a marvellous hilltop situation overlooking wooded slopes, its little tower extraordinarily rustic in shape and texture, a sort of octagon, heavily buttressed at the base and crenellated above. The ambitious W. doorway is probably of 1843 when the church was "thoroughly repaired and beautified". Broad Purbeck font, 13th-century. Medieval roof creosoted. Interior walls scraped and whitewashed and much bedizened in Anglo-Catholic fashion. *Lower Hockley Hall*, an old brick house spoilt with cream plaster, stands under Plumberow Hill. *Plumberow*, oak-clad among cornfields, rises to a low peak with vestiges of Roman occupation.

Hullbridge is a large bungalow settlement, nondescript, though the doctors have built themselves a respectable central group surgery. The old *Anchor Inn*, now Anchor Cottage, bearing the date 1793, is a shade tumbledown. *Coventry Cottages*, 1 Hockley Road, are almost alone here in being built of good traditional brick.

Holland, Great (14). Church with Tudor red brick tower has lovely view across two fields to marsh, Goldmer Gat, and Gunfleet. Rest of church (A. Blomfield, 1866) large unfractured flints in lower courses, rust-coloured septaria in upper. Monument by Hinchliff to rector's son, 19, who died in Heidelberg, 1812. Rather grand Old Rectory, basically Georgian, plastered. Great Holland Lodge, very attractive white brick front with double bay windows, in marshes on way to –
Holland, Little (14), its church long perished, and now known as Holland-on-Sea, a satellite of Clacton.

Horham *see* Thaxted.

Horkesley, Great (10). Early Iron Age Camp, formerly oval, known as *Pitchbury*, double ramparts as at Clare. Horkesley was part of the big lordship of Nayland in 11th and 12th centuries. Church at Nayland end of parish, with result that diapered red brick *chapel of Our Lady* built shortly before 1500 more centrally, beside main road and near Brewood Hall, by John Brewood: served houseling population of 200 in 1548: now a cottage. Similar need met in 1837 by *St John's*, further S. amid the suburban ribbon-development; brick, with "Romanesque" chancel arch, approached by footpath between pair of gate-cottages, one round, one octagonal: charming group messed up by wire-scape. It was built by J. L. Green, farmer of Terrace Hall further S., whose very pretty rotunda gate-cottage has graceful colonnade and shield saying "J.L. and R.G. built 1835". *Windyridge Farm Home* for boys has Georgian stucco front with unrivalled views of Nayland and Stoke.

Suburban ribbon is redeemed by one or two other buildings, such as the Yew Tree, a trim cottage-pub. Old church stands aloof in wellingtonias. South-west quoins and W. window of nave Norman. Yellow brick floor. Figures carved in triple nave arcade: early 15th-century male and females. Timber figure survives on nave-roof wall-post. Fourteenth-century timber door from N. chapel to vestry: Hatchments. Font cover made up from medieval tabernacle-work. The Elizabethan/Jacobean pulpit was brought from St Margaret's, Ipswich, 1848, while curate here was Rev. Sir H. Baker, author of "The King of Love my shepherd is".
Horkesley, Little (10). The *church*, in a parkland and arable landscape, was completely demolished by a bomb in 1940. Both the foundation stone *and* the weather-vane of the present church are dated 1957. It has been rebuilt on the old lines with pleasant butter-coloured stucco exterior and interior, and clear glazing except for the E. window by Hugh Powell, 1961, richly glittering. A simple open screen crosses S. aisle and chancel.
Fortunately the magnificent larger-than-life-size carved wooden effigies of two men and a woman, each over 7½ ft. long, survived: they are assumed to represent late 13th-century members of the Horkesley family: one male face rather charred, the other two preserved in good detail: all admirably restored and presented. Likewise notable brasses were saved: two Swynborne knights (1391 and 1412) under a double canopy, and in the chancel brasses of Dame Bridget Marnay, 1549, with rich heraldic mantle and two husbands finely tabarded.
The *Hall* is a handsome house of white brick, said to have been built for Edward Parsons who died in 1736 and whose funeral monument was destroyed in 1940; but Greek-revival features, in e.g. the hall and fine drawing-room, suggest an early 19th-century date. The house just N.E. of the church is probably on the site of a very small Cluniac priory founded be-

ginning of 12th century and having only a Prior and one monk at the time of its suppression by Wolsey. *Josselyns* is a rambling old timber-framed house of *c.* 1500 beside the elmy lane down to Nayland. It has been heavily restored. Farther on, *Lower Dairy Farm*, though stripped of its plaster, has attractive carved bressummers and other old features.

Horndon, East (8). The *church* perched up above the A127 (speedway to Southend) is an essay in red brick: chancel and S. transept are late 15th-century; S. chapel (with separate gable), S. porch, W. tower, 16th-century: W. tower remodelled in the 17th century, and though squat (only 2 stages), distinctive with corner-turrets and stepped parapet. All presumably the work of the Tyrells of Heron Hall, whose monuments it contains, most notably one by Nollekens, 1766. A truly splendid incised limestone slab figures Alice wife of Sir John Tyrell, 1422, in an elaborately canopied niche flanked by children with their names on scrolls. The arcade between chancel and S. chapel is on crutches awaiting repair in 1966. There are upper galleries or ? squire's pews in the transepts.
To the north, Cockridden Farm's name took Edward Thomas's fancy. *Herongate* has a pleasant small Green and suburban houses. Heron Hall, of the Tyrells, was pulled down in 1790. Its successor occupies the beautiful moated site and inherits a deep-red brick barn to the south-east of the house, with three massive tie-beams and crown posts. The old *Dog Inn*, clapboarded, has a jolly aspect.
Horndon-on-the-Hill (8). *Grices*, at the S. edge of the village, overlooks the Thames estuary. Due east of the church, "the Wool Market" is unprepossessing: the open ground floor was bricked up in the 19th century and the first floor clapboarded, but there are 16th-century features inside. *High House* opposite has a nicely conceived Georgian front of 1728, with projecting ornamental brick window-sills.
Its small spire well in view above

the tree'd ridge from the south, the *church* is properly cared for, a low building with impressive sturdy 13th-century arcades. Massive timber cantilevers and trellis struts provide stability at the base of the belfry. Dormer-windows serve as super-clerestories. Good stained glass 1900–20 in nave, aisles and S. chancel. Lively Royal Arms of George I, 1715, are signed by William Waite of Gravesend, painter. Monumental inscription to Daniel Caldwall and wife, 1634, concludes:

And from rude hands preserve us both untill

We rise to Sion Mount from Horndon Hill.

Hullbridge *see* Hockley.

Hutton (8), like Shenfield, an expanding suburb of Brentwood, fed by main road and rail. Extensive modern housing estates tend to swamp the historic outlines. The *Hall*, moated, is evidently an interesting house of *c.* 1730 with Gothick panelling in one room. The church was partly rebuilt by George Edmund Street, 1873, but without the original Gothic thinking that distinguished so much of his work.

Hythe *see* Colchester.

Ingatestone and **Fryerning** (5) have long been intermixed. A small former market-town is at Ingatestone, which was described, 1848, as "a great thoroughfare for coaches, waggons, cattle, &c., but the traffic is now mostly drawn into the vortex of the railway". After the congestion of the early motor-age, the traffic has again been drawn off, into the A12 bypass, leaving a pleasant shopping street, its core now being rebuilt, and necessary conditions for a new estate, *Tor Bryan* (Design Planning Associates), with expensive houses of uninhibited design: e.g. with entrance and staircase in a 2-storey semicircular drum, and living-rooms with pyramidal or prismoid roofs. The great interest, however, centres on *Ingatestone*

Hall, the rich, rather unrelieved, red brick step-gabled house built by Sir William Petre in the 1540s and '50s, the S. wing of which is now the family home of Lord Petre, the N. wing leased to the Essex County Council and used for annual summer exhibition by the Essex Record Office, whose gifted staff have done so much to bring the history of Essex, and not least the story of this house, alive. The Street was recently "opened up" on the E. side to give a wider (and correspondingly less dramatic) view of St Edmund's *church*: the noble W. tower is of red brick, like the Petre chapels (which have separate roof-ridges): the Norman nave N. wall is of ironbound conglomerate. Dormers are needed: the interior seems like a low tunnel after the entrance through that monumental tower. The S.E. chapel was built in 1556, for the inhabitants of the almshouses building at that time. Monuments: south of the chancel, Sir William's fine tomb-chest, 1572, has his marble achievement suspended in ironwork above: son of a Devon (Tor Bryan) tanner, he rose through the law to be Secretary of State (his tomb is probably by Cornelius Cure). In the N. chapel there is a wall monument to his son, John, 1st Lord Petre, 1613, whose portrait in oil (by "the Master of the Earl of Essex") immediately draws attention to the very far end of the Long Gallery at the Hall: here in church his grand-children kneel (only three of his twelve children survived childhood). The bust of his servant and friend, Captain John Troughton, son of a York baker, is brilliantly carved in a wall monument presumed to be by Epiphanius Evesham. They were together at Richard Farrant's new theatre at Blackfriars in 1577. In 1600 Troughton, captain of the Lioness, was sent by Cecil to the Straight "to intercept either the Spanyardes or Portingalles in their trade".

A footpath from the church leads $\frac{1}{2}$-mile south to the *Hall*. The approach is pleasantly wooded, the entrance through a gateway with picturesque bell-turret of *c.* 1690.

The original informal quad lost its W. side (the Great Hall) *c.* 1800. The Petres were a recusant Catholic family, and there are two ingenious "hides" in the house. The Queen made a point of staying in 1561. Gallery on E. side (1st floor), one of the most attractive rooms in Essex. Easy to see why small railway station in woods, 1846, is charming red brick "Tudor" and why George Sherrin designed later Victorian houses here in this style.

The Hyde, in its way as interesting as the Hall, was burnt out and demolished *c.* 1965. Its owner Thomas Brand, in Italy, *c.* 1748–53, collecting busts, statues, vases, etc., was among the first visitors to the newly discovered Herculaneum. He left house and fortune to Rev. John Disney, a Unitarian writer, who was buried at Fryerning in 1816 (see below). Disney's son John added to the collection from Pompeii, founded the Disneian chair of archaeology at Cambridge 1851, and in 1857 left Cambridge his marbles, now part of the Fitzwilliam collection.

Fryerning (5). The *church*, built on an eminence, has remarkable colours and textures: Roman-brick quoins in walls of dark chocolate puddingstone (indurated gravel), sprinkled with bright flint pebbles, the puddingstone served in regular courses in the nave, which is early Norman. The W. tower of romantic 15th-century brickwork has battlements and a corbel-table related perhaps to Faulkbourne Hall as well as to Ingatestone church. On the N. side of the churchyard, the Disney tomb with urn and column is skilfully silhouetted against pines: see Ingatestone.

The post-windmill at Mill Green is now part of a suburban fantasy: the mill-house windows are diamond-leaded! The mill is in egregiously good order. *Huskards* is a red-brick Georgian house with a big red-brick Victorian wing and curved gables.

Ingrave (8) amalgamated with West Horndon, 1734, when Lord Petre (himself R.C.) built a new church to replace two taken down.

Felix Hall, KELVEDON. The portico was modelled, c. *1830, on the temple of Fortuna Virilis in Rome*

Severely plain red brick church with tower of massive Romanesque proportions. Twin rather ugly turrets, one for stair, other for clock-mechanism. Brasses with notably well preserved figures in sanctuary: Fitzleweses owned Thorndon before Petres. John Fitzlewes is shown with four wives all in heraldic dress. His great grandson died with his bride when West Horndon Hall burnt down on their wedding-night.

Thorndon Hall was built 1764–70 to the design of James Paine for the 9th Lord Petre, whose Roman Catholicism did not deter George III from visiting him here in 1778. It was burnt out in 1878. The central block, eleven bays, is now a vast warehouse for television-sets! From it, long curved colonnades, with a series of plaster-niches over, decaying like a subject for Piranesi, reach sizeable pavilions on either side. In one, the Petres' chapel, its orders of columns still gilded, serves as the Mixed Lounge of Thorndon Park Golf Club. The ground floor is rusticated; the rest camel-coloured brick, except the grand portico of six Corinthian columns and pediment in silver-grey stone thought to have been designed by Leoni for the old Hall. It looks S. over the fairways to the site of that

previous great Tudor house (West Horndon Hall) a mile away. Five hundred yards along a woodland walk south-west of the house, Pugin's enchanted little mausoleum and chantry chapel, ragstone, with beautifully detailed "Dec" window-tracery and immensely steep roof, stands in clearing. Delicate angels kneel over the W. door, Virgin and child in a niche beside. Under the E. window there are scenes of Crucifixion, Burial and Resurrection. At Thorndon Gate, a small priest's house, of early-Victorian brick, is now a small school: it has a large niche with Puginesque sculpture of the Virgin and Child.

Inworth (13). The *Hall* is in an attractive small park unfenced on the Kelvedon–Tiptree road. The *church* is approached through a lime avenue, a goat grazing in the churchyard. Red brick "Tudor" tower rebuilt and church restored by Rev. A. H. Bridges 1876–7: brick inscription on S. wall suggests he was its architect, though Joseph Clarke (London!) was apparently employed. There are rich dark-brown puddingstone dressings on the early Norman work in the chancel walls. On either side of the low Romanesque chancel-arch, and in the nave

walls, are 13th-century blank arches. Thirteenth-century paintings fade above the chancel-arch. There is a small medieval screen, and medieval tiles. Opposite the church, *Hill House*, Georgian, is now a "Save the Children" home.

Jaywick (14). Shackery by the sea, though the sea is obscured from Jaywick streets by the sea-defence wall. It is divided from the Clacton Butlins by a few hundred yards of real country, a Martello tower and a golf course.

Kelvedon (6/13) stands on the site of a Belgic village and Roman settlement, probably Canonium: there have been rich finds east of Freemasons Hall. The by-pass was opened in March 1967, only just in time to relieve this large thoroughfare-village of the A12 traffic that had been its greatest asset since Roman times. Rebuilding, e.g. of the *Angel*, far back behind the old building-line shows how traffic was prevailing over the character of the village street, where Mr Spetley, the grocer, happily still serves his customers from a counter with gleaming brass scales. The varied street includes the small white brick cottage where Spurgeon the preacher was born in 1834, and

Brington House, early Victorian in similar brick. *Ormonde House* with an early 17th-century chimney stack is cased and parapeted in early Georgian red brick and has a rather grand doorcase. Much too much shingly rough-cast everywhere; some only recently done by the Spastics Society at *the Grange* and adjacent *Oakwood* Centre.

On the E. side of Church Street, cottages and *Red House* set the tone of the whole village: pleasant old buildings refronted in the Georgian age. New Road (residential estate, at least taking form of street) has now looped round behind, and the W. side of Church Street has been subjected to a new curbed pavement in 1967! Rural qualities must be re-asserted in large residential villages.

The church fabric was much restored in 1877, but retains a well-weathered flint texture outside (including a parapeted clerestory and engaging small shingled spire). Within, there are very notable 13th-century N. and S. arcades, of solid round piers except one which has four shafts interestingly battered by former woodwork insertions. Above the first column, and not *in situ*, is a shield of 15th-century royal arms, England quartering France. The Tudor brick N. aisle chapel (with external stepped gable), has a solid roof, much restored, with eight large original timber figures. There is a white marble memorial with carved curtains to Sir Thos. Abdy, 1689, of *Felix Hall*, now a spectacularly handsome ruin among cedars in a park. The portico, added to the earlier house *c.* 1830 by Lord Western, the Whig M.P. for Maldon, is approached by a grand flight of steps: it was modelled from Desgodetz's drawings of the so-called Temple of Fortuna Virilis, thought to be "the purest specimen in Rome" of the Ionic order, and itself completed not in travertine but in hard stucco, like this romantic copy at Kelvedon.

Kelvedon Hatch (5). Hatch is a medieval word for forest-gate. This is a woodland area still, with three old parks. The most interesting, Kelvedon Hall's, contains the old parish church, rebuilt 1750–3 without disturbing the old floor-slabs, but then abandoned for a more populous site at Hatch Common, in 1895. The old church overgrown, and damaged by a German rocket 1945, is now pronounced unsafe. Nevertheless it still (1956) had ledger-slabs and wall monuments, notably of Wright and Luther families, including one to John Luther, M.P., 1786, by the elder Westmacott. The Luthers lived at *Myles's*, of which only the service-wing and stables survive in grounds provided with a lake and a nice brick bridge in 1771 by the Essex landscaper Richard Woods. The present *Kelvedon Hall* was built by the eighth successive John Wright who died in 1751, exactly 200 years after the first John Wright. They were buried in the church, though as R.C. recusants they maintained a chapel in the house, which is severe, but with Palladian pavilions on either side of the central block, also a scrolly ironwork staircase and rococo plasterwork representing good Handelian subjects: Music, War, and the Chase. The S. wing contains the former private R.C. chapel.

The 1895 church, red brick, by a local architect, has an apse like a suburban bay-window and the 15th-century font from the old church. At *Hatch Farm*, opposite, square Queen Anne brick walls cloak an Elizabethan interior based on the great central chimney-stack. *Brizes*, a very grand house of *c.* 1720, followed Myles's in having its grounds laid out by Richard Woods. *Priors* is said to be the house where Richard and Anthony Luther esquires lived near 40 years joint housekeepers together till 1627. A smock windmill was pulled down in 1916: thought to be landmark for zeppelins.

Kirby-le-Soken (14), part of the ancient soke (liberty) of St Paul's, London. *Hill House*, white-washed brick, with ilexes on slight slope, looks over a mustard field to church, Kirby Creek and Horsey Island. The good 15th-century W. tower is East Anglian, like Brightlingsea: silvery grey and dark grey flint with pleasant smooth finish. The rest largely of 1870: the S. nave aisle is of buff septaria. Original N. aisle of septaria too, with traceried parapet: graceful niches above buttresses. *Waterloo House*, north of the church, has rococo wooden swags over the door. Traditional old thatched and plastered house among ribbon development on Halstead Road, north of Kirby Cross.

Laindon *see* Basildon.

Lamarsh (10). Glorious valley-views at south end of parish. In the valley bottom, *Orchard House*, a nice old building is in strange company. The church exterior is delightful: the Norman round tower has lately been stucco'd: its Rhineland fairy-tale conic (and comic) roof was acquired in 1869. The S. porch glows with old red brick-work: a quotation from Ecclesiastes, V, is prettily painted on plaster over inner door. Paraphrased, it might read: "Listen, and don't behave like a fool in church". Simple broad interior, chancel and nave divided only by traceried 15th-century wooden screen of ten bays. The E. wall with lancets was entirely rebuilt in the 19th century. *Hall*, Tudor, with exposed timber frame, just N. of church. Farther north, *Daw's Hall* (now a wildfowl farm) is basically Tudor with an extremely attractive Georgian front.

Lambourne (8) is outflanked by Loughton and Romford, yet occupies completely rural wooded slopes northwards to the Roding river.

Abridge is a small thoroughfare settlement at the old river-crossing between Epping and Romford (known as "Aeffa's bridge" in King John's day, the bridge itself is now Georgian red-brick). The main thoroughfare of the Ongar–London motor-traffic zigzags past three pubs: *White Hart* beside bridge, *Blue Boar* with heavy Victorian Tuscan porch, *Maltsters*

LAYER MARNEY. Henry, 1st Lord Marney, 1523, with his ancestor Sir William Marney, 1414, in the background

Arms weatherboarded, with Georgian Tuscan doorway. The hamlet's *chapel-of-ease* is a simple barn, with clock of 1902 and glass signed William Morris, 1954. The brick parish-room was built in 1833 as a chapel by Methodists: they claimed they had reformed Abridge, which "was usually called the Little Sodom". Alas, twenty-five years later the Congregational agent reported that the village still had that name. The lane up to the mother-church leads past *Lambourne Place* (the sparkling red-brick early-Georgian old rectory, also known as *Priors*), a house of immense charm behind its ha-ha, with a staircase from Dews Hall.

Lambourne church has a short leaded spire and a Norman N. doorway with lopped columns. The W. doorway, of 1726, part of a great restoration and redecoration promoted by Churchwarden Thorogood of *Dews Hall*, leads under the W. gallery given by Wm. Walker, a London ironmonger, of *Bishop's Hall*. Both houses, now demolished, were lived in by generations of Lockwoods, whose hatchments and monuments fill much of the church. Thorogood's redecoration was at its most ingenious in transforming the appearance of the internal roof-structure. The best monument is a classical lamp, carved by Flaxman, 1801. An-

other to John Lockwood, 1778, is by Joseph Wilton. The angel on that of Captain George Lockwood, Cardigan's A.D.C., who died in the charge of the Light Brigade at Balaclava, points up to a head and shoulders of St Christopher, painted in the 14th century and superbly repainted *c.* 1500. Five brilliant miniature stained glass pictures from Basel, 1623–37, were brought here in 1817. Well conceived small modern sculptured figures by T. B. Huxley-Jones take the place of a reredos.

Langdon Hills *see* Basildon.

Langenhoe *see* Abberton.

Langford (6/13) at the junction of Chelmer and Blackwater rivers, above Maldon. Near the mill, the church of St Giles is a great oddity: at first sight of 1882, but then one spots a Norman apse at the *wrong end* of the church! South-west porch leads into it. Next one notices that Langford formerly had an apse at the east end as well: it can be seen in puddingstone at the beginning of its curve in the outside of the S. wall, 34 ft. east of the E. edge of the S. door. Unique in England, and rare in Europe. *Langford Grove* was one of John Johnson's urbane Essex houses, 1782, that, alas, our age demolished, *c.* 1953.

Langham (10). The church has Constable associations: his friend Rev. Jas. Hurlock stood in here as curate while John Fisher was rector – later bishop of Salisbury: hence Constable's great friendship with the Fishers and great paintings of Salisbury. Later Hurlock's son, Rev. J. T. Hurlock, became rector; in whose time (1832) the little church school for poor girls of the parish was built in the churchyard, where it now houses funeral and lawn-mowing equipment. Also from Rev. J. T.'s time, is the cast-iron "Dumb Animals Petition", urging drivers to rest their horses on nearby steep "Gun" hill, lately by-passed. One of Constable's favourite views of Dedham Vale was from a position just N. of church, where the old Hall is familiar as "The Glebe Farm" (National Gallery), painted in 1826–7 as a memorial to the bishop. *Valley House* down by the river is interesting in its own right, a timber-framed Tudor house with remarkable Jacobean additions: porch with brackets voluted like baby elephants' trunks, and staircase with tall carved newels like totems.

Langley (1). Heavily restored church on a platform above surrounding fields, next to *Hall* with stripped timber frame. South doorway has Early English columns and capitals and round arch. Tudor brick chancel, late Stuart Royal Arms in glass shield in E.

LAYER MARNEY

window saying "Dieu et Mon Droit". Georgian pulpit. *Rumberry Hill* is associated with Roman finds.

Latchingdon-and-Snoreham (13) run right across the neck of Dengie peninsula. *Snoreham* church decayed "several centuries" ago near the *Hall*, where an annual sermon used to be preached under a tree. *Uleham's Farm* represents Uleham, an owl-haunted hamlet already in 1086. *Latchingdon* has two churches, one of 1857, with steep roofs and "Essex" bell-cote, and St Michael's old church is on a fine hill-top site, with just nave and porch. North *wall* is reminiscent of A Midsummer Night's

Dream: "Mathew Bets and Robert Peirc mad this wall, 1618". Old fashioned 4-light chink. Brick floor. Leather-covered back-to-back seating (? from a station waiting-room).

Latton *see* Harlow.

The Lavers (5). Laver is old English for "ford" which suggests that the earliest settlement was at one of the crossings of the Cripsey Brook.

— High (5). Norman and 13th-century church with E. lancets and 14th-century tower which has whole S.W. corner neatly stitched in in red brick, 1737. A board inside says "a benefactor whose

name by some misfortune or neglect is now unknown" gave a field for perpetual repair of the church. Nicely kept now. Among pleasant tablets note that to John Locke, 1632–1704, the great philosopher, composed by himself in Latin. For £1 a week he and a manservant lodged here at "Otes", with the Mashams. Here he had a library of 4,000 books, a specially designed chair, and his meteorological instruments set up in the drawing-room, and here he died. Bits of moat, wall and ornamental lake survive. *Church Farm* and *Travellers Joy* have good old houses. Livery-buttons have been dug up at Travellers Joy.
— **Little** (5). The old manorhouse, pink washed, Victorianized and now "The Grange", seems to date from 1587. Date re-cut in great chimney. The church, in front of it, is unusual in having no sign of tower or bell-cote. Agreeably remodelled with apse, 1872 (Turner & Son, Wilton Street). Ambitious interior, with three E. windows seen through slender arcade (alabaster, or pink veined marble). Late 12th-century font with whorl and crescent disk (sun and moon?), recut in 1872. Roman remains, now at Chelmsford Museum.
— **Magdalen** (5). The church, with a very picturesque "Essex" timber bell-tower (possibly early Elizabethan) is approached through a meadow with small islanded lake. Horizontal weatherboarding on top of the tower has been neatly redone in cedar, the bottom white-painted: apparently a plaster finish was originally intended (V.C.H.). Outside the S. doorway is a charming tomb with cherubs: Wm. Cole, 1729, several years Treasurer of St Thomas's Hospital. Oak W. door very ancient. Tower inaccessible. Early 14th-century oak screen was reconstructed in the 17th century. Beautifully painted reredos (Ten Commandments), c. Queen Anne. *Wynter's Armourie*, originally "Winter's", a large timber-framed house restored since 1937, contains part of a medieval aisled hall; c. 1450 it was a tenement of Richard Wynter called "Ar-

maerer". The roof has been renewed since a serious fire in 1961.

Lawford (11) is merged at its edge with Manningtree, and Lawford Place is a plastics research station, but it preserves fine things of its own. Church has a prodigiously carved chancel of the 14th century, and a tower with the richest patchwork of building-materials in Essex: ginger septaria, coffee-coloured puddingstone, dark-grey almost black flint, silver-grey freestone and at least three different shades of red brick. Heavy restorations, especially 1887–9. Nearby in park, an old timbered Elizabethan house, 1583, lives gamely behind handsome red brick mask of 1756: the true age of this "Georgian beauty" is given away by the high roof-ridge and soaring shafts of end-wall chimney stacks. Field-glasses help full enjoyment of the stone-carving in the chancel: the great windows N. and S. of the chancel, four a side, are designed with high virtuosity: not only is the window-tracery designed with much originality, there is delightful detail in the voussoirs round the upper windows, the sort of detail for which Southwell Chapter-house is famous, and of which one begins to get a taste at Widdington, in Essex, and at All Saints, Maldon: birds lurk in the foliage, and men clamber on top of one another.

Lawrence, Saint *see* Saint Lawrence.

The Layers (13). Layer probably represents a Celtic river-name.
— **Breton** (13). *Hall*, c. 1700, was re-topped after the 1884 earthquake. The simple old church stood opposite, see 1909 watercolour in simple new church erected up on the Heath, 1923, by James Round, P.C. Cattle tethered outside. Monument 1392: Alice, wife of Nicholas Breton. Wooden sculpture (Italian "Mannerist"), Virgin playing with Child, given by Mrs De Zoete, 1934. Also fine fragment of 16th-century woodcarving of Abram, Isaac and the ram, said to be from Upminster Church.

— **De-La-Haye** (13). Church has exchanged view over tributary of Roman river for lake-land view over Abberton Reservoir. Purbeck marble tomb-chest, 1500, lost effigies of Thomas Tey and wife during past century. Kentish rag tower: Roman-brick quoins. In churchyard, tribute to Marlborough on General Brown's fine obelisk.
— **Marney** (13). The *Hall* is usually known as "the Tower"; a spectacular red brick gate-house of c. 1520. The church of c. 1524, also of red brick, has very fine monuments.
The Marneys were already here, it seems, c. 1166. The alabaster effigy of Sir William Marney, M.P. 1408, died 1414, lies solitary on a tomb-chest in the church, rebuilt by his descendant. Henry, 1st Lord Marney, a staunch supporter of Henry VII from 1485, was at Spurs and the Field of the Cloth of Gold with Henry VIII, whose Keeper of the Privy Seal he became in 1522, the year before his death. Connexion with the Court explains "latest" Italianate decoration on Tower and tombs, which remain in basic design ineluctably Gothic. The Tower is a direct successor of Oxburgh, Norfolk (1483) and of Hadleigh Deanery, Suffolk (1495), improving on them only in its additional height, in the profusion of windows in the polygonal turrets (facing S. over Layer Brook, so that this is one of the earliest "prospect" houses in England), and in the decoration. The most striking new decorative feature is the replacement of battlements by small semicircular scollop-shells with dolphins. The central feature of "the English Palace" in the Hampton Court painting of the Field of the Cloth of Gold is a semicircular pediment fluted into a scollop-shell! Less noticeable from a distance, but very impressive at close-quarters, main windows in the Tower and in the block running W. from it have terracotta transoms and mullions,

LINDSELL Hall

Heybridge, near MALDON

the heads cusped by delightful dolphins in scrolls and counter-scrolls. This terracotta is honey coloured and very fine.

The idea of working in terracotta seems to have been brought here by Italians, either by Girolamo da Trevizi, as Nathaniel Lloyd noted in his *History of English Brickwork*, or by Torrigiani, a Florentine, at the end of Henry VII's reign. Tombs of 1st Lord Marney, 1523, and 2nd Lord, whose death in 1525 ended male line, may be the work of an Englishman trained under Torrigiani. 2nd Lord, knighted at Tournai, and with his father at the Field of the Cloth of Gold, left £250 towards rebuilding of church. The entire church, including good W. tower,

N. (Marney) chapel, and *two* S. porches, is of red brick with blue diapering. Unluckily much of it was plastered over until fairly recently. It is happily still lit by oil, 1965. "Partially renovated 1870, restored and re-opened 1911" by a rector, whose son died at Rio in the Merchant Navy, is depicted in a simple brass at prayer beside bunk. Large St Christopher on N. wall *quite* un-influenced by Italy! Terracotta tombs not *wholly* Renaissance: 1st Lord's tomb a bit like a most ornate 4-poster bed. Effigies superbly carved in black marble, apparently Catacusan, i.e. Cornish marble. 1st Lord shared the strong nose and bleak ascetic countenance of Henry VII. By

contrast, the face of the 2nd Lord is that of a wide-eyed, round-cheeked young man of 32. His widow's tomb is at Little Horkesley. Grey and white marble to Nicholas Corsellis, d. 1678, aged 40, with Latin inscription claiming that the printer's art was taught to the English by a Corsellis at the behest of Henry VI.

Duke's Farm, an attractive brick house, has a middle-Tudor gabled wing, with stone mullioned windows (10 lights, with 2 more at right angles in side walls), and "up-to-date" wing of *c.* 1700 adjoining. Foundations of the rest of the Tudor house are visible beneath the lawn. Glass roundels with rose and crown and initials E.R. The house now bears the arms of Round, who owned it in the 19th century. Duke family owned in 15th. A handsome medallion of Archduke Ferdinand, 1560, has lately been found in garden.

Leez Priory *see* Leighs.

Leigh-on-Sea *see* Southend-on-Sea.

Leighs, Great and **Little** (6), meadows along the shallow Ter Valley, dammed just east of Leez Priory to create a reservoir, 1967: 110 million gallons, stocked with trout so that fishing-rents offset capital outlay: £125,000, to irrigate 1,000 acres.
Great Leighs has a well-tended church with stout round W. tower of flint, with some ironstone conglomerate, the lower stage buttressed, and flattened on the E. side at the junction with the nave. A delightful Regency S. porch, ceiled, leads straight onto a big zigzag Romanesque doorway with deal Gothick-panelled door. Nave floor of red pamments. A west gallery. Rich 14th-century chancel with rich Victorian glass. Small Regency barrel-organ, Wm. Phillips. Good oak pews.
Little Leighs church has preserved a true rustic feel. Nave full of pleasant medieval grooved oak benches. Successful simple 20th-century screen and pulpit. An early 14th-century recess (with external tiled quoins) contains the absolutely beautiful carved wooden figure of a 14th-century priest in cope, scarf and alb.
Leighs (or Leez) *Priory*, of Austin canons, founded probably in the 12th century and soon well endowed, fell to Lord Rich at the Dissolution. The last prior, Thos. Ellys, given Blackmore vicarage, practised alchemy, for which he was prosecuted in the Star Chamber. Lord Rich built a vast diapered red brick house, preserving much of the site-plan of the priory, i.e. his great hall was on the nave of the priory-church, his main quadrangle on the site of the cloister. Most of his house was demolished *c.* 1753, and, in the grounds, the outlines of the medieval and Tudor buildings are confusing. The most impressive part of the house preserved is the inner three-storey gatehouse, leading through the former W. range of cloister: no Layer Marney, it is more like the entrance to a Cambridge college. To west and south two sides of the outer quadrangle survive, with lower, two-storey, outer gatehouse on the south side, all in warm red brick and tile. It is a private house but in winter months one sees the top storeys of the inner gatehouse, its windows glinting in afternoon sun, across the still, tree-grown monastic millponds from the road.

Lexden *see* Colchester.

Lindsell (2). One of the most delightful small churches in England stands among farm buildings of the Hall. Nave and S. aisle add up to a square plan. The flint Elizabethan tower, edged in red brick, rises in the S.W. corner. Perfectly rustic interior. The broad semicircular chancel-arch is possibly the work of Henry, a clerk skilled in medicine and favourite guest at Walden Abbey, who held this living many years from 1154. The chancel wall contains the aperture of an anchorites' cell of the same period, communicating with the sanctuary. Dugout chest. Brass, 1514. "Pater noster" graffito at child height.
Simpkins Farmhouse, modest beside a quiet pond, has main-rooms fashioned *c.* 1500 into two storeys, the ground-floor room ceiled in solid oak by the beams, joists and boards of the first floor.

Liston (10). The *Mill House*, white-boarded, stands in the Stour bottom, near Melford Roman villa-site. The early Tudor church-tower is of deep red brick with black brick patterns. The fabric of the Palmer S. chapel is beautiful gauged flintwork, 1867 (with pleasant decorative interior ironwork). Nave floor of pamments. Very original tympanum over the chancel-arch: pargeting with Prince-of-Wales' feather moulds, dated 1701, and initials I.S. The whole nave ceiling is faintly pargeted. The extremely good solid oak chancel ceiling, *c.* 1500, houses four carved angels. The window glass is brightly coloured in the W. window, 1923 (after Kempe), with good traditional roundels; 1932 in N. window, with fragments of four 15th-century lights above. There is a spirited but unsigned marble to Dr Poley Clopton, 1730, founder of handsome almshouses in Bury Abbey cemetery-site. A tablet commemorates members of the Thornhill family massacred at Cawnpore, 1857.

Littlebury (2). The original little *burh* (fortified Saxon settlement) may, perhaps, have occupied the ring hill Iron Age camp immediately W. of Audley End, crowned quite appropriately by Robert Adam's Ionic temple celebrating the triumphs of the Seven Years War. The village now nestles on the ancient Granta-valley route, with the S. doorway of its church going back to the 12th century. *Mill House* below the church to the east, a tall mansard-roofed house of *c.* 1700. *Gatehouse Farm*, beside A11, with walnut-tree by the gate, a beautiful plastered 16th-century hall-house, timber-framed, with an original stone fireplace at rear. *Granta House*, just west of the church, basically 16th-century with an open courtyard at rear, white plastered, slated, and given handsome projecting pediments above the wings early in the 19th century, keeps its original floor-levels: face-lift reveals them behind ground-floor windows. The church, much rebuilt 1870–5, has tall 16th-century porches, with vestiges of fan-vaulting; the font, completely boxed in early Tudor linenfold panelling, has a crocketed and finialled crown; the neo-Renaissance N. chapel screen, 1911, was done by Rev. H. J. Burrell. Impressive, slightly lurid painting, described by Dr Pevsner as "kneeling angel", is captioned "Ecce mulier quae erat in civitate peccatrix"! It commemorates a vicar's wife, 1881. Near the sharp corner on the road to Catmere End, a remarkable pit contains chalk weathered to the most vivid hues, scarlet and yellow.

Loughton (7). The first syllable rhymes with cow, and trees hold their own about this otherwise suburban town. A family of Loughton woodmen called Willingale took a memorable stand against the enclosures that were steadily wiping out Forest in 1860s. Their action, and the Commons Preservation Society led by E. N. Buxton, secured recognition of the ancient lopping rights of the inhabitants of Loughton; finally the Epping Forest Act of 1878 appointed the City of London Conservators of Forest.

Part of the £7,000 the City paid for the extinction of lopping rights went to build Lopping Hall, 1884 (at the corner of High Road and Station Road), provided with reading and lecture rooms, and later extended to make room for the Midland Bank. W. R. Fisher, author of an authoritative history of *The Forest of Essex*, 1887, regretted the extinction of Loughton's lopping rights, "a relic of antiquity not less worthy of preservation than . . . Ambresbury Banks" (see Waltham Abbey). In 1900, Loughton became an Urban District, in 1933 united with Buckhurst Hill and Chigwell to form Chigwell U.D. Hence the confusion to strangers who see Loughton labelled Chigwell and anyway find the buildings uninteresting. At least they are grateful for the trees, and for the hilly situation, which give what character there is. If the thin-spired Victorian churches were granite instead of Kentish rag, Loughton would seem more like somewhere urban in the Scottish lowlands than an Essex town.

St Mary's church, 1871, just below Lopping Hall on High Road, has a lush profusion of stone foliage on its aisle arcades. The R.C. church farther north, beyond the dip, was designed by an accomplished Loughton firm, Tooley & Foster, 1958. The old church of St Nicholas (rebuilt 1877) is hardly worth pursuing out on the road to Debden Station (the Central line): an 1860 copy of Edward the Confessor's shrine stands uneasily in the churchyard. Eden Nesfield's large essay in "Queen Anne" domestic, *Loughton Hall*, 1878, rears its cupola behind the churchyard wall. (Back on the High Road, south-west of Lopping Hall, "St Margaret's", is a perfect example of the influence of Nesfield and Norman Shaw all over England, a modest version of Loughton Hall and now a school of the remedial kind.) The Hall itself is now a "Community Centre". An elegant little library by County Architect just below, and big new College of Further Education. Opposite, *the Broadway*, comprehensive shopping centre for the *Debden* Estate, unspeakably nasty in scale and entire conception, 1958. *Alderton Hall*, many gabled, weatherboarded like a rambling old water-mill, and tree-screened, is worth tracking down in Alderton Hall Lane, off Alderton Hill, for it helps to keep Loughton in perspective. There are very good examples of modern architectural engineering: *Loughton Station*, 1940 (Murray Easton); the *Bus Garage* at Goldings Hill (Yorke, Rosenberg & Mardall); and the *Bank of England Printing Works*, 1953–6, with superb skylit vault (Easton & Robertson).

Maldon (6). Saxon for "cross-hill", the name may mean that this fine site above the Blackwater was landmarked by a cross in its early days, or more prosaically was already at an important crossroads on the hill controlling the lowest fordable points above the estuary – Fullbridge and Heybridge. Today as you stand down at Fullbridge looking up at this ancient borough, its roofs still well interspersed among trees, only three buildings, two of them churches, break the natural skyline of the hilltop: the sharp-pointed spire of All Saints (presumably the mother-church), the red brick tower, stair-turret and comic bell-cage of the 15th century Moot Hall, and the medieval flint tower of St Peter's, serving as vestibule to the public library that was built in place of the church in time of Queen Anne.

Lay-out of town agreeably simple. From medieval Fullbridge Street, two alternative roads climb very steeply up to High Street, the main spine of the old Town. High Street descends gradually from All Saints, in the west, down to the Hythe, beside the estuary, in the east, where St Mary's church, with its large 12th-century nave, betokens centuries of coastal trade. The medieval fish-market lay just west of All Saints (in front of the Blue Boar!), the corn-market in the wide part of High Street south of the church; this part of the street was formerly occupied by a row of buildings that were presumably the usual encroachments on a market-place. Farther to the west, just beyond Gate Street, lying plumb across the road to Beeleigh, some outlines of the Saxon *burh* can still be made out.

A fortress was built here in 916 by Edward the Elder to protect his great fort at Witham from flank attack in the campaign in which he brought Danish England to terms. An imperishable 10th-century poem, *The Battle of Maldon*, records the heroic stand in the summer of 991 by Byrhtnoth's Anglo-Danish defence-force against Viking invaders camped on Northey Island, in the estuary: perhaps sportingly, he allowed them to cross narrow causeway and form up on mainland, but then he lost the battle. The causeway still breaks surface at low tide, the scene now idyllic rather than epic.

Domesday Book records a borough of 180 houses, perhaps over 1,000 people, with its own mint since early 10th century. It returned two M.P.s from 1329. Over 3,000 freemen voted in 1826 election: the Reform Act reduced the number of registered voters to 876. The Moot Hall is basically a defensible red brick tower of c. 1435 (sometimes called D'Arcy Tower, it became the Moot Hall only after being sold by the D'Arcys to an alderman, 1575). In the Council Chamber there are portraits of an Elizabethan lady,

of Queen Anne and of Dr Thos. Plume. A late Georgian porch provides a balcony (with ironwork) right out over the pavement, useful at election times. The "Georgian" fenestration is in fact late Victorian. *Circa* 1704, when several small parochial libraries were being founded, Dr Plume provided 6,000 volumes and housed them on the site of St Peter's church, apparently disused since the Reformation: first catalogue published 1959. Best street-scenery west up High Street from here, notably *King's Head*, with pleasant irregular Georgian front, and, immediately west of All Saints, the *Blue Boar*, with 15th-century stable range on S. side of carriageway, and on N. side a front room 'probably' of the 14th century (R.C.). Silver Street's façades create a Georgian illusion still. *All Saints*, has two particularly interesting features: its 13th-century tower, ingeniously constructed on a triangular plan to fit the acute angle between the old S. wall of the nave and the line of the old fishmarket (Silver Street)

Near MALDON

EAST MERSEA

on the west; and its great S. aisle, built out c. 1330. This aisle is richly carved, with a splendid ogee-headed arcade all along the S. wall at sedilia level, though the sixth surviving arch from the east marks a drop in the level, and provides a doorway down into the crypt. (Was this a great chantry?) Then high above all this, the windows have elaborately carved frames, the large W. window of the aisle seeming much less "restored" than the rest, and has touchingly expressive, though mutilated, heads as label-stops. The S. aisle has a dignified, tall barrel-ceiling, leaving tie-beams exposed, also the arch into S. chancel-aisle. Nave united to N. aisle by low curved ceiling, 1728, the low level providing a pleasantly "domestic" air. Small and pretty Charles II Arms. The Arms and monuments are beautifully coloured. John Vernon's white gravestone, 1653, he found among the ruins of Smyrna; a merchant, he also brought home MSS. from that antique city. All Saints *vicarage*, with over-restored timber-frame, contains old wall-painting.

Ruins of a 12th-century *leper-hospital* stand half a mile S. of All Saints. The lower end of High Street is fast going to pot, with the building-line being relentlessly forced back from the street. The N. side of Wantz Road, 48–76, including *The Star*, forms an early 19th-century terrace. At *The Hythe*, with muddy inlets and moored barges, and *the Jolly Sailor* snuggling into the river side of the churchyard, a slight spire on a slender octagon adds grace to the sturdiness of the W. tower of *St Mary the Virgin*: heavily buttressed, its upper stage is of Tudor brickwork. The whole interior is too thoroughly restored and spruce to feel like an ancient church. Vestiges of the Norman chancel-arch demonstrate impressive width of that Norman nave. Out along Marine Parade, widened and extended in 1925, and past the Marine Lake opened at Mid-

WEST MERSEA

summer 1905 by Lady Rayleigh, moorings of barges, fishing-boats and yachts give way to open fairways of the estuary, marsh walls, and long views with unforgettable sunsets. Maldon's own contribution to barge-design was the very shallow broad kind for moving whole corn-stacks up inland creeks. They were generally known as "Stackies". Beyond Fullbridge, where a plaque marks the burning of Stephen Knight at the stake, in 1555, lies

Heybridge. The church is almost wholly Norman with a great squat W. tower and original projecting turret-stair, all capped by a tiled pyramid roof: above the nave N. door, a Norman tympanum filled with primitive notched stone lozenges. The ancient S. door has iron scrollwork and hinges probably Norman. Thos. Freshwater's Master's gown was well carved in 1638; his wife is seen wearing an enormous neck-ruff. Magnificent buff-brick Ironworks like an enormous classical temple were built by Bentalls, 1863, with an adjacent small hall of the same period for the "Essex Engineer Volunteers". Maldon managed to stave off schemes for canalizing Chelmer and Blackwater till the Act was passed in 1793. Rennie surveyed the cut from Heybridge Hill to the new basin at Colliers Reach, now an active Timber Wharf, with the *Old Ship Inn* and agreeable weatherboarded cottages, lock-gates and barge-traffic. *Millbeach*, beyond, has a tawdry site for caravans.

Beeleigh. Remains of a Premonstratensian Abbey, inhabited and often open to the public, lie in the lush Blackwater valley. One block survives from the W. side of the cloister: the chapter-house and 1st-floor dormitory with its undercroft. These are both 13th-century buildings, the ground-floor vaults resting on slender Purbeck marble piers; they date perhaps from a large bequest by the Bishop of London in 1262. They are entered through a picturesque 3-storey timber-framed domestic building, brick-nogged, put up at the S. end of the monastic range soon after the Dissolution. The Undercroft,

probably used by the canons as a warming-house, has remains of 13th-century painting, also a very heraldic, flamboyant cock, possibly 16th-century. The vault here is of chalk. The dormitory over has a lavishly timbered waggon-vault roof and the late Mr Foyle's library, looking rather unused.

Manningtree see Mistley.

Manuden (2). Beautiful approach from Clavering along Stort valley to *Pinchpools* farmhouse, its Elizabethan core reduced to a panelled plaster-ceiled bedroom and three-shafted chimney stack. *Manuden House*, Queen Anne behind its 19th-century stucco front, has ironwork railings with gilded owls, and noble Wellingtonias planted in 1855: good panelling, staircase and 3-arched arcade on fluted columns with exuberant caps. The Georgian parsonage stands next, then the *church* with an external appearance of 1862, except the medieval N. transept. Inside brick-floored; a medieval screen; four ancient tie-beams and crown-posts (one in the transept, where the memorial of Sir Wm. Waad, 1636, says his father Armigel, clerk of council to Henry VIII and Edward VI, was reputed the first Englishman to find the continent of America and was called "the English Columbus": Sir William was clerk of council to Elizabeth I and James I). In 1430, the vicar, John Bagley, believed the consecrated host remained "bread in its own nature" and so he was burnt as a Wycliffite heretic.

Waad lived at *Battles Hall*, nicely remodelled c. 1660, presumably by his grandson, William, Captain of the trained bands, later murdered in a nearby field. South of the churchyard, *Benrose Cottages* have a carved Tudor bressumer and good internal timbers. *The Bury*, beyond, makes a pleasant thatched group with own farm-buildings. At the *Hall*, nearby, the great chimney-stack and four Tudor brick step-gables alone survived incendiarism in 1888: the flames were watched by a man who in his nineties still remembers it as the work of a "drunken little tyke" never prosecuted.

Maplestead, Great (3). The abrupt stout square Norman church tower, slightly recessed in the top stage, had its E. wall and much of the S. wall rebuilt in Tudor brick: the W. wall of the S. aisle is also rebuilt with much old red brick. Interior dark, despite whitewash. The little Norman apse, impressive within, is lit by a tiny Victorian skylight. The reredos is a pleasant Victorian triptych. Two remarkable monuments in the S. transept were restored for Mr Hart of Dynes Hall by Beryl Hardman and François Angello-del-Cauchferta in 1964. One shows Sir John Deane of Dynes Hall, 1625, stiff on one elbow, his widow and children in perfectly realistic costumes, on the shelf above, with an inscription composed by his eldest daughter: "His parts and person were admirable: Desarte and hee were twins". He "mach't with Mrs Anne Drury of the Honorable tribe of Druries of Riddlesworth, Norfolk", whose famous memorial, by William Wright, of Charing Cross, faces Sir John's across the transept. It shows her upright in her shroud, a pair of very natural angels waiting above a split arch to crown her as she rises through it: her son reclines below. *Dynes Hall* goes back to their day, though mostly of 1689, and with distinguished Gothick fenestration. *Chelmshoe House*, of lovely red early Georgian brick, has thick glazing-bars and a Gibbs surround to the front door.

Maplestead, Little (3) is remarkable for having one of the five round churches of the Knights Templars left in England; it was built in the early 14th century, whereas the others are Norman. It is a disappointment after seeing the irresistible engraving of Greig's drawing of the interior in *Excursions in the County of Essex*, 1819. Restored to death in the 1850s, the interior is white and chilly. The exterior, too, is an anticlimax, for there is a chancel to the E. of the round nave, which looks there-

fore, at first sight, only like a rather large round W. tower.

Margaretting (5/6). (Just "Ing" in the 11th century, but St Margaret's Ing by the 13th.) St Margaret's church, now beside main railway line, rears her tall slender shingled spire above one of the great timber-framed "Essex" belfries. This one is on ten posts, like Blackmore, and probably of the 15th century; with the usual cross-struts. One of the four bells is by Robert Burford, *c.* 1392–1418. Good timber porch and roofs, especially the embattled early Tudor wall-plates in the chancel. The E. window contains a complete 15th-century glass Jesse window. The E. wall of the chancel exuberantly pargeted at an indeterminate date, is too much like wedding-cake. Tudor brass shows Robert Sedge and wife, of Killigrews: a monument over the N. door commemorates Tanfields, *c.* 1625. *Killigrews* is a basically Tudor moated house. *Peacocks* is Regency, a stucco'd villa with portico that distracts the eye from the main road.

Marks Hall (6/13). Church down in 1932, house in 1951. *Cradle House* beside Robin's Brook is a cottage with a grand diapered Elizabethan chimney-stack.

Mashbury (5) at dead end, with Hall and very large pond. Tudor brick S. porch on basically Norman fabric: small nave and chancel. Medieval N. and S. doors in Norman doorways: in the south, two orders and zigzag. Four large belfry posts no longer support anything.

Matching (5). The church is part of a delightful village group, sighted over arable fields from the north-west or over the large pond. Beside the pond a Regency fishing-lodge backs on to Hall-grounds with old oaks. The church contains a pulpit of 1624 and a well-carved wall monument of 1716, to Nicholas Ashton. Hall moated, roughcast, pink-washed, among pleasant outbuildings. There is a dovehouse here and at

Kingston's farm. A 15th-century "Marriage Feast Room", seen beyond a handsome urn in the churchyard, preserves its external plaster. It is not known how long the room has been used for this purpose: it seems very consonant with the village name.

Mayland (13). Holiday settlement beside Mundon Creek. Church of 1867.

Mersea Island (13) is oval in shape, 4½ miles by 2, lying east between the mouths of the Colne and the Blackwater and separated from the mainland by Pyefleet, a creek. One road, the Strood (pronounced Strode) crosses to Mersea, which rises from marsh level as high as 70 ft. An east–west road along the spine gives lovely views. It is divided into two medieval parishes: *East* and *West.*
East Mersea is still visually much as it must have been when Sabine Baring-Gould was rector (1870–81). He wrote, among over 100 books, *Mahalah*, a story never forgotten by people who love these marshlands that provided its setting. He is said to have had W. Mersea's six bells in mind when he composed "Now the Day is Over". The lovely whitewashed interior of his church (and St Edmund's) has lost its box-pews since 1912; but it is still lit by oil-lamps; and his 17th-century pulpit, with its tester, is still perched up on a stone base, and with no visible means of access! There is a brass doggerel to Mawdlyn Owtred, 1572, and a painted wooden tablet to Lt. Col. Edward Bellamie, citizen and fishmonger, 1656. The font wears a pretty modern cap. Medieval S. door. All looking especially nice in evening light, now the day is over.
West Mersea. Crossing the Strood one's first impression of Mersea is marred by massed caravans away to the west. In fact W. Mersea has tucked away or avoided most of the unsightliness that goes with seaside popularity. Mr Hervey Benham's book, *Two Cheers for the Town Hall*, shows memorably how since the 1920s the large oyster-fishing and bathing village,

MESSING. The east window: Acts of Mercy

discovered by yachtsmen and exposed to the people of Colchester by cut-price bus fares, has become a community of 3½ thousand swelling to 10 thousand in summer with the caravanners, hut-owners, etc., and all this controlled by a staff of 4½ council officials. Yachtsmen, Dabchick Sailing Club, etc., concentrated at the W. tip of the island, leaving the secluded S.-facing shore, with almost Mediterranean gardens like that at the West Hold, to fortunate permanent residents.

Near the church, *Hall Barn* is a brash-looking "country club" and *New Orleans* flats appear to be composed of some synthetic rock; but *Yew Tree House*, to the south-west, is of very striking early Georgian brick, and west from there stands a pleasant close of clapboard fishing cottages, modern flats (*Rosebank*) and two or three Georgian brick cottages. There are Georgian elements at *Myrtle Cottage* and *Bocking Hall*. Roman elements at Mersea (they picked good sites) are now mostly underground. The base of a structure thought to be possibly a Roman lighthouse is now built

137

MISTLEY: The Strand. The swans are attracted by the waste from the maltings

over in Beach Road, off Yorick Road, that leads to *Pharos*, i.e. lighthouse, Lane. *The Mount*, part of yard pecked over by chickens, is a 20 ft. high Romano-British burial mound that has yielded its lead casket and glass bowlful of human ashes. (It was cleared of the poultry in 1967.)

The *church* (St Peter) on a Roman site (remains are beneath the churchyard east of church), is thought to be a 7th-century foundation built as a collegiate minster in the 10th century: the base of the big square W. tower, with Roman brick quoins, may be part of this rebuilding. The medieval nave, heightened in brick in 1833, has a charming Gothic interior corbel-frieze and painted cartouches. There is a piece of sculpture after della Robbia. The S. aisle is unhappily scraped bare.

Messing (13). Never confuse it with Mucking, near Tilbury, nor be deterred by church's ugly red brick W. tower of 1840. It has a most remarkable chancel, much as it was when completely fitted out in 1634, for the vicar, Nehemiah Rogers, a supporter of Archbishop Laud. His parishioners, the Chibbornes of Har-

MISTLEY: The Swan: the former spa-pavilion designed as part of Richard Rigby's model river-port

borough Hall, who were connected by marriage with Juxon, Laud's successor, presented a set of communion plate in the same year: their arms and sentiments appear on the carved Royal Arms, also of 1634, now suspended in the S. transept. It carries a quotation from *Proverbs*, 24: "My son, Fear thou the Lord and the King . . . and meddle not with them that are given to change". Rich wood-panelling round the chancel, plaster-panelling in the ceiling. Contemporary glass in the E. window, six of the seven Works of Mercy, in predominant Prussian blue and gold, with some purple, attributed by Pevsner to Abraham Van Linge by comparison with his work at Peterhouse. Alas for all this royalism: the church registers include a transcript list of the parish's arms out at the Parliament's "Leaguer before Colchester", 1648, and its expenses that year in quartering Fairfax's army.

Middleton (10). Delectable village of wooded slopes and footpaths. The small church stands beside the large white-brick Victorian parsonage, a rushy pond, beeches and crumbly urns, and the motto *Cave Stagnum*. The Norman S. doorway is set in a little Tudor porch unsophisticated as a country bonnet, much remade, and containing a carved medieval door

of silvery oak. Impressive semi-circular chancel arch with zigzag and lozenge ornament. Abaci continue across to N. and S. walls. Badly worn incised slab to priest, James Samson, 1349, perhaps a victim of the Black Death. A painting of the Annunciation, 16th-century Venetian (Andrea Schiavone ?), needs care. Small carved Tudor Royal Arms. The lane to Henny Street has views over the Stour.

Mile End *see* Colchester.

Mistley and **Manningtree** (11) two of the best-looking places in Essex, partly for their old buildings, but mostly for their situation beside the quiet estuary, a mile wide at high water. As you walk east along Manningtree's main street it bends sharply into sudden view of the Strand, a green waterside frequented by swans. Further delights lie ahead: the remaining Georgian buildings of the small model port begun by Richard Rigby (d. 1730) and improved with church, terraces and quay-side offices by his son and name-sake, the notorious political jobber, Paymaster of the Forces, 1768–84, whose handsome mural tablet, 1788, in the (Victorian) church omits his most famous achievement – that he died leaving "near half a million of public money". Garrick, who stayed

139

here, liked to say Rigby fixed his abode in a swamp to excuse himself for using brandy as the rest of the world used small-beer: in fact Garrick loved the situation, especially being able to look out of his dressing-room window at 50 vessels under sail; and "one, half an hour ago, saluted us with thirteen guns". Sail mostly those of pleasure-yachts now, and Mistley's business mostly maltings, with buildings topped by characteristic tall ventilated pyramids – those of Ind Coope, between cliff and water's edge, a spectacular finish to the little river-front town.

Manningtree ("many trees") emerged in the 14th century from Mistley ("wood where mistletoe grew"), and not surprisingly took to shipbuilding. Its chapel suffered badly at the Reformation (Manningtree over zealous then): it was rebuilt on a new site in the main street in 1616. Mistley register records "Old George Pegrime of Maintree by whose labour and care the chapel there was built under God and King James". A S. aisle was built in 1821, a new chancel in 1839, and all dismantled in 1965; its N. wall and buttresses were preserved to form a valuable part of enclosed street-scene, but now Manningtree is allowing this to be scrapped in 1968. Constable's fine painting for this chapel is now safely at Feering (q.v.): the parish has gone back to Mistley. 38 High Street, next door, contains a massive early 17th-century chimney stack. The street's character is derived from Georgian and Victorian fronts. Former Corn Exchange, with Ionic portico, has been very skilfully converted into R.C. church by Raymond Erith, making the most of round-headed arcading. The pleasantest Georgian buildings are to be found up South Street and South Hill from the main crossing in High Street: mostly in white brick, e.g. *Hill House* and *Prospect House*, with behind it the *Independents' chapel*, 1818, now British Legion Social Club. Hill House is duplicated higher up South Hill (*No. 59*), at right-angles to the *Methodist*

church, 1807, whose cupola makes it the most eminent building in the town.

Mistley. The medieval village church is now represented only by a handsome, neglected, flush-work S. porch, on Mistley Heath, given *c.* 1520 by Richard Darnell, whose mark survives prominently in the spandrels: it was roofed in as the Rigby mausoleum and contains medieval altar-slabs. The church's roofs fell in *c.* 1710, and it was replaced by a simple building on a new site at Mistley Thorn (spur in the river), *c.* 1735. In 1776, this was given Tuscan porticos on the (ritual) N. and S. sides, and twin square towers, supported by freestanding Tuscan columns and surmounted by cupolas with Ionic colonnades; one serving as W. tower, the other still containing the reredos (with Ten Commandments), an azure ceiling with gilt emblem of the Trinity, and the plans of Robert Adam engraved by John Roberts. These two towers were saved as mausoleums (though never used as such) when the rest of the church was found eaten with dry rot and sold to a builder in part exchange for the erection, in 1870, of a Victorian Gothic church with spire, on yet another site. It contains an incised slab of Jhone Boner, 1533, an early Georgian memorial to Thos. Osmond, fuller, who was burnt in 1555, and late Georgian memorials to Thos. Tusser and the Rt. Hon. Richard Rigby. Rigby's house was pulled down in 1844, but two lodges by Adam survive. So does much of Rigby's village, with terraces, the Thorn pub, and the small quay-side building with circular pond and inelegant swan, spellbound by its own reflection.

Moreton (5) is in the gravel, with quarrying west and south of the church, and the old buildings commonly now roughcast with gravel. Church tower rebuilt upon the model of the old one in 1787, by, it is said, Jas. Marrable. Tablet on its east wall merely names church-warden at time. Harry Marrable was a bell-ringer in 1919. Chancel a sorry clutter.

Former guildhall opposite, *c.* 1473. To the east, *Hill Farm* is a small 15th-century hall-house in country indistinguishable from High Suffolk. The post-mill belonging to Society for Protection of Ancient Buildings is down.

Moulsham see Chelmsford.

Mountnessing (8). The church is perched up high, alongside a pond and the Hall, which has a Georgian red-brick façade. A tall humped-up nave with broad aisles accommodates the great timber posts and braces of an "Essex" belfry. Odd-looking brick W. front: the W. wall of the nave was built in 1653, and that of the aisles to north and south is Georgian. The chancel, of 1805, houses a nice reredos and communion rails of *c.* 1730. Prominent post-mill on ridge, W. of A12: dilapidated weatherboarding. Two arches mark site of chancel of *Thoby Priory*, small house of Austin canons who probably took name of their first prior, Tobias, *c.* 1150.

Mucking (9) not the same thing as Messing, but both are very agreeable in their ways. The church, much rebuilt 1852–7, with castellated low tower and S. aisle, is approached through a young chestnut avenue, past a pleasant room (1855 "Perp.") in the churchyard. The church retains good 13th-century features. A Perp. (15th-century) green-man, or woodwose, frequents the forest leaves of the capital of the S.-aisle pier. Eliz. Downes kneels in alabaster, 1607.

Mundon (13). A most romantically beautiful little church is set beside the great lily-covered moat of the Hall. It is not surprising to see in Domesday Book that Eudo Dapifer had planted a small vineyard here by 1086. All is now hidden among oak trees. At the time of writing, the church is overgrown

with elder and brambles, the chancel wide open on the N. side, dangerously ruinous. Happily its rescue is undertaken by Mr Bulmer-Thomas and the Friends of Friendless Churches, who deserve all support. The W. view is most unusual: a tiled-roofed and weatherboarded belfry of the distinctive "Essex" kind is supported on great posts stabilized by a broader outshot base, over which a tiled penthouse slopes outwards to cover a sort of W. ambulatory. This is early 16th-century according to the Royal Commission, but contains a bell of c. 1400. Inevitably one thinks of the small pagoda. The 2-light low W. window is very domestic looking. The Tudor timber N. porch is well carved with spandrels and pendants. The chancel, rebuilt c. 1750, contains trompe-l'oeil paintings of curtains and Creed and Commandments on E. wall, all badly spattered with bird-lime. There is a cheap 19th-century Gothick screen.

Navestock (8). Uneventful slope down from S. Weald: wide wooded views. The needle of Navestock's spire extends as you approach. The farm-track beside the church led to a grand park, now barley-fields: lake and swans survive. The spire surmounts one of the finest of the "Essex" belfries in which the swing of the steeple is steadied, as at Mundon, by a broad outshot base of "aisles" on the three sides away from the nave, which provides its own contribution to the stability of the belfry. Stability was certainly needed here during the Battle of Britain. On 21 September, 1940, a land-mine fell in elms near the churchyard gate: the site was marked by a suburban rose-garden at the re-dedication fifteen years later.
The great belfry, re-covered in unattractive brown cement, serves as a vestry in its base: inner posts run up to a key central boss as at W. Hanningfield, here carved with

oak-leaves. A photo in the vestry shows the S. side hideously blasted open. An etching shows Bishop Stubbs, who had young Swinburne to stay here in the summer of 1859, when the vicarage was the scene of two dramatic episodes recounted in Gosse's *Swinburne*. The interior plaster walls, and the stone and timber of the main piers (and even the organ-case at the W. end) are all dazzling white, which shows up the lambent red brick pamments on the floor, and old broken stone slabs recording that Mr James Jeggins departed this life in 1757 and Mr John North, gun-stock maker, in 1768; and poor Jane Radcliffe, only 15:

"So faire a blossome so
 exquisitely good
That I want words to make
 it understood."
How the clear uncoloured glass enhances everything inside! The 4th pier of the nave is of timber thrillingly fluted like some antique column in Sicily. Memorials include a martial series, with young Edward Waldegrave, by Jn. Bacon, junior, shipwrecked off Falmouth after surviving the retreat with Moore to Corunna.
The "site of palace" so firmly marked on our map is dubious.

Nazeing (4). The church, set up on the naze (spur) of the original settlement, presides now over the

The Essex landscape: MOUNTNESSING windmill

low Lea valley in which acres of market-garden glasshouses are distinguishable from the shimmering river only in summer-time, when the river is signalled by the sails of dozens of small boats. The Tudor brick church-tower is a rich dark red, with black diaper. In the timber-framed S. porch, the bricks have been laid regularly instead of "nogged" (? at the 1928 restoration). The porch is floored with tiles set on edge and worn into a very attractive condition. The whole interior, Victorianized, gleams with polish. *Nazeing Park*, "lately rebuilt" in 1814, its 2-storey wings masked by bay windows and joined across the 3-storey front by a balustrated Ionic colonnade, is now an E.C.C. Special School. *Upper Park Town Post Office* is a moated, weather-boarded late medieval house. *Nazeingwood Common*, on which a golf-club was founded in 1890, is now great arable open fields, very impressive to the south.

Netteswell *see* Harlow.

Nevendon *see* Basildon.

Newport (2) had its market removed to Saffron Walden in the 12th century; what looks like the ancient market-place survives, east of the church. But fairs went on, and 13th-century records show Newport with glovers, grocers, furriers, carpenters, vintners, coopers, dyers, goldsmiths and a moneylender. This rich village owed everything to its thoroughfare position, including rupture by railway and the current purgation by A11.
Starting at the north end, *Short-grove Hall*, secluded in its own grounds, was built by Giles Dent (his monument, of 1670, in church is specific on this point): wings and 3-arched stone bridge added by Earl of Thomond (d. 1714): it was being converted into a hotel when gutted by fire, 5 June 1966. Attractive wrought-iron gates mark the entrance. Nearby is a

BLACK NOTLEY

vast erratic boulder, then an ancient group of buildings, including *Crown House*, pargeted with a crown in high relief, 1692. An unusually good 15th-century range (*The Priory*), now cottages, with an original moulded oak oriel-window, abuts the railway bridge. Across the main road, the *Grammar School* building by Eden Nesfield is impressive in a Charles II style. Then comes a little toll-bridge with scale of charges: "For every ass . . . $\frac{1}{2}$d.": that would still bring in a good sum. And then *The Links*, the former House of Correction (1775), with elegantly carved shackles on the Georgian white brick front. After that, the attention is drawn to *Monks Barn*, timber-framed, with a "Wealden" over-hang, brick-nogging and a fast-decaying carving of crowned Virgin and Child with attendant musical angels.
The *church*'s best externals are a 15th-century porch and handsome Tudor brick chancel-clerestory. It was collegiate. The present stalls are mostly Victorian renewals. Next to Dent's, a monument to Joseph Smith, of Shortgrove, records that he was the younger Pitt's private secretary during "the whole of that arduous administration", and nevertheless lived to be 65 in 1822. Nicely fretted medieval screen. In the roomy S. transept, a 13th-century chest is used as an altar, its lid painted as reredos with crucifix and four saints. Noble 13th-century font. The 14th-century glass was bought early in the 20th century for the N. transept lancets. Brasses.

Norton, Cold (9/16). On the hills above North Fambridge and Stow Maries: thus "cold". Exhilarating views to north, east and south from the church, a building of 1855 which has neither tower nor bell-cote. A Tudor lady engraved in brass is without inscription. A separate inscription on slate says, presumably of another, "Here lyeth Maude that was the comfortable wife of Robert Cammocke of Layer Marnie", and died 1599, leaving a son living and having here a daughter buried with her.

Norton Mandeville (5). Hall, barns and two cottages are all of Victorian brickwork beside a screen of Victorian firs, and set with a small church of the 1180s among wide farmlands. Church oil-lit, rather neglected: simple Norman font set round with surviving medieval slipware tiles. The small belfry rests on a tie-beam with three posts; *Norton Manor House*, at Norton Heath, is many gabled, white-fronted, with three good chimney-stacks, one dated in brick 1610.

Notley, Black (6). Why the Notleys were distinguished by Black and White early in the Middle Ages is uncertain. Black N. is becoming a suburb of Braintree, with ribbon development along both Chelmsford and Witham Roads. There is a large hospital, and just south of it *Stanton's Farm*, with one of the medieval aisled halls that have lately been more widely recognized (plan and section in R.C., 1921). B.N. *Lodge*, a symmetrical early-Georgian red and blue brick house with curved gables (parapet unhappily cemented) was built for William Rayment in place of Balls Farm which belonged to John Ray (1628–1705) the eminent naturalist. Ray, born here the son of a blacksmith, is commemorated by a small obelisk in the churchyard just south of the nave. In Morant's day it was moved into church to stop injury by weather. Now outside again, but with his friend Benjamin Allen's table-tomb moved alongside and both lately restored by the Essex Field Club. A new Junior School, on the brink of Braintree, opposite B.N. Lodge, is named after Ray. The church, grouped with the great barns of the Hall, has Royal Arms of 1802, charmingly painted with a rose garland.

Notley, White (6). White Colne, not far away, took its distinguishing name from a Domesday owner, Dimidius Blancus, who *may*, conceivably, have acquired an estate here after the Domesday records were completed. White Notley's elegant thin shingled broach spire rises from a white weatherboarded belfry of the early 16th century. The Romanesque semicircular chancel arch is dressed with red Roman brick: the chancel was apsidal until a 13th-century rebuilding. Vestry contains a fragment of 13th-century glass set in an 11th-century window, itself cut from a Saxon headstone. The many-gabled Hall is of Henry VIII's reign; the W. end, including the hall-chimney, was rebuilt in brick in Elizabeth I's reign.

Oakley, Great (11). The church is set beautifully on a sloping churchyard amid trees and headstones. Square medieval tower of septaria, repaired in 1766 from sale of bells, with red brick W. wall (decorated by stone memorial tablet), white weatherboarded belfry and tiled pyramid roof. The pleasant porch is of *c.* 1800. The bare barn of a 12th-century nave contains a 12th-century font. Angels are beautifully carved, though emaciated, in high relief on jambs of the N. chancel doorway. Registers record large parish-population in 17th century: mass burials of plague victims, 1666. Pretty Victorian glass in E. windows. Victorian painted reredos (? the master of Braxted).

——, **Little** (11). The church, isolated and neglected, looks over Peewit Island and creeks of Hamford Water. Plain glass and beautiful 14th-century window-tracery and steeply canopied niches and aumbry. 14th-century window-tracery, too, in the Norman nave. The Rev. George Burmester, 1794–1892, was rector here for 61 years.

Ockendon, South (8), now joined to a piece of North Ockendon apparently found indigestible by the G.L.C. when they swallowed most of that parish: the remnant includes a Tudor timber-framed house called *Baldwins*. South Ockendon *church*, on the S. side of a cheerful small Green, has a prominent round W. tower of dark flintwork with stone dressings: the upper stage is Victorian "Norman". The tremendously rich 12th-century N. doorway,

with stone zigzagging in three dimensions, is much restored. The brass effigy of Sir Ingram Bruyn, of 1400, has been foully decapitated, but an inscription is tattooed, as it were, across his breast-plate. A Lord Mayor, Sir Richard Saltonstall, kneels in alabaster effigy erected by Lady S., who kneels facing him in her furred gown and widow's veil, 1601. East of the church is one of the most interesting great moated hall-sites in Essex, though the Hall itself is Victorian; a smock windmill is part of the group. Two mounds stand on this steep scarp looking across Mar Dyke; a third has gone (R.C.). Amid acres of new housing it is worth looking for *Little Belhus*, Elizabethan, with walled garden, roughly three-quarters of a mile south-west of the church.

Ongar, Chipping (5). After 1066, the great moated castle-mound was thrown up to provide a local H.Q. for Count Eustace of Boulogne, King Stephen's father-in-law. Later it belonged to Richard de Lucy (see Great Tey), justiciar of Henry II who visited him here. A market ("chipping") grew up at the gate of the castle, probably in the 12th century, certainly by the 13th, and provided the bulging main street of the present little town, now bustling with much traffic. Smart Post Office beside Bell Inn. Brick-fronted King's Head dated 1697 over carriage-way. Opposite, the old Corner Shop, with 1642 carved on a window-frame, flanks a short lane back to the attractively secluded *parish church* of St Martin of Tours. Church interior homely, unambitious, unspoiled. West gallery for organ. Skylights just right, as most of the small aisle and chancel windows have coloured glass of various dates and qualities. The rich E. window by Leonard Walker, 1929, is very effective. (Note evidence of two tiers of 13th-century lancet windows, with interesting brickwork, in the E. wall.) Ingenious and decorative bracing of the chancel roof, with pendants dated 1647. Simple

tablet, signed Nollekens, shows cherubs disconsolate at the death of Jn. Mitford's wife, 1776. Ornately panelled Caroline pulpit. In the S. aisle (added in 1884) the altar, with 17th-century rails, has a reredos painted and gilded in neo-Italianate manner. *Art nouveau* angels in aisle roof. Font much weathered!

Wren House is nicely islanded at the edge of the market-place and the church path. Most old houses here have suffered from the insertion of shop-fronts conceived more in Harrow than in Ongar. North of the Post Office, do not let the shop-front of Baugh the chemist deflect the eye from the prodigious chimney-stack above. A few hundred yards south one comes to the *Congregational church* associated with the young David Livingstone, who trained under the pastor to be a missionary, 1838–9. At the approach to the castle, up Castle Street (a lane), *White House* (large with old red chimneys) is surrounded by a good old red wall growing wall-flowers. *Castle House*, tall, Victorianized, has byres full of Friesian cattle. The great castle mound is moated, and the moat is actively patrolled by a flotilla of red-crested pochards.

——, **High**, includes *Marden Ash*, a suburb of Chipping Ongar with two nice old houses Georgian-cased: *Marden Ash House*, and *Newhouse Farm*. There is a rectory of solid, dignified Georgian red brick. Just east of the church, *Nash Hall*, weatherboarded, has stout Elizabethan chimney-stacks. The church's small Victorian white brick S. tower-porch shelters a very rich Norman doorway, with tympanum and hood-mould. The interior is rather dull.

Orsett (8). The name goes back to 957, and means place of either "bogore pits" or "chalybeate springs". An admirably trim large village: see, e.g. the spruce appearance of the row of old-people's cottages along Malting Lane. A large impressive new school and hospital are sited together south of *Orsett House* (tall Georgian red brick). *Orsett Hall* retains a room that was elaborately decorated in the middle of the 17th century: its stone over-mantel has two arched bays, each with a carved female figure, apparently Hope and Charity. "Bishop Bonner's Palace" is a ring-and-bailey earthwork, presumably the site of a former castle: adjoining it, *Hall Farm*'s early Tudor wing is an interesting example of timber-framing never plastered over; the upper floor is jettied, and each storey has an original window of eight lights with pointed heads.

Just west of the church, are the former Swan Inn and an adjoining red brick Georgian house now a shop. The large flint *church* has a low tower of dark brick, stone-buttressed and supporting a little white-boarded pyramid and gilded vane. The noble Norman S. doorway shelters in a porch of much-restored 14th-century timber: an early Norman window is just east of it. The rood-screen by J. N. Comper, 1911, was made from the timber of a frigate in which a Bonham of Orsett House served. The N. and S. chancel screens by Nicholson are less graceful than Comper's work. The N. choirscreen is best, 14th-century work well restored. Monuments include the semi-recumbent figure of John Hatt, life-size, 1658; a handsome Baker marble of 1784, and two more monuments to the Baker family by Sir Richard Westmacott. There is an array of a dozen funeral-hatchments unusually well painted. At the W. end of the S. aisle, below rich Kempe glass, are five panels of 18th-century Italian plaster-work, high relief, beautifully "nervous": Annunciation, Holy Family, Mourning the Dead Christ, the Resurrection from the Tomb, Pentecost. There is good Victorian glass, rendered slightly disconcerting by evident likenesses to persons commemorated.

Osea Island *see* Totham.

Ovington (3) absorbed Belchamp St Ethelbert in 1473. At end of a lane edged with cowslips, the pink-washed Hall has for company a small church with bits of Victorian stonework applied outside, as at neighbouring Tilbury, and a yellow brick floor.

Paglesham (16), sometimes written Packlesham, keeps a remoteness and beauty astonishing so near to Southend-on-Sea. A manor here, possibly the main one, was given to Westminster Abbey by a thegn when he set out with Harold for the battle of Stamford Bridge, his great Yorkshire victory three weeks before Hastings. At *Eastend*, the red-brick *Cupola House* and weatherboarded *Plough and Sail* are cheerful Georgian buildings, *plough* and *sail* summing-up Paglesham's life, if we overlook smuggling. Behind the Plough and Sail, a track leads down to *Paglesham Reach*, where as many as thirteen barges at once have been repairing or building on Shuttlewood's hard, now given over to yacht-building. Hervey Benham records that the present yachtsmen's car park was the saw-pit, where every plank was cut by hand. Here was a great oyster-fishery a century ago, exporting to Ostend. *Ingulf*'s is an utterly charming weatherboarded cottage behind ash-trees and a great lawn. The village cluster alongside the tall hipped-roofed pub, *Paglesham Punch-bowl*, comes into view unforgettably across an open cornfield. This is *Churchend*, a small grey buttressed tower rising from the churchyard with old scrolly headstones, skulls, crossbones, cherubs. George III's arms still hang over the chancel arch. Mason's marks in tower-arch and doorways. The N. wall is Norman. Monument to a benefactor, John Massue, 1807. The small red-brick *Hall* with Georgian front adjoins the churchyard.

Panfield (6), beside the river Pant, is rather bungaloid, but the small Tudor red-brick *Hall* is in beautiful condition. The *Hall* runs east–west and may once have been quadrangular. The oldest part is in the W. end, the original great hall, *c.* 1500, with hammerbeam roof and diapered N. wall. Subsequent improvements apparently include one by George and Frances Cotton, 1583, whose initials appear in mantelpiece. Bought in 1641 by Richard FitzSymonds (see Gt. Yeldham), whose shield of arms appears over the main entrance in the porch-tower at the E. end. This was formerly 4 storeys high; now 3, and crowned with a lead pepper-pot top. At the Restoration, in 1660, FitzSymonds had the Royal Arms pargeted in an upper room, on the former end-wall.

A small cell of St Stephen, Caen, founded by one of the Conqueror's men *c.* 1066, has left traces in a field north of *Great Priory Farm*. The parish *church* has a medieval porch and the usual stout timber belfry-posts inside.

Parndon *see* Harlow.

Pattiswick (6). Farmland plateau above Stane Street. The small medieval *church*, with sentinel yews, is scarcely distinguishable from a Victorian copy of a small Essex church. Bare interior. It stands beside a former Green, a gabled Elizabethan *Hall* to the west.

Pebmarsh (10). In the gulley of a stream, surrounded by cornfields and oaks. Too many crude restorations and insensitively designed modern cottages. Nice group of buildings near the *King's Head*. The pink roughcast mill-house, down the lane south of the church, is where Courtauld's silk mill started in 1798 (the mill itself came down *c.* 1900). *Stanley Hall*, beside a delectable lane towards Halstead, and moated, has had the plaster stripped from its timber frame, the fillings between the timber studs pargeted and brick-nogged. In the windows are small panels of European 17th-century glass, much of it heraldic: the rural setting is lovely.

The church has an elaborately step-gabled mellow red brick porch; the tower parapet has corners that are *crocketed* in red brick and meant to look like small pepper-pot finials; a slender cupola on top is just a shade askew. Sir Ronald Storrs, "urbane and artful Governor of Jerusalem", and (also in T. E. Lawrence's words) "the most brilliant Englishman in the Near East", lies buried before this porch. An ikon from Jerusalem hangs inside. Spacious interior. One advantage of ancient flint-rubble church walls was that Victorians usually resisted the temptation to scrape all plaster from the inner faces: but not here. The large brass of a cross-legged knight, Sir Wm. Fitzralph, c. 1323, is interesting for its age rather than its beauty. Fourteenth-century stained glass heraldic shields have been reset in the N.W. window of the chancel: Fitzralph's is the top one in the E. light.

Peldon (13). The sensational first view of the church from the south, across a small Green, derives from the smouldering red Tudor brick of clerestory, and nave-buttresses, and a small diapered external rood-staircase. The brickwork has acquired a most beautiful texture, set off by the dull grey of the rest of the fabric. The broad tower is of Kentish rag, decorated with crosses in flint. A very modest early-Victorian chancel is of white brick, and the rest septaria and limestone rubble. The E. wall of the nave is tile-hung. Interior a flop. A new village hall, 1966, is marred by the use of ludicrous synthetic stone. Pleasant cottages on the W. side of the Green. Böcker and the crew of his crashed zeppelin (see Wigborough) were arrested in Peldon Post Office.

Pentlow (3). Farmlands with old names, like *Larks in the Wood*, slope down to the Stour-side group of Norman church with round tower, timber-framed fine Tudor Hall, with big oriel window in view from churchyard, and the long old red brick range of the watermill. A slender tower on the ridge commemorates rector Bull's parents, 1858. In *church*, the square Norman font is exuberantly carved with cross, star, etc.: its 15th-century canopied wooden cover, much restored, was doubtless formerly painted, the whole thing looking like a holy conduit. The tomb-chest in the chancel is of Edmund Felton and wife, 1542:

heraldic shields include Felton impaling six escallops, which ties up with heraldry in the fine windows of the Hall. Feltons were here from 1490s, gone by 1570; they were succeeded by George Kempe, who lies with son and daughter-in-law in the N. chapel with its tall, panelled tunnel vault, and external step-gables over E. and W. walls.

Pleshey (6). Here one of the most impressive Norman baronial castle-earthworks in England embraces the entire village within its great outer rampart and ditch. Its name "pleissis" is a Norman–French word for a part of the forest that was enclosed by a "pleached" tree fence, presumably c. 1100, when Geoffrey de Mandeville (or "Magna Villa") was building here, in the manor of High Easter. This was the H.Q. of the second biggest block of Norman estates in Essex; very compact, but with a subsidiary H.Q. and castle at Saffron Walden. J. H. Round thought Mandeville was already based at Plessis by 1086, from the fact that a vineyard was already growing in adjacent Great Waltham. The Mandevilles were extinct by 1189, but their earldom of Essex went on in the female line, and Pleshey with it, till 1372. Through Eleanor de Bohun it came to Richard II's "Uncle Gloucester", who founded a college of nine chaplains here, in 1394; its foundations are visible in a field south of the parish church in hot dry summers. Uncle Gloucester was liquidated in 1397, and Shakespeare imagined his widow amid Pleshey's "empty lodgings and unfurnished walls, unpeopled offices, untrodden stones". Still emptier today, the castle-site is open, to be trodden by the public, from April to September.
To get the full effect of this strange place, it is most important to arrive by the lane leading in from the east, not over the flat plateau from the west. After crossing the outer enclosure of the village, the lane becomes the village-street and climbs steadily up past the N. side of the great flat-topped mount,

with views between apple-trees and cottages of the dramatic 15th-century red brick bridge canted across from bailey to mount: the entrance to the bailey on the S. side. A distinct air of decay still pervades the village, whose outer rampart well repays walking. The *church* was largely rebuilt in 1868, preserving only the crossing-arches of the cruciform collegiate building. The churchyard paths look completely unused, and the church is found locked though Pleshey is now a place of Diocesan Retreat. Inside, the stone inscription, RICARDUS REX, is a brief reminder that Richard took the castle into royal possession before his own removal. The top of an altar-tomb, now upright, south of the chancel-arch, is probably that of the founder's grandson, Buckingham, killed in 1460 in the battle of Northampton, and his wife, c. 1480. A monument to Wm. Joliffe, 1749, is by Cheere, and another to his nephew Samuel Tufnell, of Langleys, Gt. Waltham, 1758, is also probably by Cheere.

Prittlewell *see* Southend.

Purfleet *see* Thurrock.

Purleigh (6). Hilltop village-centre, with *Bell Inn* at edge of churchyard, and *church* with tremendous view all round. Well-restored 14th-century tracery in the W. tower, which is buttressed and machicolated. Handsome polished pulpit, c. 1700, and communion rails. A Georgian reredos is in the baptistry. Painting of Moses and Aaron is signed by I. Fairchild. The Royal Arms are painted with a medallion profile of the young George III. The large parish stretches down to Mundon Wash near the Blackwater, and its name implies "a clearing where the bittern booms". The hamlet of *Cock Larks* has changed its name to Cock Clarks, which is meaningless.

Quendon and **Rickling** (2). *Quendon* church, almost entirely rebuilt in 1861, stands high above A11, its decorous bell-cote of 1963 a

RADWINTER. William Harrison's old rectory re-coated by Eden Nesfield

landmark for miles. The steep sweep of the nave roof is dappled with brown and peach-coloured tiles as in Cambs. and Hunts. Gilded interior a touch overdone, perhaps, remembering the difficulty of keeping Gt. Sampford's great church (not far off) even watertight. The chancel roof is brightly painted: from its N. and S. windows and plinths in its E. corners (one barley-sugar curly), it must be early Tudor. Contrast the ornate monument of Thos. Turner, 1681 (of Newman Hall, now Quendon Hall), with the chaste marble to charitable T. F. Forster, 1806, who had a well sunk for the use of his neighbours. The nave roof was panelled and gilt in 1963. The *art-nouveau* alabaster lectern, 1906, takes the form of an angel with spreading locks. The Georgian organ-case is said to be from Jesus College, Cambridge. *Quendon Court*, 1750-ish, red-brick, is mercifully set back from the racket along A11: a good timber-framed house adjacent. *Rickling House*, opposite, with billowing twin 2-storey bows on W. front, is secluded in a

glorious garden. *Quendon Hall*'s timbered core dates from the ownership of Thos. Newman, *c.* 1540, and now presents the splendid red-and-blue brick S. front from the time of Thos. Turner, *c.* 1680, pilastered like a 2-decker colonnade, a row of pedimented dormers above. Nice brick dovehouse, too.

Rickling. The *Hall* occupies a large moated site just below a Norman motte. This steep little mound was presumably thrown up for the Conqueror, whose manor it was, by the thoughtful sheriff Geoffrey de Mandeville to whose family it came! The medieval quadrangular plan of the present Hall is almost intact. Walls 3 ft. 6 in. thick. Stone dressings to the main gateway (filled in) in the N. side. The rest of the fabric on the N. and S. sides is cased in red brick of *c.* 1500: the E. side (present dwelling-house) is early 17th-century, with an external staircase added in the courtyard: the S.E. room was panelled about the time of Queen Anne.

The *church* has an early 14th-

century chancel complete with graceful screen. West tower and S. aisle added at the same time. Tomb (presumably of the donor of the 14th-century building). Fifteenth-century traceried pulpit. The interior is seen to best advantage from the sanctuary.

Radwinter (2). The Old Rectory, to the south of the churchyard, was the home of William Harrison, rector from 1559 till his death in 1593, and author of a vivid description of England: the Anthony Sampson of his day. His celebrated tilt at Elizabethan men's dress serves for the men of Elizabeth II: "except it were a dog in a doublet, you shall not see anie so disguised as are my countrie men of England". His dislike of young men back from Italy full of the wisdom of Machiavelli, and his approval of the English "artificer and the husbandman . . . verie freendlie at their tables; and when they meet, they are so merie without malice, and plaine without inward Italian or French craft and subtiltie", helps us to understand the

149

"lateness" of the Italian renaissance in England. As we look over from the churchyard into his garden (now largely devoted to excellent cabbages) we particularly remember: "let me boast a little of my garden . . . little above 300 foot of ground, and yet, such hath beene my good lucke in purchase of the varietie of simples . . . there are verie neere three hundred of one sort and other . . . no one of them being common or usuallie to bee had". And since the rectory was probably rebuilt in his day, we read his chapter "Of the manner of Building and Furniture of our Houses" with renewed interest.

By an odd coincidence, Radwinter owes most of its present look to Eden Nesfield, who rebuilt much of it in the 1870s and 80s, applying to it what he had learnt of local traditional building materials and methods, knowledge that seemed irrelevant to most Victorian architects (and, alas, their successors). So, for instance, the good sparkling flintwork of the church is relieved by thin horizontal red brick bands, of various lengths (the tower and lead spire were added later by Temple Moore). But he has come adrift with the S. porch, originally an astonishing timber-framed building of *c.* 1350 with 1st-floor chamber oversailing the open post-structure below. The timbers he merely renewed, where necessary, but the texture of the "plaster" filling between the studs is entirely his own, a spurious cement-mixture crudely "pargeted". If only he had asked a local builder for the recipe for lime-plaster!

He has done the same to poor Harrison's house: preserved the outline (and the panelled interior), but coated it over in parge-work of his own devising. The school he enlarged and the shops and cottages he built just east of the church have the same flaw: good traditional outlines marred by the

RAYNE. Diapered brickwork of c. 1510 has been largely supplanted during 1841 rebuilding

150

refusal of "cement plaster" to weather. A reading of Harrison would have helped (see pp. 39-40 above).

The cottages, including *Travellers Joy*, along the long lane to Ashdon are unaffected by Nesfield: the best buildings here are *Bendysh Hall*, with two roof-materials and a dated chimney stack, 1659, and the farmhouse opposite, with Gothick windows.

Ramsden Bellhouse (9). The church, in lovely open country, beautifully disposed against the oaks of a park, is best seen in westering sun, for the walls of the red-brick choir and the ragstone nave were rebuilt in 1880, but the (?) early Tudor "Essex" belfry, with outshot "aisles" except on the nave side, is clad in handsome white weatherboarding; it wears a respectable shingled spire, and retains an early Tudor W. door. In 1200 the manor was held by Richard de Belhus, whose name might presumably be a reference to this bell-house (belfry) or a predecessor.

Ramsden Crays (9) is now known as "Crays Hill" and in danger of sinking identity in "Billericay U.D.". Its church, at the end of a very long lane, is locked and disused.

Ramsey (11). *Michaelstow Hall*, 1902 "Georgian", has a gateway with lovely tall heraldic lions sejant. An elegant post-windmill is dilapidating on the skyline. The large church tower is basically of septaria: its W. wall, pleasantly patched with grey pebbles, has good 15th-century tracery; the S. wall, including the staircase, is buttressed and handsomely repaired in Georgian brickwork, with a round-headed belfry-louvre. Outside the S. porch, the prominent draped urn to E. F. Burbidge, aged 24, 1854, is fenced round with 24 iron anchors. Enter by the beautifully carved 15th-century S. doorway and door. (There is a Norman N. doorway). Interior bare. Notice the curious Elizabethan curved brackets in main chancel rafters (cf. the rood-beam at Dovercourt), also the domestic square fenestration of chancel. The Royal Arms, of 1727, are over the E. window. There is charmingly simple Victorian glass, 1871, in the early 14th-century S.E. nave window. Late 14th-century capitals with figures in the chancel-arch.

Ramsey Island *see* Steeple.

Rawreth (9) means herons' stream. This stream joins the Roach below the church and above *Battlesbridge*, which is at the head of the navigable estuary. Here the sight of barges' brown sails sticking up in the middle of the landscape pleased James Agate in 1936, and Hervey Benham (in his book *Down Tops'l*, 1949) was delighted still with the great mills, the bargemen's weatherboarded homes and the *Barge Inn*, whose sign in 1968 serves as a reminder of what a barge looked like in full sail. For two decades of ever-multiplying Chelmsford–Southend motor-traffic, fuming and jockeying across the bridge, have dispelled the slow-pace landscape of brown barge-sails and grey-winged heron-flight. The *church* is a tour-de-force by the Master of Little Braxted, the Rev. Ernest Geldart, in his prime, 1882. Edward Tyrell, 1576, in plate armour, with his wife: their brasses are in a nice architectural frame. Two early 14th-century bells hang in the 15th-century tower.

Rayleigh (9). The town-centre shares its fine hilltop site with tree-shaded walks and with the ponds of a magnificent earthwork, the motte-and-bailey castle that brought a town into being. The castle was built by Suain, whose father Robert had built at Clavering one of the few pre-Norman castles. After 1066 Suain moved here to keep an eye on things: his coastal marshland was reckoned enough for 4,000 sheep. A tower windmill now stands just below the inner bailey, on the W. side, but not very striking visually. Approaching the W. end of the church from the east and north sides of the town, the atmosphere remains that of a country lane. South of the church, subtopia immediately appears. Still, it is an unusual sensation in Essex or E. Anglia to be in a small town-centre perched up well above 200 ft. The *church* has a stout 15th-century tower, and a Norman chancel. The best feature, the S. porch, is one of those demonstrations of Tudor bricklayers' virtuosity in these parts – with stepped battlements and a corbel-table. Wm. Alleyn's tomb-chest stands in the chapel he built south of the chancel, *c.* 1517.

Rayne (6) along Stane Street. The dominant church-tower, red-brick and idiosyncratic, was erected *c.* 1510 for Sir William Capel: the W. doorway and windows form part of a projection crowned with a crow-step gable and a single pinnacle. On the S. front of the tower, an exuberant stairturret culminates in a tiered pyramid, a stubby brick pinnacle sticking out above the tower itself. The church forms part of a picturesque group on the untidy Green. The *Hall*, going back, perhaps, to the 14th century, was largely rebuilt by Sir Wm. Capel's son, Sir Giles, who cut a dash with Henry VIII in France in 1520, and died in 1556. It is now spoilt visually by roughcast. Along the N. side of the Street, *Rayne House*, of Georgian red brick, has a Trafalgar balcony; *Rayne Place* of 19th-century white brick, has a bow-window to the east. West of the *Cherry Tree*, a late medieval hall-house now forms three cottages.

Rettendon (9), over 4,000 acres, includes much of *Battlesbridge* and stretches east along the Crouch as far as Fenn Creek. The 15th-century W. tower of the church presides over Victorian *Rettendon Place* and a Tudor-brick gabled barn: to the west a deep valley contains Runwell Mental Hospital. The church contains one of the most elaborate and attractive marble monuments in Essex, in a good position at the E. end of the N. aisle. Carved in agreeably veined marble, 1727, and signed Samuell Chandler, it represents two life-size figures standing beneath a central arch (almost as if at their front-door), another on either side under smaller arches, a fifth figure semi-recumbent, addressing a pair of cherubs: this is presumably the Edmund Humphrey commemorated, who died a bachelor and left all his estate here to Wm. Fytche of Danbury Place, and his W. Hanningfield estate to Humphrey Sidney of Margaretting: the standing figures are presumably the two beneficiaries and their wives.

There are also several nice brasses, and old oak benches, and a priest's chamber, in this well-kept church.

Rickling *see* Quendon.

Ridgewell (3) was granted a Tuesday market in 1318 and a fair on the eve of St Lawrence. St Lawrence's *church* is prosperous Perp., unusual in Essex; its tower, with two 14th-century bells, stands proudly at the end of a lane, beyond an insensitively conceived new brick village school. The parish was ordered to take down a north chapel – presumably a former guild chapel – by a late 17th-century bishop. This order may help to explain either the odd way the north wall of the N. aisle swerves to the north-east or the re-setting of a Norman doorway in the N. wall of the N. vestry. The initial of the Pannel family is in the E. window glass. *Ridgewell Hill Farm* also has their initials, with "1589", carved in a bressumer.

Rivenhall (6). *Hall*, a simple early-Tudor farmhouse north of the church. As the road slopes down from the church, then rises, antique bumps in the cow-pasture in front of the Hall mark the site of a Roman villa, never properly examined. Hall was farmed a century ago by the brothers Hutley; sons of a blacksmith, they started with £40 and built up to 4,000 acres by seeing how to apply chemistry to farming: the posthumous influence of Thomas Tusser, Tudor agricultural propagandist, born in this parish.

The church was completely refurbished and given a stucco texture and tall corner-turrets on W. tower, c. 1838, at cost of Lord Western of Felix Hall, Kelvedon. In 1840 the rector came back from a continental tour with very remarkable stained glass, bought, apparently, from the curé of Chênu, near Tours. Here in the E. window, however inappropriately, it provides the chief interest of the place. It was re-arranged in 1948.

Most reproduced section, small square in bottom of S. light, shows a 13th-century knight, Robert Lemaire, in silvery chain-mail and amber-coloured banded helmet, riding a caparisoned steed and waving a sword: caparison a deep coffee-brown, may need cleaning. In next light, at bottom, a late 12th-century roundel with entombment of ? the Virgin by light of cresset-lamp. Nice Annunciation above. Two other contemporary roundels and two large figures, abbots or bishops. Western monuments, also Wyseman. *Rivenhall Place*, early 18th-century, has a core of 1558, a Repton park (his earliest Essex commission, 1789), and a bridge by William Wilkins. It was the home of Kitty O'Shea, the *femme fatale* of Irish Home Rule. Trollope often stayed here with her father, Sir John Page Wood. *Hoo Hall*, also, is of charming Georgian red brick. *Durwards Hall* is now an Antiques Emporium, open only to "the Trade".

Silver End. Neat horizontal flat-roofed housing, begun in 1926 by Crittall with a factory for the disabled, is almost the earliest instance in England of what Pevsner called the "International Modern Style". Its merit here is that it was part of a carefully planned village, focused on "The Chateau", now the 65 Club, its walls shabby. Craig Angus opposite, and No. 77, pleasant; also at the Circus, small R.C. church (1966) by Martin Evans, screened by lilacs. The trouble here as elsewhere is that the controlled design of village housing has given way to the usual banal suburban stuff.

Rochford (16: lowest road-crossing of Roach). An agreeable little old market town; but Southend airport, beside Rochford Hall and golf course, causes a constant scream of planes. The celebrated "Whispering" or "Lawless" court is now scarcely feasible, albeit held from midnight to cock-crow. (Tenants were alleged to have conspired against Lord of Manor: thereafter the manor-court held in open-air on King's Hill, 1st Wednesday after Michaelmas: steward opened in conspiratorial whisper, and the tenants who failed to answer were fined!) A sect here, known as "The Peculiar People", is unexpectedly dormant.

The *Market-place*, where John Simson of Great Wigborough was burnt for his convictions, is a regular rectangle, with the English feel of, say, Halesworth. *Hartley's saddlery and cobblery* ("est. 1777") is an engaging exercise in unbridled self-advertisement. Calm red-brick domestic Georgian *Connaught House* stands on the W. side. The E. side is a dismal example of unimaginative uniformity, even though a self-service store duly projects on to the square on the site of the poor old Market House (demolished a century ago). North and South Streets run straight past, carrying the worst of the motor traffic. East Street runs in at an angle. The main interest is in *West Street*, preserving a pleasant domestic scale, e.g. at 46 and 48 with climbing roses. *South Street* has good Georgian red brick houses. The dominant diapered early-Tudor brick *church-tower* rises from a churchyard islanded by a low wall round which sheep graze: the arms of Boteler earl of Ormonde are set over the W. doorway. The N. chancel chapel has been given domestic-looking gables and a chimney (? c. 1600). Disappointing Victorian interior. Hulk of former grand *Hall* opposite. Probably rebuilt by Rich (see Felsted and Leighs). His by 1555. Boleyns and Careys had had it since Ormonde's death, 1515. The

ABBESS RODING: Luckyn monument

E. front, facing the church, is a stucco'd late-Georgian remodelling, serving as Golf Club-house. The N. front of impressive original gables, with a single chimney-shaft erect in the apex of each, is seen from the farmyard at the W. end.

The Rodings rhyme with soothing: White Roothing insists on phonetic spelling.

Roding, Abbess (3) was owned by abbesses of Barking. The *church* (St Edmund), largely rebuilt in 1867, salutes with a lead flèche. Medieval wooden screen elaborately traceried. Georgian pulpit with handsome tester and convenient hour-glass. Fragments of 15th-century glass. Two endearing Jacobean monuments: Sir Gamaliel Capel (N. wall) and his youngest daughter (S. wall), Mildred, Lady Luckyn, receiving the Crown of Glory from flying cherubs, and being the happy mother of eight children. "We bragge no vertues and we beg no tears." *Rookwood Hall*, where they lived, is now a moated farmhouse of good Victorian brickwork, with ancient barns, and with an evocative ruined fragment of their house contained within the moat. Lady Luckyn's monument is thought to be by Evesham.

——, **Aythorpe** (5). The *church* has a small timber belfry, broach spire and weathercock. At *Gunners Green*, post windmill leaning over, *Gunners* was re-thatched early in 1966 with 4 tons of wheatstraw from Pleshey. *Yeomans* is a small thatched, timber-framed former farmhouse of *c.* 1600, much cared for.

——, **Beauchamp** (5). The *church* (St Botolph) stands alone among remote fields. A Jacobean churchwarden was in trouble because many weatherboards had been blown off the steeple by the violence of the wind and not repaired. Church newly repaired in 1965; the over-Victorianized interior cream-washed.

——, **Berners** (5) pronounced Barnish. The *church*, in the farmyard of the Hall, is pleasantly unrestored but a rather less sophisticated structure than the neighbouring barns. Chancel and nave equally small.

——, **High** (5). Extended late-medieval ribbon-development of pleasing cottages along Roman Street: deplorable wire-scape removed in 1967. 1966 housing all right. *Porters*, a delightful small hall-house still has medieval doorways from hall-screen to dairy and kitchen at the N. end, and at the S. end an external staircase, added presumably in 1652, the date formerly painted on one of two bay-windows at this end. *New Hall* gone, but its barn displays fine brick nogging. *Church* door bound with medieval ironwork.

——, **Leaden** (5). First perhaps to get its church-roof leaden? Yew-path to Norman S. doorway. Pre-Reformation pulpit on (renewed) pedestal. Interesting jumble of roofs and old buildings at *Hall*.

——, **Margaret** (5). St Margaret's church has a well-restored Norman doorway, zigzag elaborate. Scheme of Victorian painting all round the inside of the chancel: seen from the nave, it resembles tapestry. There is a great old chest. *Garnish Hall*, adjacent, is fronted by a vast pediment.

——, **White** (5). The church has a Norman Romanesque nave with Roman bricks in quoins and in the round heads of windows. A 13th-century door, with ironwork, is set in a plain Norman doorway which lies within a Jacobean

153

open-timber porch. Semi-circular chancel arch. Broad nave under open-timber roof. Tablets to Rev. John Maryon, 1692–1760, who "continued here near 40 years", and his heir. *Colville Hall* has a lavishly designed oversailing barn with brick nogging. *Mascallsbury*, a splendid great old farmhouse, is faced with yellow brick, and can be compared with a careful drawing on John Walker the Younger's map, of 1609 (Essex Record Office), so detailed that it clearly shows two dog-kennels. A clay-lump cottage stands south of the crossroads near the handsome white-brick tower of a former windmill.

Rowhedge *see* Donyland.

Roxwell (5). Over 4,000 acres, once part of Writtle. The large *church* in the village is screened at its E. end from the Hall by limes. Rare arms of James II lost? Branston family monuments include Lord Chief Justice, carved with his armour, spur and sword, and Hon. Mary Byng, 1744, a corner-piece with medallion portrait in high relief, unsigned. They lived at *Skreens*. *Dukes* has three stout rectangular chimney stacks and a good modern range of farm buildings. Among outlying houses, *Newland Hall*, moated, has early Tudor brick-nogging; so has *Radley Green Farmhouse*. *Hoe-street Farm*, 1506 painted in modern numerals on front, is said to have a crown-post roof, strap-work painted on plaster, and the arms of James I.

Roydon (4) has kept tall old elmy hedges, especially on Epping Road. The *church*, beside a small Green and neglected barns, has a pleasing interior, walls cream-washed and elaborate roof-timbers all exposed to the rafters: tie-beam and crown-post form. Traceried spandrels in a *timber* chancel arch. Stout medieval screen. The late 13th-century font is supported by four jolly men in

sou'westers. Hatchments. Brasses include two Colts of Nether Hall. The churchyard lies in a deep evocative glade to the west. Low Hill Road is a tree-tunnel down to the Lea valley bottom. Cooling-towers across at Hoddesdon, but on this side at Nether Hall the romantic jagged fragment of the great 15th-century red-brick gate-house of the Colts, their fortune founded by Thos. who died in 1471, a man of Edward IV. It was the home of Sir Thomas More's first wife, Jane Colt. A good Tudor timber-framed farmhouse, with 17th-century extension, all cream-plastered, stands near the gatehouse, which proved too strong for the demolishers in 1773.

Runwell (9) easily confused with Wickford, which provides a commuter-station on the Southend line. Fine timber 15th-century porches to church, the S. one recently daubed with red and blue paint; it bears name of donor in carved letters, Johes Abbott, hard to decipher. Tablet (signed by Thos. Cartwright, jnr.) commemorates Edward Sulyard, 1692, the last of his line. They lived at *Flemings*, of which a gabled wing, c. 1600, survives, with a splendid first-floor room.

St Lawrence (13), sometimes "St Lawrence Newland". Its two main farms, *East* and *West Newlands*, were named in Domesday. It lies beside a pleasurable (muddy) bay of the Blackwater estuary with a distant view of Bradwell power-station. Lovely flat river-scenery. Church rebuilt, in 1877, on its beautiful eminence at cross-roads. A handful of square weather-boarded riverside villas at "Ramsey Island", which is partly in the parish of Steeple.

St Osyth (14) was originally called Chich, probably meaning a creek. Now it is called after the wife of a 7th-century King of Essex and pronounced Toosey. She may have founded a nunnery here, was probably martyred, and is often absurdly confused with St Sitha, the holy housemaid of Lucca to whom medieval people (e.g. at

Westhall, Suffolk) prayed when they had mislaid something in the house.

Certainly a priory of Austin canons was founded here early in the 12th century, with a distinguished scholar as first prior; and it was promoted to be an *abbey* a few years later. Now generally mis-styled St Osyth's Priory, its remains and those of the Tudor house built on the site by Lord Darcy of Chich are among the most delightful buildings to be seen in Essex. Gardens and antiquities open to public all day during summer: private apartments and art collection in August only (3–5 p.m.).

Much to see, too, in the parish-church built just across the "bury" from the abbey-gate; and at least one medieval house of note, St Claire's Hall, lies just S. of the bustling little holiday-village in a landscape of pasture-farms with names like Cocket Wick, Wigborough Wick and Lee Wick, three of ten local farms that were providing dairy products for the abbey in 1491. Alas, holiday shackery has spread from Jaywick along a shore that was enjoyable for all so long as it was built on only by an occasional Martello tower.

The Abbey. First sight unforgettable: the great gatehouse of flint-and-freestone flushwork panelling, at once probably the finest of the surviving monastic gatehouses of Essex and East Anglia, and the most brilliant display of this regional form of flint decoration. Probably built (and almost certainly paid for) in the time of Abbot John Sharp (consecrated 1482/3), it easily eclipses the gate-house of St John's Colchester (c. 1480), which has almost identical decoration. St Osyth's great gate-house has wings with large-rooms on either side of the gate-way, where St John's has mere pinnacles: furthermore these impressive wings are flanked in an almost palladian way. In the wall running south at right angles to the gate, there is plenty of red brick contrasting well with the greys of the gatehouse (the round arch in this wall not Norman, but

14th-century stonework re-set); in the range running east, the modest 13th-century gatehouse at the E. end was dressed up to form part of the new approach. In sunshine, notice the way the flint seems *alive* in these slender panels, like beds of dark sparkling oysters. Observe the fine trio of niches, two flanking, one straight above the entrance, its tall canopy infinitely graceful. Beneath the gateway do not let attractions ahead prevent you from looking up into the vault: of the carved stone bosses the main ones represent the Annunciation, the head of St Osyth in crown and veil, and a couched hart within a park-pale, a true symbol of medieval Essex. (Within the gatehouse, Mr Somerset de Chair has made his home, bringing in a Charles II staircase from Costessey Hall, Norfolk, and exhibiting much remarkable jade among his many treasures.)

Ahead, beyond broad gravel walks, lawns and peacocks, the long 2-storey red brick range is clearly Georgian to the left, but the large stone-mullioned 1st-floor oriel window straight ahead is all that remains of the abbot's own gatehouse (or gate-palace): identifiable by rebuses as the work of John Vintoner, the last abbot but one (he died in 1533, six years before his successor had to surrender the abbey to the King). Interesting that this window by an abbot, *c*. 1527, has Renaissance figures in the top band of carving, whereas his secular successors later in the 16th century left no sign of any Renaissance motif in all their rebuilding.

1st Lord Darcy bought the place in 1553, died in 1558; what he began was presumably finished by 2nd lord (d. 1581) with whom Queen Elizabeth and the Court stayed twice; but most of their work has gone the way of the monastery.

What survives is the beautiful domestic brick continuation of the abbot's work at right-angles to his oriel window, on the site of the monastic cellarer's range: this ends in a decorated S. gable and is backed by a charming clock tower. In both gable and clock-

tower, Darcy has exploited local ginger-coloured septaria as admirably as the builder of the great gate exploited local flint: his masonry is covered in an almost heraldic way by a checkered coat, freestone alternating with septaria. From the gable, a noble red brick screen-wall (providing the ruins with a sense of seclusion) runs E. through the (vanished) cloister, to point at which dormitory of abbey ran S. into (vanished) church. Norman undercroft to dormitory survives, preserved by Darcy to support his (vanished) grand new rooms to which he provided access through "Lord Darcy's Tower", the most prominent survivor after the great gate, and again covered with handsome checkers of septaria and freestone. View from top over quiet creek to sea. Back on ground, fine 13th-century passage furnished as chapel just W. of Norman undercroft. Refectory ran west from here along N. side of cloister.

3rd Lord Darcy was succeeded in 1639 by his daughter-in-law Elizabeth, Countess of Rivers: because she was Roman Catholic, a mob broke in at the outbreak of the Civil War, in 1642, "and in a few hours disfurnished it of all the goods . . . not of less value than 40,000 pounds sterling" (Clarendon). It can never have recovered. *Parish Church.* Broad nave and aisles, with handsome timber roofing. Two very remarkable features are the nave arcading, rebuilt in red brick in the 16th century, and, perhaps even more remarkable, the 13th-century transepts, with beautifully arcaded *eastern* aisles, one arch of which, at least, is also of red brick though carefully plastered so as to be indistinguishable from stone. The nave arcades were similarly plastered until 1899. It may be that the brick transept-arch is a repair of the 16th century. But it is not impossible that brick was used here in 13th century, as it was, e.g., at Coggeshall abbey. Another odd feature is the U-shaped arrangement of altar rails, apparently an 1891 replacement in stone of wooden one on same plan. Monuments to 1st Lord Darcy and his De Vere wife,

and 2nd Lord "who lived under the great Queen Elizabeth", both erected by 3rd Lord, after 1581. Another monument, by the same sculptor, to Briant Darcie, a cadet of Tolleshunt, 1587. Francis Grigs's monument to John Darcy, 1638, is not to be compared with his fine work at Framlingham.

St Claire's Hall, its great old timber frame exposed, contains one of the most complete examples of a 14th-century aisled hall.

Saffron Walden *see* Walden.

Salcott-with-Virley (13). Beside a (dammed-up) creek of the Blackwater, with a former wharf, they have seen better days. Dilapidated timber-framed cottages totter beside Salcott Street. Salcott church was much repaired after 1884 earthquake: its S. porch contains an early Tudor door in good condition. Where Anglo-Saxon place-names are the rule, Virley bears that of Robert de Verli, in Normandy, its owner in 1086. The ruins of its medieval church form part of the garden of the rectory.

Saling, Bardfield (or Little Saling) (3). Church at edge of copse, with one of Essex's six round towers. Tower, nave and aisle pre-Black Death (1348–9), chancel later (shortened and given "domestic" roof in the 19th century). The medieval building was consecrated in 1380. It has a most attractive white-plastered interior, with lofty nave ceiling and oil-lamps for evensong. Lovely example of straw-plaiting, for the altar, with naturalistic grape-vine, executed *c*. 1880 by Miss Dobson and friends. Post-windmill site. *Woolpits* has a plastered dovecote.

Saling, Great (3). Beside the church, the *Hall* is cased in red and blue brickwork with curved gables, of 1699, and seen across a pond and through poplars. The *Grove*, a large late-Georgian house, has lost its original fenestration.

GREAT SAMPFORD:
Hill Farm

SOUTHEND-ON-SEA

Sampford, Great (2/3) in area smaller, but population bigger, than Little Sampford, from which it is separated by great line of 400 k.v. pylons. Ugly council houses, but that street ends in a screen of limes, through which the great E. windows of chancel and S. transept appear among scattered headstones at the edge of sloping fields. Stone pillar by church wall erected by Col. Jonas Watson in honour of his father: he himself was killed at the siege of Cartagena, 1741, in his 78th year. Splendid early 14th-century chancel. Church in desperate need of first-aid 1966, with ancient S. door sodden and almost off its hinges, has been safeguarded, S.

aisle re-roofed, in 1967. A capital at the E. end of the S. aisle is carved with man pursued by dragon through wood.
Sampford, Little (3). Long, low-roofed nave and chancel. Red brick S. porch contrasts nicely with grey remainder. Comic little leaded flèche barely rises above well buttressed tower. Entrance through N. porch, and Georgian panelled door into broad uninterrupted nave and chancel. Very broad rustic Perp. chancel windows with bits of original coloured glass. Three old stone steps climb up to altar behind slender altar rails. Stone wall-tombs with strapwork on N. and S. walls of sanctuary: one inscribed, c. 1556:

"Lo in this tumbe combyned
   are These toe bereft of Lyfe
Sur Edward Grene a famus
   Knyghte and Margerye hys
                              wyfe."
North aisle has sweet monuments to Peck family, especially Wm. and his wife Gartrude, 1713, and their daughter Gartrude taken away in the flower of her age by the smallpox. Their house, the *Hall*, with great staircase described in R.C., was apparently demolished in the 1930s: a 19th-century white brick-fronted wing with shaped gables still stands, and what look like very stout timber-framed old barns.
Oldhouse Farm, in beautiful old plaster, has three marvellous back

158

gables, great inverted Vs that sweep down almost to ground. At Hawkin's Hill, *Clockhouse Farm*, 17th-century, also preserves its old plaster. Clock face in house front inscribed "PETTIT Watchmaker 1778". *Tewes*, a small late-medieval manor-house approached through modern farm-buildings, is open to visitors March to October, 2–6 p.m., on Thursdays, Sundays and Bank Holidays. It is a remarkably well preserved and beautiful timber-framed two-storey house (of simple tripartite plan: hall, solar and services), the external plaster faintly pargeted and white, the inside especially distinguished by the natural colours of its original carved oak beams. An old reeded window is kept, and one long side of the moat.

Sandon (6) has a new village hall, well designed. The effect of the rectory's grand new front of 1765 is spoilt by rooflines. The village Green, just E. of church, has a broad oak of no great age but astonishing spread: breadth fully twice its height. On the N. side of the Green, clean white *Sandon Place* looks like a "Wealden" house, of *c.* 1500, with a small Georgian porch.

The church fabric is laced with Roman brick, especially the quoins of nave. The S. porch and W. tower glow red with Tudor brick, very fine in the view from the west, with a bold corbel-table beneath the battlements. The tower is crowned by a flattened brick cone and a handsome stair-turret. The black diaper-pattern on the W. front makes an inept join at belfry stage. Interior spotless. From the 15th century, a pulpit of great elegance, a panelled chancel roof, and one hammer-beam truss at the E. end of the nave. A brass shows an Elizabethan parson of Sandon with a

SOUTHEND-ON-SEA.
Percy, *built at Maldon in 1894, represented Southend in the Thames barge race of 1935*

SOUTHEND-ON-SEA

159

wife in a hat, but saying, hopefully, "God's wrath is pacified". Window signed W. Hart, 1929. An agreement to rebuild the chancel in 1348, the year of the Black Death, survives at St Paul's. Thomas Rickling, of Barkway, Herts., was to have the use of the old materials, and build on the old foundations.

Sewardstone *see* Waltham Abbey.

Shalford (3), ancient ford over upper Blackwater, beside which the church stands in elmy landscape. Church 14th-century, with S. door, tall clerestory and three canopied tomb-recesses. Giles Firmin, back from Massachusetts in 1647, was ordained presbyter here: ejected in 1662, he practised medicine at Ridgewell. Stained glass here is naturally in fragments. Straw-plaiting for altar is from the 1872 exhibition. Shalford *Hall*, down in 1966, is being replaced. *Redfern's Farm* is very unusually unsophisticated: a diapered brick Tudor house glued on to a lower, earlier timber-framed house with room jettying out over porch. *Nichols' Farm* has a very stout 4-shafted chimney stack. *Bartlett's Farm*, likewise, framed in garden with poplars.

Sheering (5). *Church* stands above the castellated Gothick old rectory on rising ground above a tributary of the Stort. Late 14th-century fittings include the S. door with original oak lock, the N. chancel door, and a stained-glass Coronation of the Virgin in E. window. A vivid consecration cross, red with flowered ends, is painted on the plaster of the S.W. wall of the nave. The triple chancel arch looks 14th-century but is 19th-century, so is the triple arcade at the W. end. Head of Mrs Douglas, the rector's wife, 1947, in low relief by Gilbert Bayes. Chapel Field marks the site of St Nicholas's chapel, founded in 1278, on the road to Netherton (Lower Sheering) beside the Stort, where *Durrington House* was built about the time of the South Sea Bubble, the work, probably, of a masterbuilder. It was later stucco'd and

given its present decorative features, the bay-windows, for instance, and projecting portico – all by the time it appeared in an engraving in A. Gentleman's *History of Essex*, in 1771. It keeps dignified company with cedar, mulberry and fern-leaf beech.

Shelley (5). Church, of 1888, pleasantly grouped with Hall across fields north of Ongar.

Shell Haven *see* Coryton.

Shellow Bowells (5). Norman surname stoutly ungenteel: it might so easily have become Bowles. Little red brick church, of 1754, screened by limes in a small churchyard amid lovely level elmy farmlands. Key at Willingale rectory.

Shenfield (8) shares station with Hutton in the consequent suburbs of Brentwood. Church has light arcading of timber to N. aisle, but looking even more elegant in its copy at Upshire. Alabaster effigy of Elizabeth Robinson, 1652, with her dead babe. Victorian glass by Kempe. *Shenfield Place*, red-brick with hipped roof, 200 yards S. of church, was designed by Robert Hooke in 1689. Pleasant woodland has replaced mere scrub on the Common.

Shoebury *see* Southend-on-Sea.

Shopland *see* Sutton.

Silver End *see* Rivenhall.

Snoreham *see* Latchingdon.

Southchurch *see* Southend-on-Sea.

Southend-on-Sea (9/16). It is not much good looking bleakly at the 1st edition of the 1-inch O.S. map, of 1805, and trying to recall the days when Prittlewell, an L-shaped village with a church in one corner, and Leigh, a compact village-street alongside Leigh Creek, were the only built-up areas. A resort was established at the South End of Prittlewell. There are now seven miles of buildings from Leigh to Shoe-

buryness, most of which do not require the services of a guide. We are on the N. bank of London River. Too many people have wanted the same thing. At least the beaches remain, salty, and pleasurable, and crowds of people like crowds. "We all had our health perfectly well there", said Jane Austen's Mrs John Knightly (*Emma*, 1816), after an autumn at South End; "never found the least inconvenience from the mud". In 1848 Southend could be described as a handsome town and fashionable watering-place, in Prittlewell parish, on the side and crown of a woody eminence rising from the sands. Steam vessels plied daily in winter, 5 times a day in summer, from a wooden pier (already shown in an engraving of 1831 advancing elegantly seawards from double bow-front of Marine Library, and extended to a mile after 1835); there were 1,600 settled residents and as many visitors. The hotels then were the Royal, the Ship (starting well back in the 18th century, where men met to discuss the steeplechase), the Hope, and the Castle; the neighbourhood of the Terrace was hopefully called New Southend c. 1791, but it apparently did not get going till Prinny's unsavoury princess stayed at 7, 8 and 9: renamed Royal Terrace 1804.

Now Southend's population has grown over 100 times bigger, mostly since the end of the 19th century when the second, more direct, railway to London was built. The first and most enjoyable, 1856, winds with Thames through Purfleet and Tilbury. Easily the biggest town in Essex, a county borough, with tremendous seaside industry, especially for the day-trippers. Other "service" industries are rapidly developing, and a series of office-towers rapidly rising on the side and crown of an eminence no longer woody. With so much growth since the late 19th century, the interesting landmarks, old or

LEIGH-ON-SEA

160

new, are not easy to find. Map indispensable. Since the only pattern is that formed round ancient parishes and hamlets we still take bearings from these, starting with Prittlewell's "hamlet", Southend, and then going on alphabetically.

Parishes and hamlets in the County Borough.

Southend. Of the early resort, the yellow-brick *Royal Terrace* on the cliff is still good to look at, though a shade *too* un-smart and un-wanted-looking, which seems odd because the uniformity of a very long terrace allows here for individuality of occupier: very engaging series of 1st-floor ironwork balconies, each of slightly different pattern from neighbours. Engraving of 1832 shows two centre ones with pediment; they now have stucco pilasters and cornice. Terrace provided H.Q. from which all shipping was controlled, over 100 million tons, on approaching London docks in 2nd world war. At E. end of Terrace, Royal Hotel contained the resort's "elegant assembly-room" (behind Venetian window over bow-porch). Oyster Bar now occupies site of original library. Along Marine Parade, *Hope Hotel*, of pleasant painted stucco, with a length of 1st-floor balcony, is disfigured by tiled porch and scarlet oval brewer's sign. *Falcon Hotel* has nice ironwork screen along ground floor front. *Minerva Inn* (in Brewhouse Road, near gas works) was run by the Vandervord family who also ran Southend's trading barges; they disapproved of siting and construction of pier, and on their barge *Minerva* threatened to throw pier-dues collector overboard. Pier rebuilt 1890s, 1920s, and constantly providing new entertainment, as in bowling centre recently roofed by "inverted pyramids". Pier runs on Gothick columns of Victorian ironwork across Sea Road. Gasworks has own short pier with classical iron columns over Sea Road. As well as the longest pier in the world, Southend boasts of the longest bar. One rich old red brick Elizabethan house, *Porters*, stands inland off Southchurch

Street and is used appropriately as Mayor's Parlour: it was for long just "Porters Farm" but from its fireplaces and other fittings must originally have been a fairly opulent "Hall". New *Civic Centre* coming into shape under Borough Architect.

Cambridge Town see *Shoebury, South.*

Chalkwell see *Westcliff-on-Sea.*

Eastwood (9) retains on brink of airport its basically Norman church (see font), with tower capped by weatherboarded bell turret and comically thin spire, and with two doors (one unhinged and kept for show) bound by remarkable 13th-century ironwork. What looks from outside like gabled domestic annexe proves to be a S. aisle with unconventional roof. However, there *are* domestic arrangements – in W. end of N. aisle a 15th-century timbered priest's chamber, two storeys. Their cosy proximity undid a parishioner in puritan times: he was taken before the archdeacon for "sleeping in time of divine service upon a Sunday in the afternoon this last summer (1619), and so sat sleeping until all the people were gone forth from the church".

Leigh - on - Sea (9). Though a double-line railway has been driven through back gardens on the N. side of village street, the old fishing village somehow retains its integrity, and goes its own old way. The cockle-boats are laid up long-ways on the beach against the sheds where cockles are prepared for local and London markets. All lately doomed by Southend Council's grotesque decision to run a new main road through the fishing village instead of keeping it along N. side of rail-track. The holiday-village preserves much of its charm: at the E. end are cornfields and a view to Hadleigh castle, and up the cliff some delectable modest weatherboarded villas and terraces, past which the Church Steps climb. Steep ascent fully rewarded, first by a surprise, a Calvary among evergreen oaks and silhouetted against small moored ships in estuary below, as if in

Brittany. Then through the red Tudor-brick porch the church proves to be one of tremendous character. Tones inside set by polished unstained oak poppy-heads and panelled deal pews and by superbly theatrical E. window, another Crucifixion, this time 18th-century with great blobs of fiery gold, and Royal blue and purple. Nave roof ceiled, N. aisle open-timbered; both give long tunnelled effect. In 1818, author of *Excursions through Essex* noted: "In this church and cemetery are more monumental inscriptions than in all the hundred beside, and mostly on seafaring people". Most remarkable, the coloured bust of the right worthy and worshipful Robert Salmon, "that great instrument of God's glory and the commonwealth's good – the restorer of navigation almost lost 1614: Master of Trinity House 1617, and the glory of it 24 years". Ball in one hand and spy-glass in the other. He died 1641 in 74th year, and was interred in the chancel "with his ancestors of about 300 years continuance". Brasses.

Prittlewell (9). A red-tiled timber-framed 16th-century house with cart-way through central block stands immediately west of the parish church, which is a silvery-grey ragstone building standing back from crossroads, its battlements checkered with flint. Otherwise not much survives of Prittlewell's old village, the streets immediately west and south of church. Richly carved early 16th-century S. door. Comfortable sense of roominess inside wrecked by the way the walls have been scraped bare of their ancient plaster by the Victorians. Small blocked Norman windows in W. and S. aisle arcade.

To the north of the church, in a municipal park, are the remains of a well-endowed Cluniac priory; refectory and area round cloister were lived in after the Dissolution, and covered by very "Essex" tiled roofs and tall gables; they form a handsome group in the view from the south-west: the refectory is on the right (i.e. along S. side of cloister), its S. wall rebuilt "Perp" on the line of the original wall, its 15th-century roof and its N. wall original, late 12th-century. It contains a very early pointed arch, much restored. Range on W. side of cloister remodelled in 18th-century and also retaining 15th-century timber roof, probably that of the Prior's lodging.

Shoebury, North (6). Wide 13th-century chancel with lancets: the 13th-century arcade of the vanished S. aisle is visible outside the nave wall. Pleasant stepped pyramid roof on tower. Remarkable carved small piece of a 13th-century coffin lid. Simple tie-beam and crown-post roof. Well painted Georgian Royal Arms. Tudor brick *Hall*, reduced and the first storey weatherboarded in the early 18th century. Needs care.

Shoebury, South (16) has a basically Norman church of jumbled flint, ragstone and septaria – its tower topped in 18th-century red brick battlements. Georgian panelled S. door with brass handle. Norman chancel-arch lurks in dark interior. Tie-beam and (polygonal) crown-post roof. *Shoeburyness*: coastal "nose", or rather tip of chin that runs northeast up to lip at Foulness. Since 1858 it has had artillery barracks that were originally established to test Armstrong guns against the "ironclads". The barracks are on site of earthwork attributed to Danish chieftain of *c.* 894: Rampart Street marks its N.E. side. "Cambridge Town" grew up alongside gunnery-range.

Southchurch (16). *Hall*, fine example of a 14th-century timber-framed building, with hall open to roof, all set in moat in pleasant garden and admirably converted to use as public library.

Small Norman *church* with 15th-century chancel-arch and timber-piered belfry (with early 14th-century bell) all left as a mere S. aisle when the church expanded northwards to designs of Ninian Comper, in 1906 (new chancel of 1932 by F. C. Eden and E. window of 1956, the "Works of the Lord"). Two nave windows by Comper. Cusped late-14th century Easter sepulchre and early-14th century tomb recess in old chancel.

Thorpe Bay, part of Southchurch. St Augustine's in deep purple brick, 1934, by W. Allardyce, has an unusual "late-17th century" W. window. Thorpe *Hall* is dated 1668.

Westcliff-on-Sea (9) grew out of Milton hamlet at the beginning of this century, and includes "Chalkwell" where the *Crowstone*, a short obelisk, stands on the beach just below high-water mark, itself marking the eastern extent of City of London's jurisdiction over Thames. In 1836 it replaced an earlier obelisk now at Prittlewell priory. *St Alban's* 1898–1908, by Nicholson, has the pleasant flint and brick texture of his church at Frinton. Font from St Mary-le-Bow, London. R.C. church by Leonard Stokes in Milton Road. Very good modern library by County Architect.

Southminster (16). Great Saxon manor of Bishops of London, stretching perhaps 8 miles from E. to W. at that time, and supporting 1,000 sheep in Domesday Book, which says Cnut had taken it from the bishops, who recovered it from the Conqueror. Large church at crossroads in little town: Norman S. doorway and W. window give some idea of dimensions at that time. Exterior a promising-looking mixture of materials, e.g. the band of black flintwork W. of N. porch where nave heightened to receive N. porch, which has fine stone vault with carved bosses, including the Trinity. Interior a great let-down, or rather blow-up. Nave heightened again (sandy brick), this time after receiving a great empty pair of 1819 transepts with polygonal chancel, and ceiled over flimsily, with none of the Gothick panache so often redeems such work. The chancel and transepts, nevertheless, were designed by the resourceful Thomas Hopper. It may be that his design was compromised by the parochial decision to raise the roof!

Stambourne (3). The church has a massive early-Norman square W. tower, unbuttressed, battlemented, and looking like a small keep. Round-arched Roman-brick windows in the second stage. Tudor brick porch, plastered. Glass in E. window, 1530, shows Henry Macwilliam and first wife. The top lights are complete, painted to show family trees (engagingly arboreal) against a brickwork background. Unusual and very fine carving of Macwilliam arms in arch of chancel-chapel. Elaborate niches in two nave-window-jambs. Good roofs, especially in the N. aisle. Old low *Hall* with tall chimneys to the east of the church. South-west of the churchyard, the pub with carved bressummer was once Moone Hall.

Stambridge, Great and **Little** (16). *Little Stambridge* is a "vanished village", represented by its *Hall*, a Tudor house refaced in brick in the 18th century: a small medieval church stood nearby a century ago. *Great Stambridge church*: the square stone 15th-century tower is topped by a red brick parapet containing a small white-timbered flèche. The N. and W. walls of the nave, and the N. wall of the chancel, are Saxon – see the small round-headed windows, one blocked with septaria, in walls thinner than Normans built. Interior totally Victorianized. Pleasant white-faced Queen Anne house next to *Cherry Tree* pub. Ancient tide-mill, beside marshes and pylons, one of the last of its kind in the whole North Sea tidal area, burnt right out on 30 July 1965.

Stanesgate *see* Steeple.

Stanford - le - Hope (9). "The Hope" is a reach of the Thames. The church is signalled by its tower on the ridge. Tower (at the E. end of the N. aisle) was rebuilt in 1883 from Rev. Ernest Geldart's design based on Prittlewell's: characteristic Geldart inscription on E. face: "This tower once down To God again Rebuilded rings With pleasing strain". In its base, the E. window is by Kempe. Impressive Purbeck font. The W. windows and clerestory quatrefoils have good purples and golds,

1881 and '91. In the churchyard, James Adams's ambitious tomb, of 1765, is a pleasant country mixture of rococo and baroque: cartouches, curtains, cherubs and bones: he "obeyed the awful Summons with TRUE CHRISTIAN TEMPER". In the church there are skulls, cross-bones and a pickaxe on one Fetherstone monument, 1711. Another, of 1740, is signed by Bellamy of Camberwell. East of the church, "The Green" is now a misnomer for drab suburban expansion. The 17th-century tithe barn still in the Rectory grounds.

Stanford Rivers (5). Large church in farmyard. White weatherboarded belfry and graceful lead spire are well framed by the limewalk from the west. The inside is well lit: brasses, benches, altarrails. At *Little End*, the former Union workhouse now serves as Piggotts Brothers Works. In the empty walled site, opposite, stood the independent Chapel where young David Livingstone (see Ongar), found he had failed to memorize his sermon and fled the building; it was burnt down in 1927. *Lawns* is an Elizabethan house with noble chimneys.

Stansted Mountfitchet (2). A castle (ring and bailey) stood on the S.W.-facing spur of the 250 ft. contour, overlooking A11, the ancient north–south thoroughfare lines of the Upper Cam and Upper Stort. The Gernon family had it in 1086, with woodland for 1,000 swine: it passed to the Montfiquets early in the 12th century, together with the office of Forester of Essex. The ring looks as if it contained a circular stone keep. A small town grew up to the west of the castle, with its main street on A11, and some substantial houses: the Independents' Meeting goes back to the 17th century. The red late-Victorian church by W. D. Caroë is in this area. The *Hall*, rebuilt in 1875, was recently taken over by the Arthur Findlay College for Advancement of Physical Science. The medieval church, on the site of a Roman building

(according to R.C.), is now beautifully kept; it stands on the edge of the Park, a new Secondary School opposite. Romanesque chancel arch. Tower rebuilt (in brick), 1692. The N. aisle is good dark flintwork of 1888. Two very accomplished monuments: Hester Salusbury in her fine hat, 1614, is one of Epiphanius Evesham's appealing works (notice the escutcheon, whose "quarterings" are emblems of the Passion, the helm crowned with thorns, the supporters weeping babes); on the other monument are her parents Sir Thos. and Lady Middleton, 1631, with angels of almost baroque feeling. He published the first popular edition of the Bible in Welsh, 1630. The parish subscribed in 1644 to help the next Sir Thomas "to reduce North Wales to the obedience of Parliament". W. H. Torriano's 45 years in Madras Civil Service was commemorated in 1828. The *Austin Priory* of Thremhall, founded by Mountfitchets and built by a Scot called Daniel beside Stane Street and Hatfield Forest, is now marked only by moat: it is also beside the airport. Government's high-handed decision in 1967 to base Third (and indeed Fourth) Airport for London on 2nd World War airfield here, against findings of its own Ministerial Inquiry, roused great public anger. No less that 540 buildings of "architectural or historic interest" – excluding churches – come within the "45 NNI contour", the environment that will predictably be destroyed by noise. (At Sheppey the number so destroyed would have been 40). In Stansted itself, a wild life park of 60 acres, at Norman House, draws 15,000 visitors a year to see birds and animals in *natural* conditions! A tower windmill is at present well preserved.

Stanway (13) lies right across Stane Street and indeed across another Roman road to the south. Beside each road a medieval church was built – the S. one, All Saints, is in ruins and now finds itself in the grounds of a popular zoo; its tower contains 14th-

century brick, a porch of the early 17th-century, and much old ivy. St Albright's (dedicated to a murdered 8th-century E. Anglian King) has 12th-century walls, see its S. doorway, dressed entirely in Roman brick. There are stout medieval braces in the base of the tower. The rest is by G. G. Scott, 1880. The font bears the carving of a chalice (defaced). Three Victorian windows are by Kempe. *Olivers*, largely Georgian, was the house of John Eldred, a celebrated traveller and merchant of the early 17th century. A back wing with crown-post truss survives from the 15th century.

Stapleford Abbots (8). Tucked away in lane-end, the church is a truly ugly "Dec" building of 1861, with a tower of 1815. Collect key at Holly Cottage in lane on way up. A tiny glass figure of Edward the Confessor is early 14th-century; a medallion portrait of Sir John Abdy, 1758. Fittings of the 1620-ish and 1650s house, *Albyns*, that he repaired and sashed (with octagonal panes) in 1754 were taken to the U.S.A. between the wars. The fabric was partly destroyed by a V2 in 1945. The red brick harness-rooms now provide a house, and the coach-house garages.

Stapleford Tawney (5). The S.-facing Georgian *Hall* is red-brick with tile-hung sides and partly weatherboarded rear. Behind it, the *church* was utterly Victorianized in 1861. The very oddly pierced, vertically-weatherboarded belfry and the spire were badly damaged by fire in April 1968. Pierced 17th-century altar-rails. *Old Rectory*, ¼ mile to the north, is of early 17th-century red brick, with a delightful late-Georgian wing at right angles, and a small white bell-cote: it looks west over the valley to the great brick pediment of H.M. Hill Hall prison, in Theydon Mount. *Passingford Bridge*, on the boundary with Stapleford Abbots, was rebuilt in brick in 1785 by John Johnson. It is now threatened with demolition: it could surely be by-passed and preserved.

STANSTED: Epiphanius Evesham's effigy of Hester Salusbury dressed and ready for heaven in 1614

Stebbing (6) the Roman Stane Street marks the southern edge, and traces of a Roman building lie beneath the Green; beside it *Porters Hall*, a big moated farmhouse of *c.* 1600, is much restored. The distinguished and beautiful 14th-century church stands opposite the long range of *Church Farm*, spoilt externally by rough plastering; below, as at Kersey in Suffolk, are the huddled roofs of the village street.

In the street, the brick Quaker Meeting-house (dated 1674, but looking *c.* 1700) is now a "Social Club". The greatest delight is the further descent to the weatherboarded *Town water-mill* on the Stebbing Brook, its bank covered with aconites, the whole building still throbbing with life as Mr Hynds uses the water-wheel to hoist his sacks aloft; it was used for grinding till 1960. Last (first chronologically), there is the enormous castle-mound, higher upstream, 225 ft. in diameter, presumably built by Ranulf Peverel who had the larger manor and had planted a vineyard here by 1086. A causeway runs out across the moat to the present dwelling on the site, a tall late Elizabethan farmhouse; remains of two more causeways run over a gulley south-east towards the village.

The *church* is grouped with old cottages and houses. It has a ripe red-brick porch. The Dec. tracery of the east, south, and west windows gives good notice of the 14th-century pleasures within, though only those who know

Great Bardfield (or, apparently, Trondheim) are prepared for the excitement of the great stone rood-screen, of *c.* 1340, flowing up across the whole tall chancel-arch. The noble horizontal roofing of chancel is of *c.* 1500. From the 12th century to the Dissolution, the church belonged, like Little Maplestead, to the Knights Hospitallers of St John.

Steeple (13). This Blackwater estuary parish was distinguished by a steeple already in 1086. The present distinctive bell-tower rises tile-hung from the nave roof; the dark timbered louvres are capped by a shingled pyramid. It is a part of the engaging rebuilding of the church in 1884, by F. Chancellor, who achieved his rich texture by mixing red brick with yellowish septaria, re-used from the previous fabric (cf. Creeksea). The re-used 14th-century doorway has a carved head either side. *Stanesgate Priory*, a small Cluniac monastery beside the estuary, was also built of septaria: the priory church survived as a dilapidated barn in 1920s: now only one wall left. The priory had a watermill here – presumably a tide-mill.

Stifford (8). The ford over Mar Dyke is now bridged. Just north of it, *Ford Place* is an extremely pleasant mostly brick house, mostly dark red, with a long parapeted front (? *c.* 1700), and a rear court with curved gables dated 1655, and initialled J. and M.S., possibly by James Silverlock and wife. Of two elaborate plaster ceilings, one (of the late 17th century) has wreaths of oak and fruit and flowers and figures of the four seasons, including an early Father Christmas with beard. Graceful main staircase. The Silverlock monument is in the church tower, which is 13th-century. A corbel in the S. aisle-arcade was carved *and coloured* in the 1260s: a golden haired youth (? Henry III's son, the Lord Edward). The Norman N. doorway contains a Tudor door, held together by 13th-century ironwork. The brasses include one of a late 14th-century rector.

STISTED: a proper village-edge

Stisted (6), pronounced Stysted, means, very likely, the place where the pigs were styed in the wood. The village street is lined by several Victorian–Tudor cottages with ornamental chimneys and rather Swiss faces, the work of Squire Onley Savill Onley. *The Glen* is a singular example, just south of the village. The Onleys' house, pleasant sand-gold brick with ponderous Ionic portico (Hakewill, 1823), was the home

STEBBING

of the Colchester engineer Pax-man before becoming an old people's home.

The *church*, of Victorian dignity and composure, looks south across a low valley; the shingled broach spire is unusually sited, east of the S. aisle, where it was "rebuilt from the foundation" when the chancel was new roofed, in 1844. The church acquired its present calm atmosphere in the time of the Rev. Charles Forster, rector 1838–71, whose own composure was easily dispelled by Latitudinarians. On sunny days,

the interior is lit by excellent Victorian glass in the W. windows, and by Flemish glass in the E. windows, five stepped lancets renewed by Mr Forster, who bore ten books while his wife bore ten children. The books have been found uncommendable by one of the grand-children, Mr E. M. Forster. The novelist's biography of his great-aunt, Marianne Thornton, includes a description of the disordered rectory full of laundry and children, in 1843, that makes it the most memorable house in Stisted. In a roundel in the church, the death-mask (by Fredk. Thrupp) of one of the children, Doanie, who died at 16, shows a clear affinity at least to the physical features of his famous nephew, who looked in vain for the glimpse of a real boy in the 40 pages of poor Doanie's pious valediction.

Stock (9). Large, neat village. Tower windmill in good shape. The dignified Victorian rectory shares its great lawned garden with the church: the spectacular timber belfry, seen from W., is one of the most rewarding sights in Essex, though not enhanced by some modern ironwork gates painted Diocesan blue. Its ground-floor is vertically boarded in oak, with a spandrelled W. doorway and three well-preserved traceried square-panels over: a tiled pent roof covers the outshot "aisles" except on the E. side, where added stability is gained by carrying the belfry-stage east, flush with the W. wall of the nave. The belfry stage is in white-painted clap-boarding. All crowned by a tall spire, newly re-shingled. The main structure is thought to be late 13th-century. "1683" was carved on the N. side, perhaps when the vertical timber-case was renewed. Grotesque carved stone head in W. gable, N. aisle. Seventeenth-century brick *almshouses* lie west along the road. *Lilystone Hall*, of 1847, is an Animal Health Trust farmstock research-centre. *White-lilies Farm* is white plastered, tall, pedimented, *c.* 1700.

Stondon Massey (5), hilly and wooded, losing village coherence as the population increases. The sublime composer William Byrd (1543–1623) lived his last thirty years at *Stondon Place*, sub-sequently twice rebuilt. An MS music collection of 1591 bears the note: "Mr W. Birde *homo memorabilis*". Though he hoped to die in Stondon "where my dwelling is", he was a tiresome neighbour. He and lord of manor were recusant Catholic. His lord of the manor was replaced by a Puritan Merchant Adventurer. The small early Norman nave and chancel,

c. 1100, have lost their chancel-arch and apse. The church contains brasses to John Carre, a rich ironmonger, 1570, and Rainold Hollingworth, 1573, one of the commissioners for dealing with church goods under Edward VI. The three-decker pulpit of 1630 was divided up in 1850. John Oldham, rector 50 years, is said to have designed the old rectory himself *c.* 1800. A successor, E. H. L. Reeve (d. 1936), wrote a model parish-history.

Stow Maries (9). "Maries" = marsh. The church walls present a most promising mixture of flint, ragstone and septaria, the nave heightened with Tudor brick, fringed with a lacy corbel-table, and the chancel humped right up, its W. brick step-gable reared above the nave. A white rustic clapboard bell-turret caps the W. end. But the interior is dominated by a big reredos and crucifix on the E. wall, erected as a war-memorial 1914–18. There was an aerodrome here in 1916. And there are remains of ancient saltings.

Strethall (2). Farm and church in rolling downs on the site of a "street", a Roman road. Exterior of church at first sight Victorian, apart from the square-topped flint tower. But notice the fine long-and-short stonework of the W. quoins of the nave – Saxon workmanship, announcing some of the pleasure inside, through the sturdy late-medieval oak door. First, the narrow Saxon chancel-arch, early 11th-century. Prof. Pevsner finds it the work of a designer who did not know "what mouldings really mean". His mouldings mean Saxon work and we rejoice in its survival, for its age and its design have given it a grace missing in much Norman work. Quoins and arch show this to be a complete Saxon nave. Roof of well-preserved late medieval timbers on unusually well-carved stone corbels – especially man and wife at prayer on N. side. Base of ? 15th-century tower used as baptistry with simple handsome font: two bells of *c.*

1350. Chancel E. wall Victorian, perhaps rebuilding of original "E.E." work. In floor, the brass figure of a tonsured parson in cassock, tippett and hood, *c.* 1380, has been combined with an inscription to Maister Thomas Abbott late parson here which deceased 8 October 1539. Tomb-chest of John Gardyner, gent., 1508.

Sturmer (3). Leofsunu of Sturmer scorned flight after his leader's death in the battle against the Vikings at Maldon, 991: "the weapon shall take me, the iron sword". Can that tumulus north of the church, beside the A604, be his cenotaph? Nave and N. doorway 11th-century, with S. wall sloping like a ship's side. South doorway, apparently 12th-century, with very grotesque heads facing in from the door-jambs, and strange undeciphered cross-patterns. Tablet to Wm. Hicks, 1788–1874, rector 44 years, mid-shipman on the *Conqueror* at Trafalgar. The hammerbeam roof and deep-carved wallplate are perhaps by Thomas Loveday: see Introduction.

Sutton (16) between Rochford and Southend. *New Hall*, at end of avenue, and *Sutton Hall* have pleasant Georgian fronts. *Church:* Norman round-headed chancel-arch, splendid early 13th-century S. doorway (door ironwork dated 1869), 15th-century "Essex" timber belfry, and S. porch of 1633. Fourteenth-century military brass from *Shopland*, merged in Sutton since its church pulled down *c.* 1958. *Beauchamp's*, an elaborately pargeted house, bears the glorious date 1688.

Takeley (5). A market and fair here were granted to Waltham Abbey in 1253. The church stands apart from the main straggles of suburban housing (Takeley Street) along Stane Street. The parish stretches 2½ miles to the north, beyond Waltham Hall to Molehill Green, all horribly threatened by the Stansted airport proposals. At the *church*, a Tudor brick N.W. window has taken the place of a

GREAT TEY church

Norman doorway with Roman-brick jambs. Pleasant low 15th-century tower and S. porch. The whole interior has undergone a thorough restoration in 1966. The N. chancel window (E.E.) and the celebrated late-medieval crocketed font-cover do credit to previous restorers. *Warish Hall*, ¾ mile east of the church, occupies a moated site said to have been that of a cell of St Valéry, a thank-offering by one of William's men for that favourable S. wind on 27 September 1066, prayed for at St Valéry.

Tendring (14), a flattish plateau of good farmland near the 50 ft. contour. The Union workhouse of 1838 is now a hospital. From the north, *Brett's Hall* displays a splendid sweep of medieval roof. In the small village group, the N. side of the church (St Edmund) takes Victorian appearance from the ragstone tower, with limestone crocketed spire, built in 1876 by John Cardinall to designs of Henry Stone. Potato fields S. of church sweep down to Holland Brook. Apart from attractively traceried 14th-century timber N.

porch, main interest of church lies in massive hammerbeam roof-structure at belfry end, where lowest braces N. and S. spring from a timber gable, beautifully panelled, and supported on posts that frame original N. and S. doorways. South doorway now leads into 1876 S. aisle. Rest of roof of elegant and interesting scissor construction.

Terling (6), pronounced Tarling, in broad, elmy farming landscape. *Ringer's Farm*, at the end of a long lane west of Terling Hall, still has its original Gothic front door leading into the screens passage: oak, with quatrefoil panels carved in spandrels, and probably dating from the late 14th century. *Eyart's Farm*, Flack's Green, has a 17th-century carved figure on a bracket supporting the jettied first floor. Tall shutterless smock windmill, and deep ford. The church, its red brick tower of 1732 strongly reminiscent of New England, stands at a corner of the long Green. Across the road, old cottages, and the Congregational chapel, built *c.* 1700, and extensively restored in 1895. The road turns off the Green into a compact, uniform village-cluster of cream-washed, red-tiled old houses and shops. A Tudor manor-house, its timber frame exposed in front, faces south on to the churchyard. A tablet on the W. tower names Antony Goud as the builder. Based on Chelmsford, he was employed at Moulsham Hall under Leoni: the spelling of his name suggests a Dutchman, which might explain the handsome Dutch proportions and New England "feel". Red "stretchers" and black "headers", stone dressings, round arches, rustication: all topped by a tall slender broach spire, shingled. Interior bare and disappointing except for the fluted piers of the S. aisle, a couple of Elizabethan brasses, an Elizabethan communion table, and plain tablets to the great 3rd baron Rayleigh, O.M., 1842–1919, and Edward Gerald Strutt, C.H., the eminent agricultural improver. Small painting, Head of Christ, by David Rolt, 1951, in memory of

C. F. B. Rolt, 1920–45, killed in action. The handsome medieval timber S. porch is disused.

Terling Place, large white brick house mainly by John Johnson, 1772, turned about and extended 1819. West wing now houses laboratories of 3rd and 4th lords Rayleigh. All set in parkland and farmland, home of 1,200 cattle producing about a million gallons of milk a year, and scene of farming experiments since time of Hon. Edward Strutt. His brother the 3rd lord, Cavendish professor of experimental physics at Cambridge, 1879–84, discovered argon. A seven-vol. edition of his collected scientific papers was lately published in the U.S.A.

Tey, Great (10), pronounced Tay. St Barnabas's church stands proud as a castle-keep in its square green open churchyard. The rugged square Norman central tower is embattled (against the Devil) and topped at one corner by a round stair-turret like a look-out waving a weather-vane of 1793. The tower owes its tremendous character to its red Roman brick quoins and Romanesque triple arcading on each side, a central stone colonnette in each louvre. What an impression this church must have made down to 1829, when the Norman nave ran west, and transepts north and south! The parish's decision to demolish them is a standing lesson to the faint-hearted of all time: the estimated cost of renovation, £700, seemed too much for them. So they demolished and got a bill for £1,400. Jas. Beadel, junr., of Witham, did the 1829 work. Who built the cruciform church of the 1160s? It was probably done for Richard de Lucy, the Justiciar (see Ongar), who seems to have acquired Tey in 1162; he was one of the Normans who still, after a century, thought in terms of "us Normans". The building was conceivably a response to the rather shrill excommunication pronounced on him, 1166, by the exiled Beckett. The 14th-century rebuilding of the chancel was consonant with the dignity of the rest. Even the 1829 work produced an agreeable little

gallery with Gothick tracery and Royal arms. At the same time a few large Romanesque capitals were rebuilt in walls near the vestry. Old houses with large Tudor brick chimney-stacks lie east and west of the church, and inevitable bungalows. There is a large moat at the vicarage. *Teybrook Farm* forms a very pleasant 17th-century group with barn.

Tey, Little (13). At the end of a lane, a small Norman church. Its roof overhangs with broad eaves that project to make a square corner at the E. end, over the apse; so that it looks very top-heavy. A dreadfully complete restoration by Pudney of Colne Engaine was in progress in 1966, with entire disregard for emergent medieval wall-paintings.

Tey, Marks (13). The Norman owners came over from Marck, near Calais. At the junction of Stane Street with A12 is much hideous ribbon-development. The church is familiar to travellers on the Liverpool Street–Colchester line: the W. tower is especially memorable, with the top two stages *and* battlements composed of dark vertical oak boarding, a small shingled spire protruding above. Base of tower and rest of fabric no less interesting at close quarters, a rich mixture of Roman brick and iron-bound rust-coloured conglomerate. Bricks in small Norman window. South doorway Norman, with an iron handle that is medieval, though in Victorian fittings. Not only the tower, but the font, too, is of medieval oak, the carved panels much defaced by Puritans. During the Civil War, many of them, led by the "Curate", subscribed their names to the Solemn League and Covenant in the Elizabethan Register-book still kept in the vestry. "Marks Tey Village" is a new neighbourhood in 1967, well designed by a Basildon firm, Jan Farber & Bartholomew.

Thames Haven *see* Coryton.

Thaxted (2) originally "a place where thatch comes from", grew into town specializing in the craft of cutlery in the 14th and 15th

centuries. The consequent prosperity, transposed into a great church, a gild-hall and a collection of modest timber-framed houses, has left Thaxted high among the most popular English symbols of not just thatching (less than six roofs still wore thatch in 1966) but the whole picturesque business of vernacular building.

This is the trouble, and why the ruthless restoration of the gild-hall in 1910 ranks as a national misfortune. It is bad enough that its walls were completely stripped of panelled plasterwork they had worn for at least two centuries and that new wooden arches were fixed into the upright studs of the 1st floor to give the building a more medieval appearance! The real damage followed. Thaxted seemed to show everyone that medieval timber houses should expose their whole framework. Off came the plaster overcoat, and when the building inevitably became draughty, wattle-and-daub between uprights was replaced by filling of cement instead of lime-plaster: result, unhealthy-looking oak, its days superfluously numbered, and drab cement. The perfect example is only a few doors back from the gild-hall: 2–4 Stony Lane, fine oversailing houses (officially Grade I, no less!) with fronts that look leprous. Compare the adjacent nicely pargeted No. 7. Daily more damage is done, prefigured by the Edwardian stripping of this unforgettable late 15th-century hall of the Thaxted cutlers.

Town Street developed on the line of a Roman road running N. from Chelmsford and Dunmow to Radwinter (and Chesterford), which remained the main route from Chelmsford to Cambridge. The street north of the church is named Watling Street, but that is apparently an early distortion of the family-name Walkelyn, already here by 1348. To get full enjoyment from a visit to Thaxted, arrive from the south by Dunmow Road on a fine winter's afternoon. The old tower-mill is hunched on

THAXTED: from the west

THAXTED church

the skyline above broad brown sloping fields, the low sun drawing a flash from the precarious weather-cock on top of the marvellously slender church spire, 181 ft. up from the crest at the top of the town. That old mill, the *Church Mill*, was built by John Webb in 1805. Repairs to a predecessor on the site were recorded as early as 1377.

The main interest begins in Town Street, broad enough to hold the market when it grew too big for Fishmarket Street (the lane on the left as you face the gild-hall). The *gild-hall*, perched on arcaded stilts that provided an open market-house on ground-floor, mushrooms out astonishingly into two oversailing upper storeys: cutlers' hall and town hall. Thaxted was a manorial borough at least as early as 1348, and then a chartered borough, with a "Recorder", 1554–1684. The next best secular building, also doubly oversailing, is known as *the Recorder's House*, with a front of the 1470s, roughly dateable by Edward IV's arms on oak coves beneath the 1st-floor windows: at present a good restaurant. In 1917 Gustav Holst came to live in the house next door. His famous setting of "I vow to thee, my country", is called "Thaxted". Conrad Noel was presented to the living by Lady Warwick in 1910. Active secretary of the Church Socialist League, his thirty-two years here was one of the most celebrated incumbencies of our century.

Stony Lane, properly pebbly, leads up steeply to the S. porch of the best church in Essex: as fine and grand as Saffron Walden's, as elemental and light and redolent of a long, vanished past as Blythburgh's in Suffolk. There is much pleasure in looking at the details, e.g. carved stone figures on the N. porch and round the battlements of the adjacent stair-turret and in the oak roof of the N. aisle where a particularly appealing angel clutches a book. In rough outline, nave and S. aisle are 14th-century, tower and N. aisle 15th-century, chancel, chancel-chapels and clerestories c. 1510. The owners and patrons all through the Middle Ages were the great Clare family, whose complex descent through female lines after 1314 resolved in Cicely, duchess of York, Edward

THAXTED: a true Essex timber-framed terrace, one pair of cottages over-sailing, one with pargeting, and all with good plaster coats

IV's mother, and Elizabeth his daughter, who married Henry VII, which at least explains the presence of Edward's shield in church and town. Much fragmentary stained glass of c. 1460. Bourchier arms in S. aisle roof c. 1510 – also shield bearing woolcomb bendwise between two shuttles, which shows that the church-building was a corporate effort and that Thaxted went in for clothing as well as cutlery. The cloth-making seems to have developed with the decline of the cutlery in the 16th century, and to have coincided with the development of Newbiggen Street, north of the church.

The real glories of the church's interior are architectural, the arrangements of arcades; lofty 14th-century work in the nave, converted to Perp. by richly traceried clerestory and flat roof at perfect height; above all, the ravishing arrangement of delicate arcading on either side of chancel, the spandrels pierced, the whitewash and plain glass creating an illusion of infinity. What might have been too bleak an effect of all this light, is broken by the natural shadows on all the sculptured stonework, and additionally, with remarkable skill, by the introduction into the chancel of banners of six saints, which with the excellent Kempe glass of the E. window infuses just enough colour. Conrad Noel was helped by the architect Randall Wells in creating the whole interior atmosphere. The light is further modulated by pale green hangings in N. chapel, whose roof, incidentally, retains curiously rich original black and white stencilling. Baroque oak pulpit with sounding-board and carved sycamorewood, c. 1680. Elaborate 15th-century font-cover. Tower and spire, largely Georgian work, certainly show they could do Gothic if they tried! A tablet explains the work of Peter Platt on the S. side of tower in 1758:

Where Peter lies, 'tis fit this
    tower should show,
But for his skill, itself had
    lain as low.

Then in 1814 the spire was struck by lightning and all came down. The present spire is the work of a Warwickshire mason, "Mr Cheshire of Over Whitaker", in 1822. One wonders how long it would survive the establishment of London's 3rd airport at Stansted. The one fine Georgian house in Thaxted, *Clarance House*, just opposite the church, is dated "1715 $\begin{smallmatrix}H\\W E\end{smallmatrix}$". The old Royal Commission, by no means comprehensive, listed thirty buildings earlier than this in the town, twenty more in the large farming parish lying all round. 157 buildings are now officially listed as being of historic or architectural interest. The most remarkable of them, *Horham Hall*, lies half in Thaxted, half in Broxted. The S. wing, on the left as you face the front, stands in Broxted: it was probably the solar of a timber-framed house of c. 1470. The rest, including the great-hall with splendid oriel, is an early 16th-century red brick building, with stone dressings, for Sir John Cutte, treasurer of Henry VIII's household (see Arkesden), who got Thaxted after Catherine of Aragon's demise. The N. wing originally extended farther east and west. The S. wing is clad in brick of c. 1580. Its owners have moved out within a year of the 1967 Stansted-airport decision.

Theydon Bois (4). The wood that gave its name to the Norman owner here is now rapidly receding as housing developments eat into it. The *church*, a simple low barn (S. Smirke) of 1850, replaced a new church of 1843–4 which had to be taken down after six years as it was so unsoundly built. The most notable object inside is the arms of James I, painted on a panel and surmounted by a pediment saying God Save the King. The tower is on the south-west, its spire clad in hideous bright green copper since 1920.

Theydon Garnon (5). Largest of the Theydons. Seems remarkably rural, after Theydon Bois, at e.g. Fiddlers Hamlet, which was named after the *Merry Fiddlers* pub and was the scene of a fair till 1872. Market and fair were granted in 1305. Nothing else known of market. Blue bricks are mixed up in the red brick tower of 1520, newly repointed 1966. The effect is a sort of bruised purple. The brick N. aisle is dated in the E. gable 1644, an extraordinary date for church-building, and initialled I.H. in the W. gable. It has a timber arcade and charming panelled vaulted ceiling, blue and white, five nice hatchments and George III's arms. Queen Anne 2-decker pulpit with tester, and more recent upright piano. Communion rail 1683–4. Oak door-frame brought from priest's house lately demolished in churchyard. A fine large brass of 1450 shows the rector, Wm. Kyrkeby in his cope. Stanton's monument to John Archer (E. wall of chancel) has lost the swag from its split pediment. Handsome unsigned monument to W. E. Archer, 1739. Pieces of good Victorian glass in W. window. When *Gaynes Park* was rebuilt, of Kentish rag, in 1870 (date on gable) in a Tudor style, it incorporated Park Hall, a house of the middle 18th century. The stone is now well mellowed, and the gardens open in summer under the National Gardens scheme. For *Coopersale* see Epping.

Theydon Mount (5). Hilly, as the name suggests, and on the main hill is a small red brick Jacobean church (1611–14) and one of the most remarkable houses of the Elizabethan Renaissance, heavily disguised on its E. front (seen from church) as a grand Queen Anne house. Begun by the scholar and statesman Sir Thomas Smith near the end of his life (1513–77) it evidently embodies features of the French and Italian Renaissance that had appealed to him: he was a D.C.L. of Padua, was close to the Protector Somerset when old Somerset House was building, and it has been suggested that Hill House owes something to the château of Bournazel which he would know from two visits to Toulouse. In any case, the giant Tuscan columns in the courtyard, generally accepted as Smith's work, Pevsner describes

WEST THURROCK

as "a unique occurrence in England and indeed in Europe". Furthermore, a ravishing series of wall-paintings of the same time, the 1570s, showing the story of Cupid and Psyche with life-size figures in a classical landscape, are of an accomplishment authoritatively described as "without parallel among surviving examples in England". It is an odd comment on England that since 1952 Hill House has been very successfully run as an open prison for women.

The red brick church, its chancel full of Smith monuments, is entered through a porch with curved gable displaying bricks carved with initials W.S., W.S., T.S., E.S., B.S., F.S., within a bizarre classical frame. Sir Thomas, his lively face matching the bust on the fireplace in his great hall, lies uncomfortably in plate-armour

and the mantle of the Garter: the arch is inscribed:

What Y'earth or Sea or Skies conteyne, what Creatures in them be
My Mynde did seeke to know, my Soule the Heavens continually.

Thoby Priory see Mountnessing.

Thorndon Hall see Ingrave.

Thorpe-le-Soken (14) is part of the ancient soke (liberty) of St Paul's, London. It has distant memories of two fairs, and of Huguenots settled in the village (1683–1732); recent memories of Wednesday evening corn-markets and a large barge-wharf at Landermere; and now it is a lively thoroughfare village, visually damaged by overhead wires.

At the main corner a house named *The Abbey* is prominent, with a pinnacled porch bearing its date, 1583. Along the street are three Georgian fronts with bows. The *Bell Hotel*'s Tudor front oversails with bressummers, its Georgian back range along the edge of the churchyard. The great purple Tudor brick church-tower has diaper and zigzag patterns in blue brick: the N. aisle is also early Tudor with original roof and interesting window tracery (? Huguenot). The rest of fabric is of 1876: buff-coloured septaria: the dressings include red sandstone. The Victorian barrel-vault of the nave has main timbers that are partly medieval. The font stands on a Norman plinth. A 15th-century screen is carved with five angels, two bearing the message:

"This cost is the bachelors in ade by ales".

Comarques, Arnold Bennett's improbably beautiful Georgian country-house, has fine iron gates perhaps hung for him: three bathrooms were the result of his last visit to the States, in 1911. To the south of the village, a dignified group on the Clacton line includes tall maltings and the *King Edward VII* pub.

Thorrington (14) *church* is approached through a farmyard. The black flint W. campanile was given *c.* 1480 by Jn. and Margery Deth (see brass). Late 14th-century S. porch of septaria and pebble work. The pointed doorway has jambs and dressings entirely of ancient tile. Interior all Victorian except medieval font and altar of English marble from Bethersden, Kent. Tumbledown tide-mill at tip of Alresford Creek.

Thremhall Priory see Stansted Mountfichet.

Thundersley (9). The heathen god Thunor's clearing; on a precipitous hill, screened all round by trees. Remarkable steeply terraced graveyard in trees to the west of the church. Nave roof, of massive tie-beams and crown-posts, strengthened in 1965, as piles are driven into the churchyard for a 45 ft. extension to the east, a response to the spreading dormitory population: the work entirely in the hands of boys.

Thurrock (8), the Anglo-Saxon word for the bottom of the ship, where the bilge collects. Thurrock is grimy, but that Saxon description is now too strong. At Purfleet a thick fold of chalk rises 100 ft. above the river, and the lime-quarrying operations over the centuries, and on a big scale by the Whitbreads in the 18th and 19th centuries, greatly added to the picturesque cliff-effect: Wright's *Essex* includes a spectacular engraving, 1832. Belmont Castle, a Gothick Fort Belvedere

WEST TILBURY:
Sir Bernard de Gomme's
Water-gate

of 1795, was alas demolished *c.* 1945 at Grays.

Thurrock, Grays (8), sometimes called simply "Grays" from the medieval lords of that name, has wharves, a Wharf Hotel and a Globe Terrace. Impressive old church in well-tree'd churchyard beside a street that runs south to a screen of masts and rigging. The fabric of the church, thoroughly repaired in 1846, when the nave was extended westwards and the top of the tower rebuilt, contains the crossing of a cruciform church, with two Norman round-headed arches. The crossing is included now in the chancel, and all well paved in black and white marble. A monument to Ann Cox, 1796, with stricken girl, is signed C. Regnart. A small tablet commemorates master and boys of the training-ship Goliath, destroyed by fire at Christmas 1875.

Thurrock, Little (8). *Hangman's Wood*, beside a roundabout and large petrol-station on the hair-raising A13 speedway from Dartford Tunnel to Southend, is a 4-acre triangle of oak wood containing seventy-two of the mysterious pits known as Dane-holes, or Dene Holes. Two or more are kept open (securely fenced-round at the top: key at 41, Parkway) by the Essex Field Club, who organize occasional descents. Narrow shafts go down vertically 50 to 100 ft. through Thanet sand to chalk, then broaden out into chambers about 20 ft. long. Date and purpose extremely obscure. Apparently "post-Neolithic". Hardly for mining chalk, when there is abundance of chalk on the surface only a mile away; and there are good reasons against most quarrying theories, though that did not prevent someone having a shot at floating a company "to rework pits for gold" during the South Sea Bubble *c.* 1720. Possibly secret storehouses for grain in times of invasion? The church contains a broad round-headed Norman chancel-arch (restored) and a tall Victorian triple arcade between tower and nave. Pretty monument with painted shield of arms, 1808.

Thurrock, West (8) including

Purfleet. West Thurrock church almost holds its own, its 15th-century tower is so distinctively faced with horizontal stripes of black flint and light grey ragstone, and retopped in brick in 1640; but in scale it is dwarfed by *Procter & Gamble's* massive works to the east, and by the superb W. Thurrock *Generating Station* to the west. In 1912, what seems to have been a round nave was excavated on site of present tower: it had a W. porch and aisleless chancel. At *Purfleet, High House*, a great old farmhouse of late 17th-century appearance, is well set up but wedged between quarries and works. It has a large octagonal dovecote of dark red brick, with dark blue tiled roof. The *Royal Hotel*, formerly Bricklayers Arms, is a riverside Trust House with a marvellous view and an ilex. Government *Powder Magazine* and Purfleet *Barracks*, in Tank Lane were established with handsome brick buildings of the 1760s. The Ministry of Defence is letting these excellent buildings become derelict since they were evacuated in 1962.

Tilbury-juxta-Clare (3). *Church* remote, though not forlorn: it bears marks of the unsophisticated care of a Victorian parson, who has stuck bits of carved stone into the flaking outer coat of the chancel, and very primitive emblems of Elizabeth, countess of Oxford, inside the fine diapered red brick W. tower that she paid for in 1519. Also a primitive plaster dragon adorns the tower, which contains, as well, a very ancient ironbound chest. The old plaster walls have been white-washed, except over patches of red medieval painting – one on the nave N. wall, though faded, showing a Tudor man with white horse in front of house of contemporary brick-nogging. Victorian red stencilling round the chancel-arch is agreeably un-doctrinaire.

Tilbury, East (9). The grim square grey walls of *Coal House Fort* were built on this bend of

the Thames at Coalhouse Point by Gordon of Khartoum, O.C. Royal Engineers at Gravesend in 1869. Its construction has the happy indirect result that old Tilbury Fort (West Tilbury) was never refitted with heavy Victorian guns, and so survives intact from the 17th century. The church, just above the fort, could have done with protection on 23 July 1667 when the Dutch landed and destroyed the vicarage, the S. aisle and the 13th century tower. The bells now hang in a timber frame W. of church. A new tower, begun as a war-memorial by 2 Coy., The London Electrical Engineers, 1917, never rose above one storey. Inside, a beautiful trio of lancets at the E. end has the right amount of colour in its 1905 glass: there is creamy plaster and stone, and a chancel-floor of good rough red brick. On the S. side of the chancel, a table-tomb of 1721 with cherubs in a side panel has lately been washed pink! The fish mosaic in the floor by the vicar's stall was done in April 1966. Oil lamps and candles in use, supplemented by electricity. Great *Bata Shoe Factory* occupies the site of the old St Clare's Hall, near E. Tilbury Station: it was begun in 1932, on the model of their buildings in Czechoslovakia. Cheerful new recreation centre in 1957.

Tilbury, West (8). The best view of the church is from the south-west, from the bottom of Gun Hill at the edge of the marshes. There one can avoid looking at the great mesh of wires, poles and pylons advancing on the power-station beside the Thames, and see how this (uninteresting) church occupies a commanding position on the crown of the slope. The earthworks on the hillside below the church have a double interest. We know from Bede that Bishop Cedd organized the first Christian mission to the East Saxons from Tilbury as well as Bradwell in the 650s: this is the most probable site of his church. Less hypothetical, and more celebrated, this is where Englishmen gathered in 1588 to see that even if the Spaniards got past Drake, they should never get nearer to London than this hill.

The slopes of the ridge, good arable fields hedged by superb elms, are as completely rural as they were in Elizabeth's day. It is easy to imagine the multitude of men and armaments gathered around the church and never possible to forget that arrival of the Queen on 8 August, crying "Lord bless you all" as men fell on their knees and prayed for her; or that speech: "Let tyrants fear . . . I have the heart and stomach of a King, and of a King of England too"; or Walsingham's wry comment: "Thus your Lordship seeth that this place breedeth courage". How much it did was remembered three years later: an unlucky Maldon man tried to wriggle out of military service on grounds of unfitness and was asked: "Who was so good a man as you when you were at Tilbury camp, for then you set forth yourself as though you could fight against 40 Spaniards".

Down below, at the river's edge, a blockhouse had been built in 1539. It is dismal to note that in 1588 the great boom of ships' masts and cables was got across the river only *after* the Armada had been routed. Similarly, the present *Tilbury Fort* was built only *after* the Dutch had landed at East Tilbury. It is now the finest example in England of an important fort of the age of Vauban; the fact that it was never put to test is perhaps the best tribute to its strength. Since 1950, open to the public *daily*, with admirable official guide-book by A. D. Saunders. The offensive batteries lined the river *outside* the water-gate. Defence was provided by the two complex concentric moats with a star-shaped system of earthwork-bastions. What one always remembers is the *Water-gate*, a romantic nonsense, as Sheridan was thinking when, at the lowest point of the war against the Americans, French and Spaniards, he made one of his characters exclaim: "Tilbury Fort! Very fine indeed!" Its engineer-architect, Sir Bernard de Gomme, was more concerned to cover up the gable

of the guard-house than to provide academic 2-dimensional satisfaction: so an endearing *arc de triomphe* that looks as if it has sunk into the marsh is crowned by a large round pediment on Corinthian columns, the sides stacked up with stone trophies that looked best in the 19th century, with two chimneys sticking up through them.

Gravesend looks surprisingly close across the river, which provides endless entertainment. The old ferry-house nearby, rebuilt in 1788, is now the *World's End* pub. British Railways have fixed themselves up with a new signal-box like a super one-man grandstand, at "Tilbury Riverside". The great *docks* were constructed in the 1880s.

Tillingham (13). Marshes down to the sea, and wild fowl decoys. A large village; the manor belongs to the Dean and Chapter of St Paul's, and possibly has done since the foundation of St Paul's, *c.* 604, as cathedral of the E. Saxons! It is relevant that Bishop Cedd settled in an adjacent fort (see Bradwell). Bishop Theodred, leaving St Paul's his Tillingham lands in the middle of the 10th century, may well have been repeating an earlier, pre-Danish, endowment. In any case, this makes the dean and chapter easily the oldest county family!

There is a Norman doorway into the church (St Nicholas), and a Norman font with fine carved acanthus leaves; beautiful lancet windows in the 13th-century chancel. In 1297 an inventory showed this church to have a rood with Mary and John, and images of the Virgin, St Paul, St Nicholas, St Edmund and seven other saints; but a fly-fan (*muscarium*) and iron for stamping wafers were missing. An old farmhouse, *East Hyde*, was handsomely refronted in saffron-coloured brick and single-pane fenestration in the 1950s.

Tilty (2), a Cistercian abbey-site, blissfully pastoral as usual, in the upper Chelmer vale. The fine lofty "Chapel-outside-the-Gates" survives as the parish church. All else

is gone except a long fragment of wall that formed the W. side of the cloister, and outlines in the ground that "read" clearly in air-photographs. Picturesque pond with oak stands at the S.E. corner of the S. transept of the (vanished) great church, on the scale of St Mary's, Saffron Walden. The medieval fishponds were lower down, by the mill. The view north-east to Duton Hill, Easton, is covered with new housing, but their colours blend with the landscape.

The chapel hints at the nobility of the buildings destroyed. A modest 13th-century nave leads into a prodigious early 14th-century chancel: its height and grace are matched by the beauty of the window-tracery, especially in the E. window. The E. wall is flanked by buttresses, each with an ornamental niche and part of a most memorable composition. It rises to a gable that flattens out above the E. window, candidly revealing the form of the chancel-roof within. Textures important: chancel flint and freestone, nave stucco agreeably butter-coloured, with simple rustic porch and delicate little cupola over the W. end. The inside is gloriously light. Fine W. lancets. Well-preserved brasses: note, especially, the rhyming Latin epitaph of abbot Thomas Takeley, 1459–75, which says, not surprisingly, that he loved this place.

Tiptree (13). A great heath here was "waste" of the Essex Forest, in which freeholders and tenants of *sixteen* neighbouring parishes had common rights of grazing and use of wood for repairing houses. By the 19th century, the heath had been divided among all these parishes in "radiating slips" which explains the present maze of roads. *Tiptree Hall Farm* was the scene of the first successful reclamation from waste, by J. J. Mechi, in the 1840s. Messrs Wilkin & Son's famous jam-factory is on the site, surrounded by strawberry fields, orchards and mulberry groves. *Tiptree House* is strikingly tall,

TOLLESBURY

part of a mansion Brian Darcy built c. 1560 in place of a priory of Austin canons. A famous fair was held on the portion of heath embodied in Messing. The 1855 parish-church is like a large Victorian schoolroom. Ugly interwar housing sprawls everywhere. A tower wind-mill needs attention.

Tollesbury (13) is a place of wild-fowlers and oystermen with, at its centre, above the marshy peninsula, a quiet square of old houses and shops and the (former) village lock-up. The church alongside, possibly on a Roman site, has an impressive square, squat tower, the Norman lower stage septaria, short upper stages and buttresses of Elizabethan or Jacobean brick, all dressed with clunch. Georgian font with a roughly carved penitential of John Norman, whose fine paid for it: "Good people all I pray take care, that in yᵉ church you do not sware, As this man did". Rich E. window and two (12th-century) nave windows glazed by Kempe. A handsome monument commemorates Jane Gardiner, 1654, of *Bourchiers Hall*. Bourchiers held the main manor from 1329 to 1570. Their beautiful white plastered house contains clear evidence in the attic and one bedroom that its W. side is that of the original aisled 14th-century hall, though the aisle-posts have all been cut away on the ground-floor. The roof-timbers are smoke-blackened from the days of the open-fire in the middle of the hall. Cottages at Old Hall Creek were licensed as *The Hoy* when trading barges nosed up through these saltings. *Guisnes Court* now a "Country Club".

Tolleshunt D'Arcy (13) shelves gently down six miles from Tiptree in the north to the Blackwater estuary, with views of a tidy Dutch kind from the north. The church is approached through a brick-floored, light-grey Kentish-rag S. porch and medieval doors. Georgian coved nave-ceiling, the panels of the choir ceiling charmingly painted (E. Geldart, 1897). West end occupied by a big new organ gallery. Pleasant lighting by two unobtrusive "chandeliers" of slender modern shape. Six brasses. The neatly carved marble to Thomas d'Arcy, 1593, says he left his wife Camilla a sorrowful and greeved widow who by her father is descended from the noble house of GVYCCIARDYNES within the dukedom of Florence. Darcys succeeded the Tregoz and Bois families here in the late 15th century. The late 15th-century part of their L-shaped moated house, admirably preserved, faces the brick and silvery-stonework bridge that is inscribed: Anno Regny Regina Elyzabeth 27: 1585. A 17th-century wing at right-angles, which in the early 18th century faced a parallel wing, now provides a stone-floored hall. This hall is lined with the most magnificently carved early 16th-century panelling (bearing initials of Anthony Darcy, died 1540, whose odd brass in the church was long ago skied), and ceiled with re-used carved ribbing. At present it houses a modern harpsichord and a Clementi piano of c. 1815. In the village, *Darcy Cottage* and an adjacent house have nice Georgian fronts. Small new school: Franks, Saunders & Partners, 1966. There is a Red Hill (see Introduction) down beside the Blackwater at Lauriston Farm. Long marsh views and walks.

Tolleshunt Knights (13). The old Rectory has been a cell of the Orthodox church since 1959. They have the loan of the old parish church (standing beside an un-made lane at Manifold Wick), and use it to minister to busloads of Cypriots and others. Tolleshunt had no use for the building. The manor was presumably held by Knight's service in 1238 when the surname first appears. A knight of c. 1380 is carved in effigy in the church, with heart in hands, mutilated.

Tolleshunt Major (13). Not so large as the others, it takes its name from the Domesday tenant "Malgerus" (Mauger). The church-tower, of really beautiful diapered brickwork, deep red, contains a late 14th-century bell inscribed "Vox Edwardi sonet in Aure Dei". The rest of the fabric is of puddingstone and septaria. Good S. porch, 1888, by E. Geldart, the Master of Braxted. Tie-beam and crown-post in the nave, the south and north walls of which each have a small terra-cotta (or brick) canopied niche. Nearby, *Beckingham Hall*, an unremarkable old farmhouse with a slate roof, is fronted by very fine red Tudor brick walled enclosure with round thin turrets at the corners and a square gateway in the middle (which also has round thin corner turrets). This is dated c. 1540s from a piece of fine panelling from the former house, now in the Victoria and Albert Museum. The farmer says there are old foundations in the front lawn and all round his house. The front wall at Erwarton, Suffolk, is comparable.

Toppesfield (3). The village has been filled up with characterless modern bungalows. Church-tower beautiful, red and black brick, 1699, "to the memory of Mr Robert Wilde, late rector, who gave £100 towards the building of the steeple. Dan Hills, Bricklayer". Nice to have the builder's and donor's names on a plaque. Delightfully original parapet, very lively with inverted arches. The top stage has lately been re-pointed with too much mortar. The rest of the church is covered with old cement stucco. Interior beautifully kept, washed cream and white. Pamment floors. Georgian W. gallery and plain pulpit. Fragments of 15th-century glass in the E. end S. aisle, and an excellent carved S. aisle roof. Small memorials in the narrow chancel. There is a legend that valerian was planted round the E. front, in 1649, at time of Charles I's execution, that its colour might remind men.

Totham, Great (13). The churchyard is kept mown like a lawn amid flat fruitful fields and distant woods, like a Dutch scene. The base of the tower is of ginger septaria; puddingstone higher; then the recent shingled belfry. Early 17th-century armorial glass exactly fits the W. window. In the time of James I, John Newton was in trouble with the arch-deacon here for persistently refusing to sit in any pew save where gentlewomen sat. The *Hall*, early 17th-century, was modernized in 1825. *Osea Island*, in the Black-water, was held with Totham in Domesday Book (a fishery and pasture for 60 sheep), and seems to have remained with Totham till recently. Up for sale in 1968, its surprisingly shingly beaches are crowded in summer.

Totham, Little (13). Church-tower unusual: the top two-thirds cream-painted clap-boarding and a pyramid of tiles, on an entirely flint base with great buttresses and the date 1527 over the W. door. The cottagey clapboard S. porch contains an astonishing rich late-Norman doorway, and a door with medieval ironwork. Bare inside but for a charming marble monument with kneeling figures of Sir John and Lady Samms, he in armour, she in weeds, erected by her brother: Sir John, Captain of ISENDIKE in Flanders, lies buried out there: mid 17th-century.

Twinstead (10). Beautiful undulating country, savagely trampled by the Sizewell–Sundon 400 k.v. pylons. Picturesque old house on Twinstead Green. *Church* 1860, very red brick, with pattern of soot-coloured bricks outside, and fantastic brickwork trellis-pattern inside. Triple "E.E." chancel arch with iron tracery. Splendid rich blues and purples in E. window. There is a sketch of the previous church, 1858, with a procession of children.

Ugley (2) *church* is approached from the west past a thatched huddle of cottages and laurels and limes. Early 16th-century brick tower, a beautiful red, but not in good order. The S. chapel was built from the ruins of Bolington church, formerly a separate parish. The rest is of 1866. Nice headstone to Elizabeth Mumford, 1771. *Orford House*, red brick, *c.* 1700, behind gates with handsome stone urns, is very close to the main road, which probably explains the slightly derelict look.

Wades Hall, away to the west of A11, entirely derelict, still had Elizabethan panelling in its W. room in 1966.

Ulting (6). The small church is set beside the river-bank. Mainly 13th-century, it has nothing to commend it but situation. It was drastically restored in 1873. No trace of any gild "in a lady chapel in the churchyard", founded in 1481 by Henry Bourchier, earl of Essex. *Church House*, attractive Victorian "Tudor", in pale sandy-coloured brick, with elaborate window-glazing. *Tanhouse Farm* has a fine Elizabethan chimney-stack: similar shafts on the chimneys of *Ulting Hall*, which has nice Georgian additions.

Upshire (4), the upland edge of Waltham Forest, hived off from Waltham Holy Cross. On St Thomas's day, 1901, Sir Thomas Fowell Buxton's wife laid the foundation of Freeman & Ogilvy's beautiful copy of Shenfield church. Here, the handsome N. arcade of *timber* piers, and the massive belfry-structure, are housed in a yellow-brick building, roughcast like a Voysey villa. The chancel ceiling is plaster-panelled, an *art-nouveau* design in lower panels the year after the Paris Exposition. *Art-nouveau* furnishings include communion-rails in form of two long prayer-desks; two priests' chairs with inlaid backs; a green and beige sanctuary carpet; cross, candlesticks and vases of beaten brass. Memorial to Fowell Buxton, 1915 (the Liberator's grandson), carved in oak. (A steel engraving shows his small daughter presenting her godmother Queen Victoria with bouquet when she came to High Beach in 1882 to declare the Forest liberated "for the enjoyment of my people for ever".) War-memorial oak font, 1919.
East of the church, *Blue Row Cottages* form a nice weather-boarded terrace; the builders left bark on the roof-timbers. Down in the bottom below the church, *Warlies*, the Buxtons' house, has been Dr Barnardo's since 1915. There is an ornamental rotunda,

of *c.* 1780, on "Temple Hill". The stucco'd red brick obelisk at Obelisk Farm is commemorative: "That's where Queen Boadicea took her poison" a girl affirmed, as though she had been present and happened to notice. At *Breach Barns* a second obelisk marks the spot where that queen expired, but neither location seems even remotely plausible to modern antiquaries!

Vange *see* Basildon.

Virley *see* Salcott.

Wakering, Great (16). A farming village, it includes marsh-grazing, also Potton island and Rushley island in the Roach archipelago. Its peaceful barging days are over. The *church*, of ragstone-rubble, septaria and flint, is basically early Norman, with a late Norman stout square tower and round-headed arch. A homely, not at all rectilinear, late 15th-century gabled porch with chamber over was clapped on to the W. end. Two-storey W. porches were rather a pre-Conquest fashion; in the 15th-century porches usually went S. or N. of the nave. But, for that, a tall, clerestoried nave was needed, so this went up against the tower instead, which has a rather ponderous broad-bottomed spire. Prettily restored late Georgian creed and commandment boards are properly each side of the E. window. A good Norman font and some old wall-paintings have disappeared. The village street is disastrously "infilled" and now part of big ugly ribbon development. At Landwick Police Lodge, Foulness island is barred off as security area.

Wakering, Little (16). The slightly crooked needle of the shingled spire is on a tower that was apparently the gift of a bishop of Norwich (1416–25) who took his name from here; see his arms on the W. doorway. Dark little Norman nave and chancel. Nicely painted Royal Arms, with "Laus Deo", 1769, are stowed away with the pillory in the base of the tower. *Hall*, inaccessible, Guard Dogs on prowl. Apparently a 15th-century house with improvements of 1599 and a fine early Georgian fireplace. Fleet Head and the ferry to Potton island are part of an Army prohibited zone.

Walden, Little, one of four outlying hamlets of

Walden, Saffron (2), probably the best looking small town anywhere in Essex or E. Anglia, and the chief of all its attractions is the way it merges immediately in surrounding fields and parkland without hindrance of suburbs. From London (40 miles away) the road arrives suddenly at the S. end of High Street on the ridge at the S.W. corner of the town. A straight broad thoroughfare lined with pollarded plane-trees, High Street swoops down and up and then down again to Bridge End, marking the W. edge of the town. Walking west from High Street, one quickly enters the very pastoral and partly arable park of Audley End, the vast Jacobean palace that supplanted Walden Abbey as a dominant influence on the life (and appearance) of the town. And continuing north across the bridge at Bridge End, the road climbs straight out into the country, the broad open arable downland. Running east from the High Street, and at right angles to it, George Street, King Street, Church Street and Castle Street mark the medieval grid on which the town is built. George Street in the south, Castle Street in the north, do lead through small suburban ribbons before reaching the fields on their way to the ancient hamlets of Seward's End and Little Walden. But the other roads east from High Street are blocked by the castle-site in the north (known as Bury Hill), and by the market place established just below the castle to the south. Along the east side of the castle and market place lies the great square green open common, contributing impressively to the definition of the built-up area, though a small piece has (only temporarily, one hopes) been sacrificed to the parking of cars.

Just west of the castle-gate, on slightly lower ground, at respectful distance from the ruined keep, the great medieval church of St Mary rears its long line of decorous battlements in all-round defence against the forces of darkness, and with its great spire (12 ft. taller even than Thaxted's) points finely upwards in a gesture visible for miles. This tower is the work of 1831 (Rickman and Hutchinson), and like the splendid designers of nave in late 15th and early 16th centuries (probably Simon Clerk and John Wastell) the architects were doing famous work at Cambridge, 14 miles away. Thos. Wright (of Trinity) in his *History and Topography of Essex* (2 vols., 1831–5) mentions that the cost of the spire, £3–4,000, was voted by the parishioners to be raised from church rates. Notice, too, that almost £8,000 had been spent on restoring the church in the years 1791–3. Late-Georgian indifference to splendours of Gothic is too often assumed.

Three sentences of Wright in 1835 still apply: "Footpaths, on different roads near the town, have been made or improved, by which pleasant promenades have been furnished to the inhabitants, especially towards Littlebury and Audley End. In addition to horticultural and other societies, an Institution has lately been formed to encourage the cultivation of literature and science. A small museum has been already collected." Walden's museum, at the castle, is one of the liveliest little museums in England. And though the Walden Institution is at present in peril, Walden remains gloriously a place for *walks.*

Walden's name means (from its earliest forms of spelling) "valley of Britons (*Wealh*)", not "wealden" as might be assumed. Whether or not this original valley-settlement was down beside the Cam at Audley End (called Brookwalden till the 16th century) or near Bridge End in the present town (which was known as Cheping or Chipping Walden all through the Middle Ages, from its market), the name "valley of Britons" argues a continuity of settlement here from Romano–British times right through to ours. "Saffron" replaced "Cheping" not through lapse of market, but because the town specialized in the growing of autumn-flowering saffron crocus at the end of the Middle Ages – for use in dyeing and in medicine: the dyeing may well have been used in conjunction with one of the town's other late-medieval mainstays, clothmaking. Saffron is no longer cultivated at Walden, but notice the saffron crocus carved *c.* 1495 in spandrels of an arch of the S. aisle of the church, facing the S. door. Walks in Walden show abundant evidence of medieval prosperity, continued evenly through to the present. The patronage goes back to the Norman Mandevilles, who had a castle here as well as Pleshey, and who founded a priory down beside the Cam; it was advanced to the status of abbey in 1190, acquired by Lord Chancellor Audley at the Dissolution, and descended through his daughter to the Howard earls of Suffolk, lords Howard de Walden, and lords Braybrooke; the house named Audley End, built by the Jacobean earl of Suffolk, was made over to Ministry of Public Building and Works in 1948.

Walks. Start at the *Castle.* Remains of the 11th or 12th-century square keep dull, though oak-shaded, and the adjacent *museum* full of interest, especially for local collections. Notice the shape of the castle-bailey, preserved in the curve where Museum Street joins Castle Street. Nicely plastered cottages on this curve have incredibly low front doors. *Castle Street* is full of medieval cottages. Some (e.g. 1 and 2) have early Victorian embellishments, and the old Railway Mission, now Snowflakes Laundry, is a castellated "folly". There are prospects north from this street, into the country, and one of the pleasantest surprises in Walden, especially on hot summer days, is *Bridge End Garden,* shady with ilexes and clipped box and yew, and with a Georgian domed summerhouse: accessible from Castle Street and from beside the bridge. Bridge

SAFFRON WALDEN Market

End includes some of the most interesting timber-framed housing, especially the *Eight Bells*, well pargeted, and Y.H.A. Hostel, L-shaped, at corner of *Myddelton Place*: late 15th-century, it preserves an oak screen of most unusual design; a big wide arch, almost like a carriage-way, in the middle, and a small doorway each side, all with carved spandrels: the big arch blocked-in with square Tudor panelling. 17th century tapestry, much cut and reshaped, on S. side of screen. The dormitory above the S. wing is open to the rafters and wind braces: this is said to have been used as an old malting, and the oak wheel-hoist is still in position. Outside this wing are two moulded oak oriels: all the plaster has been stripped off to show studs, a particular pity at the east end, where the eaves retain pleasant plaster coving and where the windows

are Georgian. *Myddelton House*, Georgian red brick-fronted is, presumably where Myddelton family lived: their rebus is on a fireplace, *c.* 1534. Next along Myddelton Place is the entrance to *Walden Place*, best seen from the west, from a buttercup meadow in Freshwell Street. It is a plain dignified Georgian red-brick house, behind a stout medieval and Tudor garden wall: it was the manor house (presumably the steward's house), and with that great spire in the background and willows in front one thinks of Salisbury for a moment.

1 Freshwell Street round to 5 Bridge Street is all highly picturesque. Bridge Street merges S. into High Street, and there is a tempting footpath east to the churchyard. 7 High Street has a most elegant Georgian front of flattish bays (there are other examples of these window-bays in town, indeed opposite, in 4–12, which include the Saffron Hotel). Turn left up *Church Street*, quiet, with Georgian fronts, very reminiscent of Bury St Edmunds (though that town, bent on expansion, is no longer quiet).

The S. view of the *church* from Church Street was recently opened up to create a more formal approach: hitherto approached only by agreeable smaller paths across churchyard-close from north, west and south. From outside, the most impressive features apart from the spire, are the length of the building – nearly 200 ft.; the sense of richness and depth created by the way the clerestory windows are coupled by outer delicate traceried stone arcade; and the big glazed S. porch, with sham turrets. The Bourchier emblem (a knot) is in the stone cornice above the clerestory. The stone turrets are topped like crowns at the E. end of the nave clerestory, an obvious link with King's College Chapel (Wastell): it was repeated on the corners of the tower (? in 1831). The main glories, though, are inside. Tall arcading with ornate spandrels is surmounted by a superbly designed clerestory with lower panels like blind lights: all reminiscent of rich late Gothic in many

SAFFRON WALDEN. Market Hill leads direct from the market up to the castle-site

places (Stratford-on-Avon, for example) but especially in Cambridge. Do notice two extremely beautiful E. bays of the nave roof, and the way the three E. window-bays of the N. aisle have blank arcading with carved angels joining hands, and the Tudor rose, crown, and portcullis, by way of reminder whose splendid age this was. The choir roof, magnificent 15th-century carpentry, is painted delightfully (? in the 1790s). Monuments: a few surviving brasses are lined up dejectedly on the N. wall of the N. aisle. At the E. end of the S. choir-aisle, the black marble tomb-chest of Lord Chancellor Audley who acquired the abbey-site at Dissolution: very impressive coat of arms carved by Cornelius Harman: Fuller (*Worthies*) thought this

marble not blacker than the soul, nor harder than the heart, of the man whose bones lie beneath it. (Another tomb-chest and two Jacobean monuments are in the N. aisle.) In the S. aisle, one Braybrooke monument commemorates two young officers who died in one Crimean November week, of 1854; another, the 8th baron's two sons, one killed at sea in 1941, an able seaman, the other in Tunisia, 1943. The state claims full death-duties even in such cases, and so acquired Audley End.

We resume the walk along Church Street. *Old Sun Inn* has almost the best surviving pargeting in England; Gog and Magog over carriage-entrance, and swags and birds on the next gable to left. From here a steep drop down

Market Hill, as from the castle, leads to Chipping Walden's *market-place* which is still the town's centre, as you see on market-days, Tuesday (cattle) and Saturday, when it is thronged: Sunday is the day to look at the buildings in the empty piazza. Originally, the market-place probably stretched along King Street to Cross Street and Market Row, whose shops presumably represent the usual gradual encroachments on ancient stall-sites. King Street, with Hepworth's Georgian shop jutting out at right-angles still feels part of the market-place, which has two dominant buildings on the E. side: the 3-storey cream-stucco'd front, *c.* 1700, of the *Crown* Trust House, with vast dangling emblem of hospitality suspended over its canopied front door – a bunch of

SAFFRON WALDEN: South end of the High Street

golden grapes. The hotel was re-pargeted in his own style by Eden Nesfield, 1874 (see date on black down-pipes), who designed the adjacent red brick bank with "Tudor great-hall" stone windows and late Gothic stone entrance, 1878 on down-pipe. At right-angles on the S. side, the Town Hall was rebuilt in 1879 as the gift of Mr Alderman Gibson. (The Gibsons lived at the S. end of High Street, No. 75, great benefactors of the town, and G.S., the Quaker banker, compiled the *Flora* of Essex, 1862.) Newsagents alongside, with a splendid little Corinthian portico-front. The W. side of the square is occupied by the low, single-storey, *Corn Exchange* with central portico and clock tower, in early-Victorian "Vanbrugh" style, by R. Tress;

the stone colonnaded effect makes a good transition to King Street, where the Literary Institution continues it. Before going down King Street, leave the market-place by the N.E. corner and walk over to the E. side of the Common to see one of the half-dozen surviving *Troy Towns* or *Mazes* of Britain. It deserves careful preservation. When Titania said:

"And the quaint mazes in the
wanton green
For lack of tread are
undistinguishable"

she was describing the present condition of this one: the green not noticeably wanton, but the maze overgrown. Its plan is reproduced in the Royal Commission's volume. Treading-the-maze is one of those unsophisticated medieval

entertainments that may, like Walden itself, represent a survival from Romano–British times. Back in King Street, turn left down Cross Street, where early Tudor shop-windows remain on the side of 17 King Street, also opposite, at the side of *The Hoops*. Cross into Gold Street, an untroubled street of old houses and cottages of different periods, climbing the hill with stepped roof-ridges and pleasant natural curve in middle. A sharp bend at the top, where a russet plastered cottage terminates the view. From the bend look back at one of best views of the church. Gold Street leads into the upper, southern, end of High Street.

Gold Street and the S. end of High Street are apparently part of a very interesting town extension in the 13th century: a rectangular earthwork 300 yards to the west, known as Pell, Paille, or Re-pell Ditches, seems to have marked this new enclosure. Observe well-preserved houses of the 18th, 17th and 16th centuries descending High Street. The *Cross Keys* is impressive at the corner of King Street; and higher up, No. 18, stripped of plaster on 1st floor, but with pretty pargeting below, and kiln in rear. West from High Street the pleasantest approach to Audley End is on foot along

Abbey Lane. The lane demonstrates the range of 19th-century building-fashions: Congregational Church, 1811, an unusually "fashionable" classical temple of the Lord; Jubilee Sunday Schools, 1861, show extraordinary Gothic thoughts of fifty years later, red-and-black brick window-arches very instructive; then the "Edward VI Almshouses" (in fact instituted in 1400 by Archbishop Roger Walden of Canterbury), handsome "collegiate Tudor" of those 1830s, that saw such good work in Walden, with separate

wings of 1840 and 1881 (given by the Gibson family). The bottom of the "Pell Ditches" is visible opposite the almshouses. Inside the Park Gate look back at St Mary's spire and Walden Place. Take the footpath forking left, for *Audley End village,* blissfully rural, Georgian farm-houses and one street, which starts with the farm-cottage Post Office (kept by a nephew of the preacher Spurgeon), and goes on to two infinitely attractive long ranges of old cottages, following the slight curve of the lane, each with a window on either side of the front door and two dormers over. At the end, *St Mark's College,* designed as almshouses *c.* 1600 on a collegiate plan, two quadrangles of ten dwellings, divided down the middle by the taller range of chapel, hall and kitchen. One quad became a farmhouse, but all was restored, and the E. end of the chapel rebuilt to the old design, *c.* 1948–51, to the great benefit now of retired clergy. The mantelpiece of the dining-room is fitted with a magnificent late

17th-century wooden overmantel carved with (extremely secular) masks and swags of fruit. The E. window of the chapel and other windows of the central block are fitted with scattered fragments of fine 14th- and 15th-century stained glass (Norwich School), possibly from the abbey. A crowned Virgin with child is in the central light.

Audley End. Open daily April–October 10.30–5.30: guides a.m., roam p.m. The abbey was sited west of the town "at the confluence of two streams and meeting of four roads, for the convenience of the poor and of travellers". The deep red Tudor-brick building known as the Stables, between the river and A11, just possibly may, as at Eye priory, Suffolk, have survived the Dissolution as a recent rebuilding of the monastic guest-house; at least on ground floor and 1st floor. Otherwise nothing monastic remains but mill-race and riverside (enhanced by Capability Brown and Adam). The house, so palatial, faced with stone from Wiltshire and Rutland, is nevertheless

SAFFRON WALDEN, Audley End: the chapel

only the heart of the great quadrangular series laid out 1603–16 for Thomas Howard, 1st earl of Suffolk, who ruined himself by spending public funds on it. His uncle, Northampton, and the mason and sculptor Bernard Janssen may have designed the building, of which the present front looked W. into another (principal) court! Behind the present building, the wings were closed by a great gallery, from which more wings, including a chapel, projected east. The vast forecourts came down in 1721, with the advice of Vanbrugh who designed the brilliantly theatrical stone screen in the S. end of the Jacobean great-hall. The great-hall occupies 2 storeys of the main front, its importance obscured externally by the late 18th-century picture-gallery added to the 3rd storey just in rear of the hall. Nevertheless the two 2-storey arcaded stone porches into the hall, with splendidly carved doors, do much to compensate the loss of the former grand front entrances: the N. door is carved with Peace emblems, the south, less richly, with War. Pretty Georgian ironwork garland bell-pull. Inside, the original Jacobean N. screen is carved with excesses verging on the Mexican baroque. The panelled ceiling is slightly canted: decorative medallions dangle midway between the wall-posts on the E. wall. Vanbrugh's S. screen, staircase and staircase-ceiling steal the show, lure one up before one has begun to size up the full-length Cornwallis portraits that came here, by marriage, in 1819. On the stairs, notice Pepys's Lord Sandwich, and a candid portrait of the Royalist colonel Lunsford. The ceiling of the staircase probably started the Georgian fashion that now provides the greatest aesthetic pleasure at Audley End, continuing the decoration in a "Jacobean" style. The painted fireplace in the saloon, e.g., is *Georgian* Jacobean, a great improvement on the

original Jacobean! Portraits in the saloon are mostly by Biagio Rebecca, who worked at Heveningham (Suffolk) with Wyatt, and who designed the Last Supper for the E. window in the Georgian Gothick chapel at Audley End. As engaging as anything even at Arbury (Warwicks.), this chapel is said to be by Hobcraft. Rebecca also worked in the Alcove Room, riotously pretty, a glittering toy room, 1769. In the dining-room, Pine's portrait of George II faces Beechey's magnificent Cornwallis, the two old soldiers averting their eyes from each other. Dobson's portrait of (traditionally) Charles Lucas (see Colchester) shows a worried, sensitive face and is certainly one of the most vivid evocations of the Civil War ever painted. Nearby, Lely's masterly double portrait of himself and friend Hugh May does not fail to convey the Restoration spirit.

Two downstairs rooms by Adam have lately been carefully restored: the Great drawing-room, with pink, green, and white silk wall-covering beautifully copied by Warner of Braintree, and the dining-parlour which contains the most remarkable picture in the house, Eworth's portrait of Audley's daughter, 1562, who brought the estate to the Howards; it also contains one of the most charming and sentimental, by a little-regarded painter, W. R. Bigg, showing the lodgekeeper sharpening his scythe, and his wife spinning, outside the little Doric lodge here, 1786.

For Adam's work here, creating e.g. the handsome 3-arch bridge over the Cam, 1771 (begun 1763–4), indeed for all the details – Ring Hill temple of 1771–3 (commemorating the Peace of 1763), palladian bridge and tea-house 1782–3, obelisk 1774, the Lion Gateway with Howard crest in Coade stone, 1786 – and for an insight into the life-story of the house, William Addison's book, *Audley End*, 1953, is an indispensable pleasure. For some of the building details the new dating given in this paragraph is accepted. The Temple of Concord,

SAFFRON WALDEN,
Audley End: the obelisk

SAFFRON WALDEN, *Audley End*

1790–1 (by Robert Furze Brett-ingham) is the one major orna-ment not designed by Adam.

In the environs, the hamlets of Walden, many public and private delights remain: *Cinder Hall*, for instance, on the road to Little Walden, is an astonishing Geor-gian castellated "Tudor" folly of flint and red brick liberally decorated with black cinders; *Campions*, at Seward's End, Eliza-bethan, has an elaborately painted room described in the Royal

Commission's volume; and *St Aylott's* a rectangular house of *c.* 1500, on site of a messuage of same name bought by the abbey in the 13th century, is the subject of a touching last letter from the 4th duke of Norfolk, beheaded in 1572, to his son the builder of Audley End.

Waltham Abbey (4), a small town, speaking more Cockney than Essex, lies within the large parish and U.D. of WALTHAM

HOLY CROSS. Waltham means "forest-homestead". Epping For-est was known as Waltham Forest in the Middle Ages; about a third of it lies in this parish. There is an Iron Age hill-fort at Ambresbury Banks. Early in the 11th century, a holy cross was found through a vision at Montacute in Somerset, and Tofig the Proud, Cnut's standard-bearer, built a church for

SAFFRON WALDEN:
Audley End: the hall

it at Waltham. Harold rebuilt it for a college of secular canons, and richly endowed it; he was probably buried here after Hastings, when the bishops of Durham got the manor. Henry II converted the college into a great abbey to expiate guilt for Beckett's murder. What is left has clear building-links with Durham. Activity in Domesday: 47½ plough-teams; still forest enough to feed 2,382 swine; meadows, mills and fisheries along the River Lea. Market here already, 1189; held on Tuesdays ever since 1560, at the edge of the abbey churchyard.

The *Welsh Harp Inn*, in a long timber-framed range, divides market-square from churchyard. A Co-op corner-post opposite is carved with well-preserved hermaphrodite and jug. The *Bakers Arms* is in a good group. Lychgate passage through Welsh Harp leads to churchyard and view of abbey-church.

What survives is 100 ft. of nave, saved as parish church at the Dissolution. Not Harold's work, as is often claimed, but a rebuilding of the early and middle 1100s, the W. front rebuilt again *c.* 1315 and the Lady Chapel added on S. side in 1320s. West tower 1550s, top storey 1905. In 1938, excavation showed that E. of the nave little less than *300 feet* have disappeared. The present E. wall was remodelled in 1859–60.

From the *Welsh Harp* lychgate, the height of the Norman work is impressive. So is the rich variety of building materials, from the limestone corbel-table in two E. bays of the clerestory to patches of rusty puddingstone in the earlier W. bays, and the chalky white of the 1905 belfry contrasts with the mottled buffs of the rest of the tower.

Inside, the massive Romanesque arcading is relieved by the colour and texture in Burges's E. wall and in the painted oak ceiling, a flat Victorian version of the original Norman ceiling at Peterborough, with Signs of the Zodiac in rippling lozenge-patterns. Before the Reformation, the whole interior would have glimmered with painting. Fuller, author of

Worthies and of a history of Waltham Abbey, perpetual curate here in the 1650s, reported the tradition that deep spiral grooves in some pillars were filled with brass. Unpainted, unbrass-bound, the chiselled patterns on stone look restrained, the zigzags on the outer faces of round arches like pieces of delicate mechanism.

Undivided arches of the gallery gape above these, and in the next tier the clerestory is in triple arches, like "Venetian" windows. At the W. end an attempt to link aisle and gallery arches vertically in one tall Gothic scheme was rightly discontinued. Decorative Georgian monuments and hatchments hang on the outer walls of the aisles, framed in the lower arcades. Against one grooved pier, the elegant Stuart pulpit and sounding-board rise; behind them lurks a very "antique" marble bust of Henry Wollaston, J.P., 1670, in Roman costume. Beyond him, through a traceried 14th-century screen, Captain Robert Smith's white marble altar-tomb, 1697, carved with cherubs in tears, displays his ship, *Industria*, sailing through a sea full of dolphins.

In S. aisle, Sir Edward Denny, 1599, grips the kind of sword with which he laid about him in Ireland, repainted by Miss I. Northolt, 1965. The S. chapel, raised on an undercroft, has fine window-tracery that was hidden behind 17th-century brickwork till the restoration of 1876. At the same time a painted Doom was uncovered. It has faded, but occupies the top half of the whole E. wall of the chapel like a splendid Angers tapestry.

The E. wall of the sanctuary was brilliantly remodelled by the young Victorian Gothic architect Wm. Burges within the awkward framework of the round W. arch of the former tower and a low medieval wall (to the height of the reredos) that divided abbey church from parish church. The reredos, carved by W. G. Nicholl, is gilded: 4 scenes of the Nativity. Above, a stringcourse, like a narrow coved canopy, is carved with Aesop's fables (Fox and Crane: Wolf and Crane). Above that

three single-light windows are set in a triple arcade with marble shafts that emphasize the solidity of the wall to the height that would embrace a wheel-window within the Romanesque curve. The glass in these windows, glorious blues and flame-colours, is by Burne-Jones. Sculpture, arcading and glass in this wall unite; they restore balance and vitality to a building that had suffered almost mortal truncation.

The abbey site is bare except for a brief vaulted passage, a gateway and a bridge. A beast-market is still held in Romeland, west of the church. To the south-west Paradise Road and Row have been "improved" away in 1960s. Old urban yellow-brick buildings, like 1–9 Green Yard, have given way, opposite, to placeless 3-storey flats and to suburban bungalows at Abbey Court. A little riverside sitting-place, at Cornmill, is bleakly U.D.C. The Baptist church, 1836 Gothick, survives. Powder Mill Lane, north of High Bridge Street, lately a Min. of Aviation prohibited area, marks the site of an explosives factory from the Civil War right down to 1943. About 160 acres of glasshouses literally reflect intensive market-gardening. *Sewardstone* is completely rural at *Carol's Farm*, white-weatherboarded beside its duck-pond; also at Burn Hill, with industrial views over the River Lea. It includes *High Beach* (or Beech, for it is spelt either way; there are plenty of beech-trees, but beach, meaning "bank", is equally valid), where *The Owl* is a neat weatherboarded old pub with views south over London from Lippett's Hill. Tennyson lived at *Beech Hill Park* 1837–40, still mourning Hallam. The Christmas bells of Waltham abbey released from him:

"Ring out, wild bells, to the
wild sky,
The flying cloud, the frosty light:
The year is dying in the night;
Ring out, wild bells, and let
him die."

WALTHAM ABBEY
William Burges's east wall

In 1848 Edward Stephens sculptured a Diana for the house. In 1850 the house was transformed. The spire of Sir A. Bloomfield's church, 1873, embowered in birch and beech, is a landmark for forest-walkers. It has good Victorian glass, and, alas, a carillon. These woods give joy in the four seasons. Edward Thomas, stationed near the King's Oak during the war that killed him (his wife took one of the cottages between it and *The Robin Hood*) naturally preferred the open farmland of the Essex Tyes:

"Wingle Tye and Margaretting Tye, – and Skreens, Gooshays and Cockerells".

Upshire, see separately.

Waltham, Great (6). There are eight hamlets in the parish, which stretches 5½ miles along the W. bank of the Chelmer from Felsted almost to Chelmsford. *North End*: *Brook Farmhouse*, 15th-century with tall 16th-century chimney stacks, has been stripped of plaster. *The Black Chapel*, a medieval wayside chapel, is one of the best sights in Essex. High above the farming plateau, at a road junction, among chestnuts, limes and a rookery, the outside looks domestic, with the chaplain's house built into it. It is all timber-framed and roughcast, with the windows of N. aisle and S. nave a simple early 19th-century Gothick. Inside, it is like being in an upturned boat. Box pews and double-decker pulpit all along the S. side; 15th-century oak pews down the N. side; there is a W. gallery with an old barrel-organ: a traceried screen; and the Lord's Prayer, Ten Commandments and Creed form the reredos. The Arms of Queen Anne are faded in a tympanum over the screen. Small squires' pews in the chancel give one a strong sense of sitting in a small boat. *Ford End* is dominated by St John's red brick church, of 1871–93. Evangelists look out from the corners of the belfry. Industrial buildings at Hartford Bridge are largely a 19th-century brewery, but 300 yards upstream is a fine watermill.

The original settlement is presumably at *Walthambury* up on the Pleshey road, but a village grew up around the church and Langleys manor, whose beautiful park runs from a delightful toy-like lodge, near the church, down to the river. It is an attractive village, much interrupted by motor traffic on A130. A house at the N.E. corner of the churchyard, with three pairs of tall chimney shafts and newly "dated" 1560, has been much over-restored: the Royal Commission's volume shows how it was. In

"Being, rather than seeming to be", is a good motto for the lodge of Langleys, GREAT WALTHAM, whose Georgian beauty is quite real. The arms are those of J. J. Tufnell who succeeded to Langleys in 1820

1805, the vicar authorized the carver John Challis of Braintree to supply the gravestones for this churchyard. The E. wall of the chancel is Norman (see twin windows outside). Approach from the south between old cottages on the village street, and enter by the very broad S. porch, which has a well timbered roof. The immensely broad nave and aisles contain lots of medieval pews. Tower-arch of c. 1200. Of eight bells, one goes back to the middle of the 14th century. There is a handsome marble to Richard Sorrel, 1738, and Richard Tyson, President of the Royal College of Physicians. A grey marble, showing a shipwreck on the Goodwins, 1703, relates the story of an adventurous younger son of the Everards who at 13 abandoned Felsted school for the sea, slew a Spanish commander of horse, and at 16 was drowned. A beautifully restored monument of highly original design was put up to commemorate his Barnardiston wife by Sir Anthony Everard, 1611: two small round-headed windows, with their arms in stained glass, light the monument from inside the marble frame. It is as if they recline under a window at home: anonymous babies lie on the floor beside them. The Everards had *Langleys* from the 13th century until they were forced to sell, in 1711, to Samuel Tufnell, a city magnate to whose taste the house underwent a distinguished remodelling, incorporating the library and old dining-room of the Everard house. An astonishing plasterwork fireplace of c. 1620 makes that Everard tomb look very subdued. Tufnell's own celebrated saloon (he is thought to have been his own architect) also has a fireplace of high virtuosity, by Isaac Mansfield of London, master-plasterer. The house, of great perfections, is still meticulously maintained by a Mr Tufnell.

Waltham, Little (6), across the Chelmer from Gt. Waltham. The church, on a slight rise, has a medieval flint W. tower liberally repaired in red Tudor brick that looks extremely well from due west in the evening sun. The interior is unexciting.

Walton-on-the-Naze (15), marvellously situated on a Nose, or Ness, nuzzling north into shallow sea, giving the town south-easterly sea-views from fossil-bearing red-crag cliffs, and even better westward views over winding backwaters and creeks around Horsey Island. Devoted mostly to day-trippers at summer week-ends.
It appears as "Eadwulf's ness" in Domesday Book, part of the "soken" or "liberty" of the canons of St Paul's, London, and certainly it ran much further seawards then. The medieval church was submerged in 1796, somewhere between the pier and the massive stone breakwater to the north. The worst hazard to coastal craft, *West Rocks*, lurk 4½ miles to the east of the bleak, untapered 80-ft. *Trinity House tower* (three storeys, brick, 1720, the top two rebuilt after 1810). The main sailing channel, *Goldmer Gat*, is extremely shallow, and Walton pier projects 800 ft. to obtain 6 ft. of water.
The Pier, on rustic-looking legs, began with 330 ft. in 1830, running out from the foot of the cliff. The Cliff was "thrown down on an inclined plane" in order to give a fuller view from *Kent's Family Hotel*, erected in 1832. The whole scene, with visiting steam-packet, was engraved that year. Wright's *Essex*, in 1835, advertised the pleasures, including the gathering of *eringo*, sea-holly, whose root was candied hopefully as a love-potion; and by the 1860s there were "often more than 500 visitors". Ford Madox Brown painted the place at this stage. Peter Bruff, the railway engineer, put up *Clifton Music Hall* in 1862.
Over the subsequent century Walton has gained in popularity, not in beauty. There is no single building to delight the eye. Mrs Kent's Family Hotel has become *Barker's Marine Hotel*. There is a seemly stucco terrace to the north, but most of the textures are ugly, and the cliff is edged with iron rails and stout wire mesh. The most truly "seaside-looking" buildings are back in Savile Street, off High Street. Grey ragstone Victorian church. Caravan camp

beside Martello tower: car-parks, coach-parks and pavements packed solid in summer.

Warley, Great (8), on the woodland edge south-west of Brentwood. Its medieval church of St Mary lay in ruins south of A127, and was finally demolished in 1966. This ruin had been annexed to Greater London, with much of the old parish, but not the most interesting part. Likewise, the Victorian church is in a Brentwood suburb: *Christchurch*, 1855 "E.E.", by Teulon, who also did the vicarage. All the interest in the parish is concentrated on the third church, *New St Mary's*, built 1902–4, near *Warley Elms* and several late Victorian houses by E. Heseltine, half-timbered, tile-hung, and now rather down-at-heel, unlike Mr Todd's old smithy and farrier's shop, and unlike the church.
New St Mary's must be one of the most complete "Art-nouveau" churches in England. Designed by Charles Harrison Townsend within a couple of years of the Paris Exposition, it has the comfortable feel of a middle-class Edwardian suburb outside, though the spire is surmounted by a most sinister dove: too big! The inside is glorious, decorated by Sir William Reynolds-Stephens. The nave-roof is barrel-vaulted, with silver bands, or ribs: at their base, white briars and lilies, of aluminium leaf. The walls are panelled with walnut, set with ebony, beech and mother-of-pearl; the patterns include roses of Sharon. The font is composed of two bronze angels and a cover like an ink-well. The screen is of brass trees bearing deep-red glass pomegranates, mother-of-pearl flowers, with angels of oxidized silver, all on an Irish marble base. The pulpit is simply fronted with a hammered copper cross; the reading-desk supported on a formation of bronze roses of Sharon. The Risen Christ shines silver behind the altar. Except in chancel and transept, the stained glass is

dreadfully unsuitable, like the W. wall of 1946. The church was endowed by Evelyn Heseltine in memory of his brother Arnold, 1852–97, and the foundation was laid by his wife, Minnie.

Attractive cottages of the 15th, 16th and 17th centuries are grouped round the Green: best of all, *Blake Cottage*, Georgian.

Warley, Little (8). Long, narrow north–south parish with good recent developments in edge of Barrack Wood, and stretching S. across A127, the hair-raising speedway to Southend, which renders church and Hall almost inaccessible. The little church, with 1718 red-and-black brick tower, is secluded with the *Hall*, which is on modest scale, but with an impressive 2-storey early-Tudor front porch, of diapered red brick, step-gabled, and with adjacent tall brick chimney shafts, highly ornamental, one spiral, one zigzag. Appealing monuments in the *church*: on black marble shelves, Sir Denner Strutt and his first wife lie side-by-side (she higher), carved in brown-streaked white marble, beneath white marble curtains drawn aside by rather crudely made cherubs: 1641. His third wife, Mary, in her shroud, watches them across the chancel, propped on elbow, 1658. What became of the second wife? Perhaps the well-carved alabaster Father Time, reclining on the N. side of the nave, is from her lost monument?

Back at Eagle Way, new Central Offices of Ford Motor Company have gone up on the site of the 1805 E. India Company barracks (T. P. Bennett and Son, 1964, a shade ponderous). Next to it, the *Essex Regimental Museum* and the basilica-chapel of the Essex Regiment since 1925. The museum is well kept, with letters from Waterloo, etc., and ending with a bugle captured by C. Coy., 1/4th Bn. from 164 Panzer Grenadier regt. of Afrika Korps. Vivid photo of 2nd Bn. fighting in streets of Arnhem. Replicas of keys of the watergates, Gibraltar, 1779–83. *Keys Hall* in the smart new shopping-centre is a reference to Gibraltar. First-rate housing nearby

at *Becket Close* (Clifford Culpin & Partners), and also at *Essex Way*.

Weald, North (5: usually called *North Weald Bassett*) has been largely stripped of the woodland to which it owes name: the most obvious features now are wireless masts and R.A.F. station. Bassets were 13th-century lords of manor. The 17th-century schoolhouse is by the church, which was damaged by fire in 1964, but which is interesting for having preserved not only the rood-screen but the fine under-coving of the rood-loft: the screen is inscribed "Orate pro bono statu Thome Wyher, diacon". Brick tower like Epping Upland's.

Weald, South (8). Large parish of woods and valleys, west of Brentwood. The medieval church is grouped charmingly near a corner with an early 19th-century villa distinguished by its iron-work verandah. The big grey rag-stone-faced tower is topped by prominent stair-turret. A heavy Victorian restoration by Teulon included the S. front, now mercifully rose-grown: his S. windows are so absurdly small that the inside is gloomy on the brightest day. The memorials have been collected together under the tower, but at the E. end of the S. aisle a monument to Hugh Smith, 1757, has a charming relief, and there is a most interesting brass in the N.E. corner of the S. chapel: Sir Anthony Browne, C.J. of Common Pleas, a "younger sonne", 1567, founder of Brentwood School. Opposite the church, the *Tower Arms*, brick-fronted in 1704, with Victorian diapered front-garden wall. Adjoining church, Weald Park is accessible to the public. Weald Hall and a castellated belvedere were demolished in 1950.

Rochetts, the home of Nelson's old admiral Jervis, Lord St Vincent, still has a curious undecipherable stone trophy of his at the entrance, and a rather jolly-looking large pedimented red-brick house at the end of the ancient chestnut-drive. The dead

oak still stands that he planted to commemorate Waterloo. At *St Vincent's Hamlet*, two of the original little Gothick semi-detached cottages survive. Of several good Georgian houses, *Gilstead Hall* is now owned by Queen Mary College.

Weeley (14). The low church tower is of rosy Tudor bricks, remarkably big (11¼ in. by 5¼ in.), the rest red-brick of 1881. It is attractively isolated, with a large pond to the south. Enter through the W. door past a heartbreaking photo of the interior in 1880, with glorious late 17th-century pulpit, a superbly panelled double decker with tester, swept away next year with plaster ceiling, hat-pegs, notices and other homely paraphernalia, in the interest of chilly late Victorian asepticism. Well-coloured window in memory of a Cassino casualty, 1944. *Hillside House* is astonishing Victorian Gothic, with a step-gabled gateway from the road, 1858. *Ashe Farm* is a lovely old jettied, plastered and cream-washed farmhouse.

Wenden Lofts (2), a small parish almost swallowed in the great open landscape of Elmdon. An Elizabethan quadrangular *Hall* was replaced, in 1965, by a very large neo-Georgian house (architect, Hamilton), behind the 18th-century brick wall with urns. The *church* of St Dunstan, 1845, incorporated a fine Norman doorway with chevron moulding, all fast dilapidating: the glass is now at Elmdon.

Wendens Ambo (2). The approach to the W. front of church is unforgettable, cottages on the left, glorious broad sweep of thatch on the Hall barn on the right, and the square Norman church-tower ahead, its grey flint pierced by ancient openings, the stone piers of its W. doorway crowned by a semicircular fan of Roman red brick: the whole tower topped by a graceful spire. Within, there are delightful textures: of the walls, painted with St Margaret's life, and of the medieval woodwork, especially pulpit, screen and benches: a sad, rather elephantine tiger angrily paws a mirror on one benchend. The *Hall* may originally have been an aisled building.

Westcliff-on-Sea *see* Southend-on-Sea.

Wethersfield (3) rises steeply on the E. side of the Upper Blackwater, and spreads 3 miles southwest from its formidably square-towered church, which crouches over the main village. Tower *c.* 1200: the rather Baltic-looking pyramidal roof and stubby copper spire were "modern" in 1916. The brick clerestory is perhaps Tudor, but rebuilt after the upper stage of the tower was pulled down in ? the 17th century. The brick N. porch was rebuilt in 1750. The S. porch contains the old font and a medieval door. The unattractive interior has a tomb of *c.* 1480 of perhaps Wentworths of Codham Hall (who are also to be seen at Gosfield); also a memorial to Barbara Mott, *c.* 1752, "who faithfully practised all the duties proper to her sex and station through the several stages of a long life"; and another to an astonishing dead redcoat, Everard Marsh, 1880, in a window signed by Ch. Champigneulle, of Bar-le-Duc.
Charming small villas, cottages, shops are seen through plane trees on the small triangular Green: white-brick chapel stands next to red-brick Victorian school.
Codham Mill stands 2½ miles to the south-east: cream weatherboarding, 3-storey, early 18th-century, the old mill house at right angles. Nearby, *Little Codham Hall is a* 17th-century farmhouse with tall brick chimney-stacks. *Great Codham Hall*, fronting north, has the late 14th-century hall of the Wentworths (see Gosfield) under its tall middle hipped roof. The house was modernized and extended to the east in the 16th century, to the west probably in the 17th. A cottage nearby was a medieval chapel.

Wicken Bonhunt (2). The *Coach and Horses* has a cheerful fret-work inn sign, and *Wicken House* (the Victorian rectory, now owned by Essex C.C.) is less cheerful, beside the *church*, which is twilit even on a dazzling summer's day. It has tablets to three Bradburys dead in their twenties in the 1690s, and Scheemakers' relief of that hopeful youth J. J. Bradbury, 1731, being helped into heaven by a cherub. He seems to have been the last of them. They lived at *Brick House*, beautiful red brickwork of *c.* 1600 remodelled with curved gables *c.* 1660, and still provided with a stone statue of a headless man in Roman dress on the N.E. corner of the roof parapet, and a bust of an emperor in a roundel over the front door, with Bradbury arms. Farther east, a small thatched late Norman chapel is secularized among farm buildings.

Wickford (9). Essex County Council proposes to convert suburban straggle of nearly 12,000 people (1961) into small town of 28,000 by 1981.

Wickham Bishops (13), on west-facing slopes down to the Blackwater, where the Georgian group of Wickham Mills stands, and to the south the picturesque derelict ancient church of Bartholomew and the moated *Hall* of the 17th century – presumably on the site of a manor-house of the Bishops of London. It was Simon Sudbury's favourite seat before he became archbishop in 1375. There is a meeting of boundaries with Totham, Witham and Braxted up near Beacon Hill (272 ft.), with noble views south-east to the Blackwater estuary. Up here, among continuous woods, Ewan Christian's church and spire of 1850 stand, and several pleasant houses. The most delightful, technically just in Great Totham, is *Great Ruffins*, of 1904, by Mackmurdo: a stucco'd concrete belvedere, amid a beautiful garden, its octagonal lantern is reached by iron spiral from the 1st floor. Mackmurdo lived next door (to the west) in another of his creations, and finally settled in a bungalow now named *Mackmurdo's* at the corner of Great Lodge Road and Beacon Hill.

Wickham St Paul (3). The sturdy early-Tudor church-tower is of the red brick from Gestingthorpe. It is well grouped with Wickham *Hall* (of white-painted brick) but from the north the effect is ruined by a large pylon. Farmhouses and unkempt old cottages are gathered round the village-green, with cricket pitch, pond and *Victory* pub.

Widdington (2), secluded farmlands, with lovely descent to the upper Cam. The *Hall*, cream-plastered, with three irregular gables facing the front, has an interesting great tiled sweep of roof behind that, formerly covering the medieval aisled hall. One timber arch of the aisle is still visible on the ground floor. There are two crown posts and some charring in the roof. *Priors Hall*, based on a stone house of the 13th century, has a magnificent tiled and clapboarded 15th-century barn. The *rectory* is cased in handsome Georgian brick. The *church*, much rebuilt, nevertheless retains a 14th-century oak S. door. The S. chancel window (*c.* 1280 according to the R.C.), shafted, has leaf-capitals, one with a bird carved in foliage. Wild-life reserve up the road, at Debden.

Widford *see* Chelmsford.

Wigborough, Great and **Little** (13). *Great* Wigborough church is in a fine situation, Abberton reservoir to the north, and a view across *Moulshams Farmhouse* (thought to be basically 14th-century) to Peldon church. Approach through a long lane walled with close-planted tall young limes. The fabric is mainly septaria. There are excellent 15th-century carved hammerbeam roofs, with gilded Victorian angels. The Victorian glazing is mostly good. £3,000 were spent on restoration after the 1884 earthquake. *Seaborough Farmhouse* has pretty Gothick

windows. *Little* Wigborough church, down a long lane starting with two delightful cottages, stands in a farmyard overlooking the broad Blackwater estuary. There are nice Victorian ironwork fittings, but some are lately painted sky-blue! Hit by gunfire over Wanstead, the German zeppelin raider L.33 came down in this lane on a September night in 1916. An unlucky Little Wigborough child was christened Zeppelina Clark.

The Willingales (5: still called DOE and SPAINS, after Norman lords, d'Eu and d'Epaignes). The churches stand side by side in a small village street, commanding fine views to the west, but firmly divided from each other by a screen of five limes, with noble elms beyond. *Spain's* church, the smaller, was lately saved through energies of Friends of Friendless Churches. Its Norman nave, crowned by pretty white-clapboarding on belfry and little spire, and entered through an unusual 19th-century clapboarded S. porch, is ceiled. There is an inscribed 14th-century bell. Norman S. doorway, and much 12th-century ironwork inside the modern N. door. Oolite altar slab. In the S. windowsill of the chancel is a memorial (on vellum in a folding wooden frame) to six children, 1613–52, of Edward Bewsey, D.D.: "Six blossums here lie shaken from the tree". Willingale *Doe's* church is ceiled, the chancel pleasantly light. A large 17th-century Wiseman monument has three well carved marble figures. A brass shows Thos. Torrell armour-plated in 1442. *Torrell's Hall* was extended by John Johnson who became Surveyor to the county of Essex in 1782, and also designed Willingale rectory.

Wimbish (2) divides Thaxted from Saffron Walden. *Tiptofts Farm* (near Sewards End) is one of the most spell-binding antiquities in England, as well as being

WIVENHOE

the hub of a working farm that Mr Haigh has built up to more than 600 acres in forty years, largely through his understanding of the need for thorough pipe-draining in the heavy boulder-clay. A moat surrounds the house, as usual on old clay-belt farm-houses in Essex and Suffolk. Across it, the good Victorian brick façade gives no hint of the astonishing interior – the brick floor worn by generations of feet, the two great timber roof-trusses, with capitals carved on their main posts and spandrels carved at the main joints, the original frame of (and the actual sense of being in) a great open 14th-century aisled hall. From the floor, the vast red-brick chimney inserted during the Tudor age funnels aloft through the timber trusses. An oak door-way of the original screen survives. *Broadoaks Farm* (Braddocks), *Pinkneys* and *Thunderley Hall*, all rewarding: *Broadoaks* contains the hiding-place of the Jesuit priest, John Gerard, in 1594 (cf. Northend Place, Gt. Waltham). Till 1425, *Thunderley* had its own church. Wimbish church, with a Norman S. doorway, contains delicate 14th-century oak screens, 14th-century heraldic glass (Fitz-Walters of Wimbish Hall), beautiful small brasses of Sir John de Wantone and lady, 1347 – perhaps the builder of the great hall at Tiptofts. The N. aisle roof is well carved and dated 1534.

Witham (6), pronounced Wit'm, was described in 1548 as "a thoroughfare town for the king's liege people to lodge in". That was its essential character from probably the 13th century until the middle 1960s, when the great new A12 by-pass took the through-traffic past, and when a thorough programme of industrialization began the work that will quickly quadruple the size of the town. The by-pass has come just in time. Built as a medieval and Georgian thoroughfare, *Newland Street* still bears a remarkably close resemblance to G. B. Campion's drawing of it (in Wright's *Essex*) at the end of the Georgian age. But a few more

years of heavy motor traffic would have destroyed it.

The town probably began with the massive 10th-century mound-fortress (912) with which King Edward, the Elder of Alfred's sons, forced terms on the Danes to the north. The mainline railway that reached Colchester in 1843 was driven straight through this mound, which nevertheless retains impressive proportions. It is best seen from Armond Road, off Mill Lane down in the Guithavon valley (a curious name which sounds like the invention of a local Georgian antiquary who believed the name of the town derived from this small tributary of the Blackwater).

A "new town" called Wulnesford was recorded in 1213. This may refer to the shift of business to the old A12 thoroughfare, which is still called Newland Street for most of its length. The earlier town site was presumably *Chipping Hill*, near the 10th-century fortress and beside the medieval church. Chipping means market, and the original market here of the Cressing Templars was presumably held on this hill where ancient timber-framed houses cluster round the Green. The *church* is mostly late-medieval, including a stout S. door set in an earlier doorway of *c.* 1200. A monument to Mary Hervey, 1592, whose husband Francis was one of the Queen's "honourable band of gentlemen pensioners", says they "kept house in worshipful estate and credit at Cressing Temple" twenty-seven years. Also notice a monument to an Elizabethan judge, the spirited arms of William III, and the good bust of a Middle Templer by C. Horsnaile. A tablet recalls William Henry Pattisson and his bride, drowned together in a Pyrenean lake in 1832.

Morant wrote in 1768: "The Pattissons, eminent shopkeepers here, have of late adorned this place with good brick houses, more than any other persons". Entering from the north in his day, Lord Abercorn's house, *The Grove* (lately demolished: its site marked by cedars), stood back from the road on the left, near the present police station: the Abercorns had planted a long avenue opposite, composed now of silver birches and the metal lamp-standards of inter-War housing. But *Avenue House*, looking exactly as it did in Wright's *Essex*, still has its early 18th-century glazing and fire-insurance plaque. On the left is the *Red Lion*, and then the *White Hart*, both displaying good signs: beyond that, the *Spread Eagle*, and, farther on, three banks, all occupying Georgian brick houses probably put up by the Pattissons. Opposite the White Hart, an extensive concrete-framed Wimpey "New Town Central Development" is going up in 1968. Out in "Industrial Area East", a big new Micro-electronics plant – the biggest in Europe – has been designed for Marconi & Co., by Anthony B. Davies and Associates: a clean white pile with a pert trio of grey barley-sugar chimneys.

The railway makes some amends for its initial vandalism by providing a view of a pleasant Georgian house, colour-washed ginger, beside the Guithavon stream, a contrast to the neighbouring suburban expansion. Before the Maldon branch of the Maldon–Witham–Braintree line closed in 1966, it displayed to perfection the *Blue Mills* on the Blackwater, the mill weather-boarded and *Mathyns* a Georgian house in red brick.

Wivenhoe (14), pronounced Wivv'n-ho, has a quay on the Colne river opposite Fingringhoe, to which a ferry plies. Extensively restored in 1860 and after the 1884 earthquake, the church is a dull building at close quarters though it contains the fine large early-Tudor brasses of Lord and Lady Beaumont, Lord B. provided with elephant and castle "stops"; also their chaplain. From across the river, it looks very well with its small cupola among trees on rising ground. Cooks' prominent shipbuilding yards, turning out specialized craft and expanding in 1967, follow a trade long established: a man-of-war was built

here for Cromwell's navy. A house near the quay was elaborately pargeted soon after that time. The *Old Store House* on the quay, elegantly fronted, with fig-tree beside porch, commands views of all the river-trade for which it was built, and over to the Fingringhoe fields. The parish reaches to the Colchester boundary, where since 1964 *Wivenhoe Park* has provided the setting for the new university of Essex. The home of the Rebow family in the 18th and 19th centuries, the park was landscaped by Richard Woods, and its main feature, a lake, plays the chief part in a famous picture by Constable in the National Gallery, Washington. Kenneth Capon, architect to the university, has set the Vice-chancellor's lodge *on* Richard Wood's lake. The Rebows' pleasant Georgian house was incorporated by Hopper in Victorian Tudor "improvements" in time for a visit of the Prince Consort to inspect the Colchester garrison after the Crimean War. It is now devoted to university administration. A striking series of tower-blocks in black, or dark-grey, brick stands lower down the hill to Colchester. Other buildings are rising fast, and so far as one can tell at this stage, take good advantage of a very fine site.

Wix (11). The name shows dairy-farms here before the Conquest. Children of the Norman who acquired it founded a priory of nuns: *The Abbey* with its tall step-gabled Tudor porch, is the post-Dissolution farmhouse on the site. The inconspicuous little church adjacent is merely the S. aisle of the priory church: it is much rebuilt, but there is original stonework in the W. wall and an arcade exposed in N. wall. It was fitted up *c.* 1740 after the rest had become ruinous, and contains a nice Georgian pulpit and monument. There is a large cracked medieval bell in a pathetic ivy-grown cage in churchyard: cf. Wrabness. Henry II gave the nuns coursing rights through the whole forest of Essex. Richard I gave them a Michaelmas fair, still held

here in the 19th century. In 1204, John granted them a Tuesday market, held, perhaps, near Wix Cross, where two old inns survive? The nuns were forbidden to allow javelin-play, dances or trading in the streets or open spaces of Wix to the detriment of religion.

The Woodhams (6) three parishes still much shaded by oak woods, and distinguished by names of early baronial holders: Woodham Ferrers on boulder clay with moated farmsteads between Danbury and the head of the Crouch estuary: Woodham Mortimer and Woodham Walter on gravels between Danbury and Maldon.

Woodham Ferrers (6/9). The village is on a steep hill and spoilt by motor traffic. The *church* has lost successive early-Tudor and Georgian W. towers, though flushwork stumps of the first one survive. The royal arms of 1788 are carved in the round, the mantling painted on board behind: it belongs to the carved beam over chancel arch. The monument to the "true widow" of Edwin Sandys, Archbishop of York, 1619, shows her kneeling in an arbour of climbing flowers. She survived him 22 years. Their house, *Edwin's Hall*, was named after him: three-storey, diapered red-brick with stone mullions, set high above the Crouch, it has fine prospect. In the valley below, at the head of Clementsgreen Creek, what look like burial-mounds are perhaps ancient salt-works. Off Danbury road, a gaunt stone arch in a fowl-yard looks like a medieval gate-house: it is the W. arch of the crossing of the church of *Bicknacre priory*, a house of Austin canons who were licensed to hunt hare, fox and cat in the forest, and petred out a generation before the Dissolution.

Woodham Mortimer (6). The attractive red-brick front of *Hall* has four curved "Dutch" gables at dormer level and "Wyatt" windows on the first two floors: presumably from the middle of the 17th century, and probably by Dr Peter Chamberlen, 1601–83, who bought it from the Harris family. The inscription on his tomb-chest in the churchyard repays reading: it says he was Physician in Ordinary to James I, Charles I, Charles II, but his son, erecting the monument, thought Charles I's queen was called Mary! What he does not say is that the doctor inherited his family's secret of the short midwifery forceps, to which they owed their prosperity. In 1818 several midwifery instruments were found in an old chest under the floor of the Hall. An obelisk opposite, of 1825, commemorates a lord of the manor who left the estate for the poor of the Coopers' Company. The church, with Norman doorway, contains a photo of *Hazeleigh* church, demolished in 1922, looking like an old cottage with a bellcote.

Woodham Walter (6). The first view of the church from the north, two western mellow red-brick façades of the N. aisle and nave, rising to steep crow-stepped gables, is like something conceived in Old Delft. Odd to think these red bricks were originally plastered over. The church was "consecrated" by the Archdeacon of Essex in 1564. Churches built in Elizabeth I's reign are extremely rare. Comic Royal Arms, 1660, exactly right. Severely Victorian interior; presumably the nave was ceiled originally at tie-beam height. Thomas Radcliffe, viscount FitzWalter and earl of Sussex (d. 1583) took a lead in the building. The diapered brick walls of the great sunken dry moat suggest that he also rebuilt the *Hall* (long since ruined) before moving to New Hall, Boreham. The bressummer of the *Bell Inn* is carved with acorns (or grapes?). *Hoe Mill*, with locks of the old Chelmer and Blackwater Navigation, and swans and willows, provides fishing and much beauty despite adjacent gravel works.

Wormingford (10). The church is in a proud situation, beside two good Tudor houses, *Church House* opposite, with oddly shaped gable, and *Church Hall* to the north, with Elizabeth I's badge in window-glass, and with a series of gulleys falling away to the Stour

beneath the small sturdy Norman W. tower, enriched with Roman and Tudor brick. The interior, stricken by the Victorian restorer in 1870, is very dull except for a few fragments of heraldic glass, of the 14th and 16th centuries. To the north, the descent to river and mill is one of the best visual experiences in Essex. To the south, *Rotchfords* has a remarkably pretty Georgian front and older outlines in rear. Nearby, at *Jenkins Farm*, the early Tudor timbered porch, with chamber over, leans very venerably.

Wrabness (11). Superb long quiet views over the estuary to the Royal Hospital School, Holbrook (Suffolk). Entering the 15th-century S. doorway of the small church, notice traces of a taller Norman doorway above, also a 13th-century coffin lid in porch-wall. The north doorway, too, is Norman. Whitewashed outward-sloping walls, and a stout hammerbeam roof with traceried spandrels, bereft of figures at the ends of the hammerbeams; also, the figures on the font are terribly defaced. But this church is cared for now. *Jaques Bay* is pleasant, though much encumbered with storage huts of the Ministry of Public Building and Works.

Writtle (6). A vast Domesday manor of Harold: woodland for 1,500 pigs and the men had 64 ploughs between them. The Conqueror took over, and this remained in royal hands till 1241, when it went to Robert Bruce V's wife. Their great-grandson, Robert Bruce VIII, King and liberator of Scotland, may have been born there: excavations at a great moated site, "King John's Castle", revealed traces of 13th-, 14th- and 15th-century buildings (a hunting-lodge). There are still 8,000 acres, after Roxwell (over 4,000) has hived off. Traces of ancient forest survive in *Highwood*, which starts in stockbrokerdom at Mill Green, Fryerning, and becomes real between the *Cricketers* and the *Viper* Inn. *Gorrells Farm* and *Wards Farm* have real old farmhouses, *Frithler's* a real Victorian

one on an old site. *Horsfrith* park and *Writtle Park* were two ancient parks within the Forest. There was a hermitage of St John's abbey, Colchester (see *Monk's* and *Barrow's Farm*): it was called Bedemansberg, and two monks had right of gathering nuts in forest on condition that they prayed for the safety of the King and souls of dead Kings. Highwood parish was formed in 1842: St Paul's, simple red-brick with lancets, was built by subscription (Stephen Webb, archt.).

In Writtle parish, *Newney Green* has three good houses: *Benedict Otes*, with "1644" on its trio of very tall chimneys: *Boards Farm* opposite, with plain weather-boarded front and fine chimney-stack: *Newney Green Hall*, with jettied wings, has its first-floor front hung with old red-tiles, the nicest example of a traditional Essex–Kent–Sussex use in this county. *Hylands Park's* fine wall flanks A12 for about a mile. The entrance to this great park, open all the year, lies to the south of Writtle church. The house, revealed only after a long, blissful walk, was built *c*. 1728 for Sir John Comyns (see below). It was given its lofty portico by Wm. Atkinson in 1819, and the wings got their second storey (from J. B. Papworth's design) in 1842. Unoccupied since 1962, it would make a famous county museum. At the heart of Writtle, now merging with Chelmsford, stand the *Great Green*, and the *Church*. Two approaches to church: from the north, off the Green, up Church Lane, past a prosperous Tudor timber-framed house with three blocked Tudor shop-windows on the Church Lane side; or from the east, past three sunny Georgian houses in Romans Place, with the church piling up impressively ahead, very medieval looking, though the tower was rebuilt in 1802, and much of the 13th-century N. and S. aisles renewed in 1879. Indeed the nave-roof retains one beam from an earlier renewal, in 1740 by "Reginald Branwood, Carpenter of Writtle". There are medieval stone angels with shields, musical instruments,

201

etc., below the wall-posts. A medieval St George is painted over N. door. Early Georgian choir-stall fronts are set in medieval ends. The vestry has a timber-studded W. wall and room over; its stout medieval door has iron-work with a human face. Many brasses. Of two notable marbles, the first is a spontaneous master-piece by Nicholas Stone for Sir Edward Pinchon and Dorothy Weston, 1629. A worm or serpent burrows into the rocky hill that springs out of a marvellous golden field of standing, waving wheat. An angel, wings spread, dress wafting in breeze, looks down from rock (having, alas, lost emblems she bore in either hand). Behind her, the sun, labelled SOL: JUSTITIA. Two angels in wide-brimmed shepherdess straw-hats sleep below. The inscription is in a shallow farm-basket. The other marble, to Chief Baron of the Exchequer Comyns, of Hylands, 1759, is signed by H. Cheere.

Yeldham, Great (3) is a Colne valley thoroughfare village, with the carcass of a veteran oak-tree, nestling down out of sight of Hedingham keep. A young oak was planted in 1863 beside the dead one, whose girth is almost 30 ft. De Veres got the patronage of the rectory early in the 16th century, but shared the allegiance of rector with the Bourchier earls of Essex, according to badges carved at that time in his solidly oak-ceiled 1st-floor study facing the brook. The handsome W. tower of the church, perched boldly on the edge of a slope, is partly ruddy with brick and finished with freestone battlements. A large tower-porch, less boldly sited south of the nave, had been started *c.* 1400 and perhaps never finished: it was later crowned with a (now heavily re-stored) Tudor brick step-gable, and looks like part of an old house. Medieval S. door. Interior full of pews, piano, etc. Three painted medieval screen-panels. Neo-Georgian oak-panelled reredos, 1931. J. Bacon's chaste tablet in the S. chapel commemorates Gregory Way, who bought Spencer Grange in 1783, built by Marlborough's granddaughter, and new-fronted *c.* 1820. Richard FitzSymonds, 1680 (see Panfield), has a large marble, and appears also as youngest youth in small brass plate, 1627, opposite. He had two nephews called Richard Symonds fighting on opposite sides at Naseby. The Cromwellian was killed, the Royalist was later a distinguished antiquary. The Symonds' home was the *Pool Farm*, where only a neglected brick-nogged barn remains from their day. Between it and the church, the 15th-century timbered *White Hart* offers daily luncheons for the business-man "or dinner by candle-light".

Yeldham, Little (3). The church was given a stone screen and pulpit during ruthless restorations of 1876 and 1893. There is a pargeted vine in the dormer gable of *Mashay*, a low thatched farmhouse in the northern tip of the parish.

ASHDON: Bartlow hills

INDEX